Raising the Stakes

The Vietnam Experience

Raising the Stakes

by Terrence Maitland, Stephen Weiss,
and the editors of Boston Publishing Company

Boston Publishing Company/Boston, MA

Boston Publishing Company

President and Publisher: Robert J. George
Vice President: Richard S. Perkins, Jr.
Editor-in-Chief: Robert Manning
Managing Editor: Paul Dreyfus

Staff Writers:
  Clark Dougan, Edward Doyle, Samuel
  Lipsman, Terrence Maitland, Peter
  McInerney, Stephen Weiss
Research Assistants:
  Michael T. Casey, Kerstin Gorham, Scott
  Kafker, Jane T. Merritt, Richard Schorske,
  Glenn Wallach

Senior Picture Editor: Julene Fischer
Picture Editors: Martha Davidson, Judy Poe
Picture Researchers:
  Shirley L. Green (Washington, D.C.), Wendy
  K. Johnson, Kate Lewin (Paris), Kathleen
  Reidy, Mira Schachne (New York)
Picture Assistants:
  Peter Romanow, Kathryn Steeves

Historical Consultants:
  David P. Chandler, Vincent H. Demma, Lee
  Ewing, Paul Kattenburg
Picture Consultant: Ngo Vinh Long

Assistant Editors:
  Karen E. English, Jeffrey L. Seglin

Production Coordinator: Douglas B. Rhodes
Production Editor: Patricia Leal Welch
Editorial Production:
  Pamela George, Elizabeth Hamilton, Amy P.
  Wilson

Design: Designworks, Sally Bindari

Marketing Director: Linda M. Scenna
Circulation Manager: Jane Colpoys
Business Staff:
  Darlene Keefe, James D. Burrows, Christine E.
  Geering, Jeanne C. Gibson, Kathleen A.
  Rushton, Elizabeth Schultz

About the editors and authors

Editor-in-Chief *Robert Manning*, a long-time journalist, has previously been editor-in-chief of the *Atlantic Monthly* magazine and its press. He served as assistant secretary of state for public affairs under Presidents John F. Kennedy and Lyndon B. Johnson. He has also been a fellow at the Institute of Politics at the John F. Kennedy School of Government at Harvard University.

Staff Writers: *Clark Dougan*, a former Watson and Danforth fellow, has taught history at Kenyon College. He received his M.A. and M.Phil. at Yale University. *Edward Doyle*, an historian, received his masters degree at the University of Notre Dame and his Ph.D. at Harvard University. *Samuel Lipsman*, a former Fulbright Scholar, received his M.A. and M.Phil. in history at Yale. *Terrence Maitland* has written for several publications, including *Newsweek* magazine and the *Boston Globe*. He is a graduate of Holy Cross College and has an M.S. from Boston University. *Peter McInerney* taught at the University of Pennsylvania and has published articles about literature and film of the Vietnam War. He received his M.A. and Ph.D. at the Johns Hopkins University. *Stephen Weiss* has been a fellow at the Newberry Library in Chicago. An American historian, he received his M.A. and M.Phil. at Yale.

Historical Consultants: *David P. Chandler*, a former U.S. foreign service officer, is research director of the Centre of Southeast Asian Studies at Monash University in Melbourne, Australia. His major publications include *In Search of Southeast Asia: A Modern History* (coauthor) and *The Land and People of Cambodia*. *Vincent H. Demma*, an historian with the U.S. Army Center of Military History, is currently working on the center's history of the Vietnam conflict. *Lee Ewing*, editor of *Army Times*, served two years in Vietnam as a combat intelligence officer with the U.S. Military Assistance Command, Vietnam (MACV) and the 101st Airborne Division. An expert on Southeast Asia and a former State Department officer, *Paul Kattenburg* is a professor of government and international studies at the University of South Carolina.

Picture Consultant: *Ngo Vinh Long* is a social historian specializing in China and Vietnam. Born in Vietnam, he returned there most recently in 1980. His books include *Before the Revolution: The Vietnamese Peasants Under the French* and *Report From a Vietnamese Village*.

Cover photograph:
The landing that changed the war. Combat-ready troops of the 9th Marine Expeditionary Brigade make their way ashore from landing craft beached near Da Nang in South Vietnam on March 8, 1965.

Library of Congress Catalog Card Number: 82-071280

ISBN: 0-939526-02-6

10 9 8 7 6
5 4

Contents

Chapter 1/Saigon's Year   6

Chapter 2/Nation Within a Nation   32

Chapter 3/Into the Long Tunnel   48

Chapter 4/Season of Fire   72

Chapter 5/LBJ Takes Charge   92

Chapter 6/Insurgency—Counterinsurgency   112

Chapter 7/Covert Action, Hidden War   126

Chapter 8/Predated Declaration of War   152

Chapter 9/Enter the U.S. Marines   166

Names, Acronyms, Terms   192

Picture Essays

Choppers   26
The Soldiers of South Vietnam   67
The Brutal War   107
With the Green Berets   146
The U.S. Marines Land   176

Maps

Insurgency in the South, 1962   19
The Topography of South Vietnam   22
Ap Bac, January 2, 1963   52
South Vietnam   66
U.S. Special Forces Deployment   137
Tonkin Gulf Incident   157
Thrust-Counterthrust, February
   1965   181

146544

Saigon's Year

Black smoke pouring from her single stack, the U.S. aircraft carrier *Core* steamed slowly up the Saigon River on December 11, 1961, dwarfing the sampans and other small craft that bobbed in her muddy wake. Along the city's waterfront thousands of Saigonese shouted and waved as the huge ship edged carefully into her berth in front of the Hotel Majestic. Patrons at the hotel's rooftop bar stopped sipping their Pernod for a moment to look down on the thirty-three helicopters jamming the deck of the *Core* and the 380 U.S. Army pilots and maintenance men crowded along the rails. Across the river, hidden in the thick vegetation of the far bank, other eyes also watched. The two-year-old war between the government of South Vietnam and the guerrilla fighters of the National Liberation Front had entered a new phase. By sending the pilots and helicopters, Washington had broken through the military assistance limits imposed by the 1954 Geneva accords. The Americans had raised the ante.

Fuel for the war machine. Thousands of drums of U.S. gasoline, hauled some two hundred miles into the mountainous central highlands, lie in storage next to a runway at Pleiku.

Only three weeks earlier Washington had come to the conclusion that the U.S.-sponsored regime of Ngo Dinh Diem could not survive the mounting military and political pressure of the Vietcong insurgents without substantially increased military aid and expertise. Fending off requests from Saigon and from his own advisers for an American combat task force, President John Kennedy had agreed to dispatch military personnel and equipment for advisory and combat support duties. During the next twelve months American men and machines would help halt the insurgent advance and, at least for a moment, seem to turn the tide of war for the first time in Saigon's favor.

Men and machines

By the end of 1961 the U.S. Military Advisory Assistance Group (MAAG) had more than tripled to nearly thirty-two hundred soldiers, and the numbers continued to escalate. Within six months there would be some eight thousand American military personnel in Vietnam, and by December 1962, more than eleven thousand three hundred.

Along with this growing stream of men came a flood of equipment. The U.S. provided the South Vietnamese armed forces with small arms and machine guns, radios and other communications equipment,

Preceding page. ARVN soldiers load captured guerrillas onto a boat in the Mekong Delta.

transport aircraft, naval patrol craft, production kits to manufacture low-draft assault boats, and M113 armored personnel carriers (APCs). At Saigon's Tan Son Nhut airfield huge Globemaster transport planes delivered tons of electric generators, radar equipment, trucks, and Quonset huts. The Americans sent to Vietnam a squadron of C-123 Provider aircraft and short-take-off-and-landing Caribous, to accelerate the movement of war materiel around the country, and established a joint air force operations center complete with radar locator and plotting boards.

Even more important were American units operating equipment in direct support of South Vietnamese army (ARVN) combat operations. The U.S. supplied and manned helicopters for rapid tactical transport, all-weather radar, a radio research unit with direction-finder equipment to target enemy radio installations, and an all-purpose air force squadron with B-26 and T-28 aircraft.

The greatly enhanced U.S. military role in South Vietnam required a more substantial command operation, and in February the MAAG mission was superseded by a new Military Assistance Command, Vietnam (MACV). Paul D. Harkins, the fifty-seven-year-old three-star general selected to take over the new command, had begun his army career forty years earlier in the cavalry troop of the Massachusetts National Guard. During World War II he served as assistant chief of staff to General George C. Patton. After the war there was a peace-time tour as commandant of cadets at West Point before Har-

MACV commander General Paul D. Harkins encouraged the South Vietnamese to "take more initiative in going out and finding the Vietcong," but conceded that victory depended on "winning the hearts and minds of the people."

The President

Joint Chiefs of Staff (JCS)
Chairman — General Lyman Lemnitzer*
Army Chief of Staff — General George H. Decker**
Air Force Chief of Staff — General Curtis LeMay
Chief of Naval Operations — Admiral George W. Anderson, Jr.
Commandant, U.S. Marine Corps — General David M. Shoup

Commander in Chief, Pacific (CINCPAC)
Admiral Harry D. Felt

Commander, U.S. Military Assistance Command, Vietnam (COMUSMACV)
General Paul D. Harkins

Military Assistance Advisory Group, Vietnam† (MAAG)
MAAG Chief — Major General Charles J. Timmes

U.S. Army Support Group
Colonel Marvin H. Merchant (April – August 1962)††

Air Force Section
Chief, Brigadier General
Rollen H. Anthis

Army Section
Chief, Major General
Charles J. Timmes

Navy Section
Chief, Captain
Joseph B. Drachnik

Marine Advisory Division
Senior Marine Adviser
Lieutenant Colonel
Robert E. Brown

*replaced by General Maxwell D. Taylor, October 1962.
**replaced by General Earle G. Wheeler, October 1962.
†dissolved May 1964 during MACV reorganization.
††replaced by Brigadier General Joseph W. Stilwell, August 1962.

I Corps adviser Lieutenant Colonel William Dickerson, who opposed maintaining isolated ARVN garrisons, supervises the abandonment of a jungle outpost on the Laotian border.

kins went to Korea as chief of staff of Maxwell Taylor's 8th Army, and then as commander of the army's 24th Division. Quiet, firm, diplomatic, Harkins had earned a reputation as a solid staff officer and an excellent logistical planner. His tall, spare frame, gray hair, and blue eyes made him look, thought one American magazine, "every inch the professional soldier."

Harkins was in Honolulu as deputy commander of the U.S. Army in the Pacific when presidential envoy Maxwell Taylor stopped off on his way back from South Vietnam in October 1961. How bad was it out there? Harkins wanted to know. It was bad, said Taylor, very bad. And indeed the task confronting Harkins when he arrived in Saigon was formidable. It would be his duty to bring together thousands of American advisers with their Vietnamese counterparts and oversee the build-up of American combat support units. He was also commander of the U.S. Military Assistance Command, Thailand, with responsibilities for SEATO planning and the defense of Thailand and Laos.

But Harkins was already familiar with the overall strategic situation in the region. Strongly supported by Taylor, who had recommended his protégé to the White House, he plunged into his new assignment with energy and enthusiasm, traveling around South Vietnam almost daily in his small L-23 transport plane to inspect training centers and strategic hamlets and to measure the progress of the war.

The men Harkins commanded were soon at work in every phase of South Vietnamese military operations. American soldiers trained ARVN, Ranger, and Civil Guard detachments in antiguerrilla and village defense techniques; developed ARVN airborne helicopter assault tactics; airlifted troops, supplies, and combat equipment to strategic locations; built jungle airstrips capable of handling aircraft as large as a C-47 transport; manned radio communications networks in the central highlands; and flew medical evacuation helicopters—the famous "skin ships" or "dustoffs"—through the mountain jungles of northern South Vietnam.

American air crews trained South Vietnamese air force pilots to fly T-28s, set up a tactical air control system to monitor aircraft activity throughout South Vietnam, flew reconnaissance patrols over the central highlands in F-102 jet interceptors, and began defoliation flights north of Saigon.

American marines took part in training exercises with their South Vietnamese counterparts, coordinated artillery fire and air support, and acted as liaisons with the U.S. Navy for amphibious maneuvers. A marine helicopter squadron, code named Shufly, shuttled South Vietnamese troops and equipment into battle, first from its Mekong Delta base at Soc Trang and then from the American air base at Da Nang in the north.

American naval personnel worked at the Vietnamese sea force headquarters on ship maintenance and deployment. They accompanied the sea force on sea duty, furnished advice on ship operation and patrolling techniques, and helped coordinate the Vietnamese navy's river force operations. Americans also helped to establish a paramilitary junk fleet.

The advisers

Perhaps the most striking feature of the U.S. effort in Vietnam during 1962 and 1963 was the advisory contingent—several thousand American soldiers who served alongside their Vietnamese counterparts at every level from general staff to battalion.

Harkins and his staff had their counterparts in the Vietnamese Joint General Staff (JGS), and Americans filled advisory staff positions at each of the corps and division headquarters. At the regiment level, a senior adviser with a staff of several assistants worked with the ARVN regiment commander in planning operations and was available for tactical advice once operations were underway. Like the regiment advisers, the battalion three-man U.S. advisory team—two officers and an NCO—participated in the planning and execution of operations. But they also regularly accompanied their units into the field for periods of up to six to eight weeks, becoming the primary reporters on the scene for the U.S. chain of command.

MACV made a major effort in 1962 to extend its advisory mission to provincial administration and defense. Sector advisory teams—composed of a lieutenant colonel or major, an intelligence sergeant, a light weapons adviser, an administrative specialist, a communications specialist, and a medical specialist— were dispatched to assist thirty-six of the forty-four provincial chiefs. With a broader range of responsibilities than other American advisers in Vietnam, the sector teams not only provided advice and training in the employment of local militia units but also played a major role in the implementation of local pacification plans and civic action programs.

By and large the American military men in Vietnam—the advisers, the helicopter pilots, the communications specialists, the training teams, and the rest—worked at demanding tasks with persistence, courage, and good humor. Sometimes this meant providing tactical advice to senior South Vietnamese officers. Lieutenant Colonel William Dickerson of Elizabeth, New Jersey, an adviser to the 2nd ARVN Division, spent weeks trying to persuade I Corps Commander General Tran Van Don of the futility of maintaining small, widely dispersed jungle garrisons. The outposts tied down three-fourths of the general's forces, provided little in the way of useful intelligence, and only invited Vietcong attack. In the end Don agreed, abandoning ten of the forts and freeing several thousand men for more aggressive operations.

Sometimes it meant taking the initiative when things simply had to be done. Lieutenant Colonel Marion C. "Dirty" Dalby, a marine adviser from Arlington, Texas, single-handedly set up a boat manufacturing operation to provide desperately needed swamp and canal transport in the Mekong Delta. Sometimes it meant acts of personal heroism. Major Ronald C. Good, a helicopter adviser, flew alone into Vietcong fire to retrieve the dead and wounded left behind after an enemy ambush near Dak Uc on the Laotian border. Usually, it just meant taking on a dangerous job under difficult conditions: helicopter pilots forced by frequent low ceilings to skim for hours only a few feet above the tangled jungle; or infantry advisers living with the soldiers they instructed, sharing their food, joining their patrols, and suffering their hardships.

The advice and ingenuity of the Americans were quickly brought to bear against the Vietcong. U.S. officers urged ARVN commanders to abandon their fortress mentality and take the war to the enemy. The Americans followed up their advice with a number of tactical refinements such as the "flare and strike" technique, which used aerial flares dropped from a

C–47 to permit night operations by the Vietnamese air force, or the highly successful "Eagle Flights"—four helicopters loaded with fifty soldiers each, circling above contested terrain during military operations, ready to swoop down on any Vietcong groups that managed to escape the ARVN net. And being Americans, they introduced a never-ending stream of ingenious gadgets and inventive approaches to guerrilla warfare: electrified barbed wire, defoliant chemicals, electronic sensors, and *kpung*, a poisonous nettle causing excruciating pain that lasts a week, for use as a barrier around villages subject to Vietcong attack.

The build-up of American military personnel during 1962 did not always proceed smoothly. Some complained that the American contingent was top-heavy and bureaucratic. One "rice paddy" adviser grumbled: "There are a hundred men in MAAG headquarters in Saigon for every man doing his job on a jungle patrol." And there were the inevitable frictions between the Americans and the Vietnamese. The South Vietnamese government disapproved of contact between the two groups, making mixed cocktail parties in Saigon stiff affairs. Out in the bush shared danger might reduce the tension of an awkward situation. If pressed too hard, however, the Vietnamese were apt to remind the advisers of their inexperience. "They are too new at the game," observed one top-ranking ARVN officer, "but they can learn."

Perhaps the worst problem from the American point of view was the so-called "fiction of non-involvement." As the first advisers and combat support units began arriving in Vietnam, Washington insisted that the Americans were supposed to fire only if fired upon. But as one veteran of several enemy encounters remarked: "When you see a man aim a gun at you and start to pull the trigger, what kind of damn fool would you be to let him shoot first?" The formal explanation for the American military presence in Vietnam—that U.S. soldiers were intended solely to train and advise—simply could not withstand the realities of what was happening on the ground. When an American sergeant wounded in the leg was denied the Purple Heart, Pentagon officials explained that Vietnam was not recognized as a combat zone. To the pilot putting a chopper down against heavy fire, or an adviser caught in a VC ambush, it was an absurd distinction.

In fact, there could be little doubt about the nature of the growing American commitment. "We are going to win in Vietnam," the president's brother Attorney General Robert Kennedy told reporters in Saigon in February. "We will remain here until we do win." Whether the people back home were equally prepared to sustain an indefinite military intervention in Southeast Asia was uncertain. But as U.S. soldiers and U.S. aircraft began to be shot at with increasing regularity, it became clear to those in Vietnam that the Americans were involved in the war, as many of them put it, "up to our necks."

The Green Berets

No group of American soldiers was more involved in the war than the men of the U.S. Army Special Forces, the Green Berets.

The elite counterguerrilla unit was no stranger to South Vietnam. Members of the 1st Special Forces Group had trained ARVN soldiers at the commando training center in Nha Trang during 1957, and in May 1960, thirty Special Forces instructors established a counterinsurgency program for the South Vietnamese army. The training mission would continue, and the Special Forces would also participate in advisory and operational duties. But the chief work of the Green Berets in Vietnam was the development and operation of the Civilian Irregular Defense Group program.

The CIDG was the brain child of David Nuttle, a member of the International Volunteer Service, a private forerunner of the Peace Corps. Working with primitive montagnard tribes in the central highlands, Nuttle had become concerned at the steady increase of VC strength in the area. After Nuttle mentioned his idea of a village defense program to Gilbert Layton, a paramilitary specialist working for the CIA, the agency devised a project that combined self-defense with economic and social programs designed to raise the standard of living and win the political loyalty of the mountain people. To implement the program, the CIA turned to the Special Forces. The site for the first CIDG camp was the Rhade village of Buon Enao, five miles east of Ban Me Thuot (see map, page 66).

Preliminary talks between the Rhade tribesmen and Special Forces representatives had taken place in December 1961, but it wasn't until February of the following year that a twelve-man Special Forces A-team under the command of Captain Ronald Shackleton arrived at Buon Enao to get the program underway. Within a month the village was fortified with barbed wire and gun emplacements, fifty Rhade warriors had been trained as a village strike force,

and another hundred tribesmen recruited to build bunkers, storage facilities, and dispensaries.

The Americans had little problem convincing the Rhade to volunteer for the experiment. Accustomed to the indifference and sometimes hostility of a Saigon government that had denied their wishes for political autonomy, taken their lands for Catholic refugees from the North, and then prohibited the montagnards from carrying weapons, the tribesmen responded to the Americans with enthusiasm. "Within the first week," one Green Beret remembered, "they were lining up at the front gate to get into the program."

When Shackleton's team departed in August, they left behind a network of 129 fortified villages, ten thousand armed and trained defenders, a mobile strike force of eighteen hundred men, and a staff of 280 montagnard nurses and medics to serve a protected population of over sixty thousand tribesmen. It was, by any standard, an impressive achievement. Following on the Shackleton team's heels, additional American and Vietnamese Special Forces teams were dispatched to the area, and shortly afterward the Saigon government agreed to the establishment of Special Forces camps throughout South Vietnam. By the end of the year there were twenty-six A-team camps from Da Nang in the north to the tip of the Ca Mau Peninsula.

"Ranger kill!" shout South Vietnamese Rangers at commando training exercises run by the U.S. Army Special Forces. American instructors hoped to instill not only new skills but a new esprit among the soldiers they advised.

The Vietcong had been caught by surprise at Buon Enao. By the time the insurgents realized the extent of military training and support the program had generated, the villages were strong enough to repel guerrilla attacks. But as new Special Forces camps were established, no one expected the same leeway, and camp security became a growing preoccupation. The sandbagged mud wall outer defenses of one A-team camp in the highlands were studded with machine-gun emplacements and surrounded by concertina barbed wire. Beyond the concertina, tanglefoot barbed wire stretched out into the high grass. Sandbagged log walls with barbed wire and punji sticks at their base formed the inner perimeter. The heavily sandbagged command bunker with its protected observation post made up the final defense position. Mortar emplacements pockmarked the interior of the camp, while beyond the outer wall mines and other booby traps lay concealed.

From out of these fortresses Special Forces men and their "yards," as they called the montagnard strike force troops, went on almost daily patrols trying to intercept infiltrators from the North, keeping track of the local VC, setting ambushes, destroying crops, and looking for villagers who had fled their hamlets in fear of guerrillas, or government bombers. A man could march for hours through jungles so thick that trails disappeared completely in spiky vines that shredded his trousers from ankle to groin, so thick that Vietcong soldiers could fire from three feet away without being seen. There were punji stakes smeared with human excrement and foot traps filled with fire-hardened bamboo spikes; there was the heat and the stinking dampness, the isolation, and the fear. It was a tough, dangerous, lonesome job. It was that kind of a war.

Wherever they were stationed, what American soldiers found in South Vietnam was a struggle growing more savage as each month passed. Vietcong regular forces, now numbering twenty thousand men organized into companies and battalions, conducted frequent armed attacks throughout the southern part of the country. Outside Saigon and the main provincial centers, the insurgents had extended varying degrees of control over much of the land and a sizable portion of the people of South Vietnam. The question was not whether the Diem government could defeat the insurgents, but whether it could survive.

Arc of insurgency

Operating out of almost invulnerable bases north and west of the capital, the guerrillas had for two years been drawing an ever tighter noose around Saigon. By late 1961 what the French journalist and scholar Bernard Fall called the "arc of insurgency" was almost complete. Traffic on virtually every road and railway leading from the capital was subject to constant harassment and increasingly frequent attack. Civilian movement around the country could be accomplished only by air, creating in many areas a debilitating siege psychology.

And with the end of the rainy season in late November 1961, the Vietcong launched a major offensive. Heavy fighting broke out in the northern and central provinces of Quang Nam and Phu Yen. In Kien Hoa Province far to the south, a guerrilla battalion attacked the market at Trug Ciang and was repulsed only after two days of pitched battle. Just before Christmas an insurgent unit mounted a night attack on Duc Hoa, just eighteen miles west of Saigon and the site of the nation's largest sugar refinery. Casualty figures, which reached more than nine hun-

dred government soldiers killed or wounded in November, climbed to fifteen hundred during the last month of the year.

The Vietcong had intensified military activity in the Mekong Delta hoping to insure adequate supplies of rice for their own cadres, to disrupt the flow of South Vietnam's important dollar-earning export, and to create food shortages and panic in Saigon. But ideological considerations were also at work. February 5 would mark the beginning of the Year of the Tiger, a year the Chinese Communists had dedicated to driving the "imperialists" out of Southeast Asia.

As the new year approached the fighting continued to intensify. During one day the Vietcong staged eight major actions—ambushing convoys, attacking railroads and bridges, and raiding army outposts. By the first week of February some reports had the Saigon government losing three thousand men a month. The Year of the Tiger had begun in earnest.

A new strategy

The American decision to commit advisers and provide combat support to the South Vietnamese armed forces had taken place within something of a strategic vacuum. Even as late as the end of 1961, after two years of mounting insurrection, the South Vietnamese government (GVN) had no national plan for pacification. Along with the American men and machines came increased pressure on the Diem government to devise a counterinsurgency program. The strategy that eventually emerged, however, issued neither from the Americans nor from the South Vietnamese, but from a British advisory mission headed by Sir Robert Thompson, a veteran of the British victory over Communist insurgents in nearby Malaya.

Thompson's plan revolved around the belief that "clear and hold" operations should replace the "search and destroy" sweeps that the ARVN had so far employed with such little success. The goal of the government should not be merely to destroy the insurgents but to offer the peasants of the countryside something the Communists could not: physical security and real economic development.

Under the Thompson plan peasants would be relocated into heavily defended "strategic hamlets" in areas relatively free of Vietcong activity. Protected first by the ARVN and then by locally trained self-defense militia units, the strategic hamlets would offer economic and social programs to win the hearts of the people to the government cause.

There were some American reservations about the Thompson proposal. MAAG chief General Lionel McGarr argued that Thompson's plan called for too slow an approach to the critical need for general pacification of the countryside, and General Taylor voiced concern that the defensive nature of the hamlets would tie down forces that could better be used in a more mobile offensive role. But the idea found an attentive ear in Washington where Roger Hilsman, director of the State Department's Bureau of Intelligence and Research, helped convince President Kennedy of the soundness of the Thompson approach.

Diem was also enthusiastic about the concept of fortified villages and agreed with Thompson that "sweeps" solved nothing: The objective was to hold an area and isolate the Vietcong from the rest of the population. At the same time, he was eager to undertake a military operation to demonstrate the government's new resolve. Determined to strike a blow against the insurgents and get the new pacification program off the ground all at once, Diem selected Binh Duong Province, a heavily forested region forty miles northwest of Saigon and one of the most formidable of all the VC redoubts.

The way of revolution

In the early morning darkness of March 22, 1962, a long column of trucks rumbled out from the deserted streets of Saigon toward the forests of Binh Duong. Operation Sunrise was underway. As the first light of day filtered through the thick jungle canopy, the convoy came to a halt. Six hundred men of the ARVN 5th Division, reinforced by Ranger companies, a reconnaissance company, two Civil Guard companies, and a psychological warfare company, poured from the trucks and fanned out across the paddies and rubber plantations of what had been for years an almost inviolate Vietcong sanctuary. In the face of the government troops the insurgents melted away into the surrounding forests.

With the dispersal of the VC, phase two of the operation got underway, transforming the widely scattered peasants of the Ben Cat District into a concentrated—and defensible—community. Soldiers and government officials went from hamlet to hamlet telling the assembled farmers that they were being moved to a strategic village called Ben Tuong. The new village would be equipped with a school, a medical clinic, a market, and a detachment of soldiers to protect them. The government promised new land, a twenty-one-dollar bounty for each family, and a free daily ration of dried fish to tide them over the first months.

Within two weeks a concrete administration building and a clinic were already standing, and bulldozers had cleared land for the first seventy families. The settlers were at work constructing their own thatch houses, as well as the moats and walls that would secure the village from the guerrillas. A team of U.S. military advisers had begun to recruit, train, and arm a local militia to take over defense of the hamlet when the 5th Division moved on in three months. Giving clear indication of their own concern, the Vietcong launched a night attack on the new settlement, wounding two soldiers before being driven back into the forest.

By midsummer, two more strategic hamlets had been carved out of the jungle for over three thousand Ben Cat farmers and their families. In Saigon, the government hailed Operation Sunrise as a great success, calling the Strategic Hamlet Program the definitive answer to the problem of pacification and the reconstruction of the countryside. Particularly enthusiastic was President Diem's brother and chief political adviser, Ngo Dinh Nhu.

Unlike the president, Nhu had displayed little interest in the Thompson plan until he learned that the Americans were prepared to back the Strategic Hamlet Program with substantial funds. At once he adopted the idea as his own and soon became the driving force behind implementation of the program.

The British and Americans embraced the Strategic Hamlet Program because it seemed to provide a way to isolate the guerrillas from the general population and then turn the mass of peasants to the government cause through economic development and political indoctrination. But the Ngos—and particularly Nhu—saw the hamlets in grander terms, as the vehicle for a non-Communist social and ideological transformation of the countryside revolving around a body of philosophic and political thought called Personalism. Amorphous in its details, vaguely democratic and collectivist in its intent, Personalism declared that the highest development of human personality took place in a communal context featuring the private ownership of land, personal morality, strong family life, and the merging of individual goals into a common purpose. The Personalist strategic hamlet "is a way of revolution," declared Minister of the Interior Bui Van Luong, "the work is a revolutionary work; the spirit is a revolutionary spirit, a new spirit."

Local peasant volunteers of the Self Defense Corps drill with old French rifles. These militiamen eventually took over defense of their new strategic hamlet from regular army forces.

Right. Villagers direct pilots toward Vietcong positions by pointing a "fire-arrow" to indicate the direction in which guerrillas have been seen.

Their lookout ringed with barbed wire and sandbagged against mortar attack, a pair of sentries keeps watch atop a mud-brick blockhouse in the strategic hamlet of Tan Khanh, one of the villages created during Operation Sunrise.

Year of the strategic hamlet

Whatever lofty Personalist ideals they might eventually serve, the strategic hamlets first had to be created on the ground. While the peasants of Ben Tuong were still putting up the walls of their new hamlet, the ambitious Delta Project got underway. Soon all over the delta thousands of peasants put to work by the government dug ditches, sharpened bamboo stakes, and fenced in new strategic hamlets. In the Ca Mau Peninsula at the southern tip of the delta, an area long under insurgent domination, the 31st ARVN Infantry Regiment resettled nearly eleven thousand people into nine hamlets. At the end of spring the GVN informed Washington that thirteen hundred strategic hamlets had already been completed.

During the summer, Operation Sunrise was expanded into several provinces, while a number of other programs were begun, including Operation *Dang Tien* (Let's Go) in Binh Dinh Province, with a goal of 328 hamlets in the first year, and Operation *Phuong Hoang* (Royal Phoenix) in Quang Ngai Province, with a goal of 162 hamlets completed by the end of 1962. Operation *Hai Yen* (Sea Swallow) in Phu Yen Province, with a goal of 281 hamlets, reported 157 completed within two months.

Working with the Vietnamese in several operations, U.S. teams trained the men of the new hamlets in village self-defense. The major American contribution to the Strategic Hamlet Program, however, was money and supplies. The U.S. gave three hundred thousand dollars, for instance, to fund the resettlement costs associated with Ben Tuong hamlet, while the Agency for International Development (USAID) and the Department of Defense provided the Vietnamese with strategic hamlet kits. Each kit contained building materials, barbed wire, stakes, light weapons, ammunition, and communications equipment. During the first year of the program, Defense authorized funding for fifteen hundred kits at a cost of $13 million. The U.S. also purchased and installed hundreds of radios so that each strategic hamlet would have the capacity to sound the alarm when it came under attack.

Security was the precondition of success for the strategic hamlets, but the avowed aim of the program was to bring social and economic benefits to the peasants. Once the military had cleared the area of insurgents and the hamlet had been fortified, the next task was civic action.

Organized into groups of twenty or thirty men, civic action teams received several weeks of training and indoctrination, after which they carried the government's programs and message to the hamlets. The civic action teams were to introduce agricultural cooperatives, build schools and clinics, help create hamlet militia units from among the younger men, and establish elected local councils. One of their jobs was to organize a number of associations for self-betterment. Another was to educate the peasants about the benefits that awaited them once they rid themselves of the Vietcong. By the end of the summer some six thousand teams were trained and in the field.

The Strategic Hamlet Program, even in its early stages, was not without its problems. Some argued that construction was going on at too rapid a pace, that too many hamlets were being built in areas of tenuous government control. Others pointed to the shortage of technicians to supervise school building or develop agricultural programs. The government showed reluctance to move beyond the initial phase of security, concerned that heavy investment in the hamlets would tempt Vietcong reprisal.

But by and large American officials were well pleased. In April, Undersecretary of State George Ball, who only months earlier had cautioned President Kennedy against U.S. involvement in Vietnam, now called strategic hamlets an excellent means of bringing South Vietnam under government control. General Lyman Lemnitzer, chairman of the Joint Chiefs of Staff, came away from several tours of strategic hamlets convinced that the program promised "solid benefits, and may well be the vital key to success of the pacification program." Secretary of Defense McNamara also made on-site inspections during the summer of 1962, telling members of the press that the hamlets were the "backbone of President Diem's program for countering subversion directed against his state."

Saigon was even more satisfied. In August the government put forward a priority plan for the construction of strategic hamlets on a nationwide basis. By the end of the summer the GVN claimed that 3,225 of the planned 11,316 hamlets had been constructed and that over 33 percent of the nation's total population—some 4.3 million people—were already living in the new villages. In October the government-controlled *Times of Vietnam* called 1962 "The Year of Strategic Hamlets." That same month Diem made the Strategic Hamlet Program the explicit focus and unifying concept of the entire pacification effort.

But pacification rested ultimately on the capacity of the South Vietnamese armed forces to defeat, or at least to neutralize, the Vietcong. Here, too, the year brought progress, and even talk of victory.

The war against the VC

Backed by American equipment and American-inspired reforms, the ARVN set the pace of war during 1962. With the establishment of MACV in February, the Americans centralized the South Vietnamese army's logistical functions, redesigned training programs, and improved intelligence-gathering methods. Under the overall command of Major General Duong Van "Big" Minh, ARVN operations began to receive more careful advance planning, now closely correlated with improved local intelligence.

The armed forces available to Saigon were formidable and growing. The army, one hundred and fifty thousand strong at the beginning of the year, would soon number nearly two hundred and five thousand. By year's end, expansion of the regional Civil Guard to sixty-two thousand and the local Self Defense Corps to eighty thousand brought the roster of regular military and paramilitary forces to nearly three hundred and sixty thousand men.

It was the army, however, that would bring the war most forcefully to the Vietcong during 1962. Putting to use the helicopters and M113 armored personnel carriers made available by the United States—the former operated under American control, the latter supplied directly to South Vietnamese units—ARVN commanders began for the first time in years to conduct aggressive operations into such guerrilla strongholds as War Zone D, north of Saigon, and the U Minh Forest along the Gulf of Thailand. Unfamiliar with the tactics made possible by the new equipment and unprepared for the renewed offensive spirit of the ARVN, the Vietcong were repeatedly harassed, surrounded, and—more than once—defeated.

During the second week of April, while the 21st Division was launching Operation Sunrise north of Saigon, eight thousand men of the 7th Division, supported by river boats and fighter planes, penetrated the guerrilla-held Plain of Reeds eighty miles west of Saigon. In three days of fighting through rice fields and mangrove swamps, government forces killed eighty-eight VC and captured thirty-two others. At the beginning of July ten battalions of South Vietnamese soldiers and marines were airlifted into Kien Hoa Province to hunt down guerrilla bands. During a

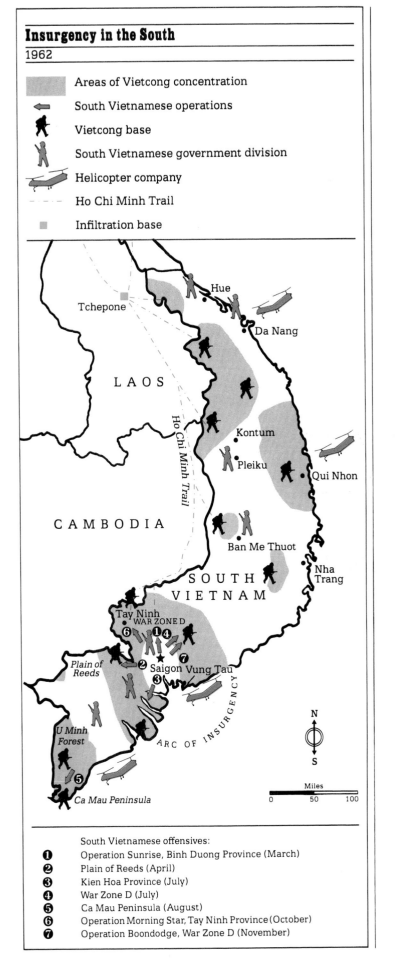

Insurgency in the South

1962

▨	Areas of Vietcong concentration
⬅	South Vietnamese operations
🏃	Vietcong base
🧍	South Vietnamese government division
🚁	Helicopter company
– · –	Ho Chi Minh Trail
▪	Infiltration base

South Vietnamese offensives:
- ❶ Operation Sunrise, Binh Duong Province (March)
- ❷ Plain of Reeds (April)
- ❸ Kien Hoa Province (July)
- ❹ War Zone D (July)
- ❺ Ca Mau Peninsula (August)
- ❻ Operation Morning Star, Tay Ninh Province (October)
- ❼ Operation Boondodge, War Zone D (November)

two-week campaign in August, seven army and marine battalions, aided by U.S. helicopters and military advisers, swept the Ca Mau Peninsula in search of enemy concentrations. In the first eleven days of the operation, government forces killed two hundred guerrillas and captured some thirteen tons of medical supplies and ammunition.

For Operation Morning Star in October, up to five thousand troops were used each day for a week against guerrilla units in Tay Ninh Province and in areas along the Cambodian border where the South Vietnamese government had not conducted military operations for several years. And in late November, some two thousand government troops, transported by more than fifty U.S. helicopters, launched Operation Boondodge, a full-scale attack against War Zone D. If American advisers were skeptical of the ultimate value of such large-scale conventional oper-

ations, they were heartened by the apparent willingness of the South Vietnamese command to take the war to the enemy.

The importance of the new American equipment in the offensive of 1962 can hardly be overemphasized. Especially in the Mekong Delta, where mile after mile of rice fields and canals made ordinary mobility impossible, helicopters and APCs made a crucial difference in hunting down the elusive Vietcong. There were problems of maintenance and reliability with the helicopters. The APCs were just as likely to get bogged down in the mud as speed through the flooded rice fields. But their deficiencies were at first less apparent than their considerable potential for destruction.

A September encounter sixty miles southwest of Saigon showed what could be done with the fast-tracked vehicles. Spotted by an observation

Saigon - 1962

Visit Saigon. Tourists still did in 1962. One traveler, on her way to the ancient Angkor Wat temple in Cambodia, asked a group of fellow Americans at a Saigon restaurant why so many Americans were on the streets. They said there was a war going on and the United States was helping the South Vietnamese. "A war? Really? Where?"

★ ★ ★

Saigon. Where's that? An American serviceman on leave in the States stood in an airport terminal on the way back to his base. A businessman noticed his uniform and asked where he was stationed. "Saigon," said the helicopter pilot. "Well," said the businessman, "you can thank your lucky star you're not out in that Vietnam."

★ ★ ★

No one knew Vietnam's cities by name in 1962. The three thousand Americans stationed in Saigon rarely made front-page news. They could go about their business in the relative calm of a famous capital in the Far East. By year's end ten thousand Americans would populate Saigon; more were on the way.

The Saigon a traveler saw in early 1962

wasn't too different from the colonial city of eight years earlier. When the French left, the tree-lined boulevards, public buildings, gardens, and squares remained to remind visitors why the town had once been called the "Paris of the Orient." The smells stayed with the sights. Seafood and Chinese and French cuisine were still renowned. Those with enough money still danced in the bars or listened to the singers in the clubs. The cafés endured as the place to have a drink and watch the beautiful Vietnamese women promenade down the Rue Catinat.

Then the Americans began to arrive in force. The streets seemed more crowded; the Americans in their sport shirts and slacks seemed to tower over the smaller Vietnamese. The streets also teemed with others: "pickpockets, moneychangers, whores, instant dentists who pull teeth for ten cents," one journalist remembered.

As the Americans poured in, the tempo of the city seemed to speed up. The sound on the street in French Saigon was the whir of bicycle wheels. Now hundreds, maybe thousands, of trucks and small Renault taxis (purchased in part with American aid) roared along the avenues. Motorbikes of all descriptions added to the chaos.

Like their French predecessors, the Americans frequented the bars and dance halls, but soon government action would end *that* colonial vestige. The Bill for the Protection of Morality, passed in early

summer, banned all dancing as "erotic, vain, and degrading." Foreigners "come here not to dance ... but to help Vietnamese fight communism," said Madame Nhu, the law's major supporter. "Dancing with death is sufficient." The law brought relative quiet to some of the clubs.

The war was never far away. Sometimes it was just a dull thump in the distance or an occasional flash in the night sky. Sometimes it was a report of Americans kidnapped or ambushed on the outskirts of the city. Hand grenades exploded in restaurants and homes in late summer. At Tan Son Nhut there were memorial services for the few Americans who had died in the field.

Still, it was a good time to be an American in Saigon. At the embassy and in the cafés U.S. officials talked optimistically about putting American know-how to work fighting communism. You could go to the American-run bowling alley or movie theater or attend a barbecue on top of one of the grand old hotels.

By fall Saigon was crowded with bars named "Texas," "21," "Miami," "Uncle Sam's," "California." France still dominated the shape of Saigon, but English began to supplant French on the streets. And in the little shops that crowded the central market you could find silk jackets with the words on the back: "When I die I'll go to heaven because I've spent my time in hell—Saigon 1961-1962." They were still laughing at the joke—in 1962.

The new ARVN aggressiveness of 1962 inevitably meant more casualties. These troops carry their wounded platoon leader out of the range of guerrilla fire after an unsuccessful attack on a Vietcong jungle camp.

plane and flushed into the open by ARVN infantry, two companies of guerrillas tried to escape across the paddies in shallow-draft sampans. In the past, this would have been the end of the day's hunt, another vain attempt to close with the enemy and destroy him. But this time things were different. Alerted by the observation plane, ten of the huge green APCs raced to the scene, running headlong into the fleeing Vietcong. Smashing through the sampans, the "ducks" swept whole boatloads of guerrillas under their steel treads, while army troops protected by heavy plating machine-gunned the survivors. The toll: 154 Vietcong killed, 38 captured, 12 government soldiers wounded.

More than anything else, however, it was the helicopter that altered the face of war in Vietnam. Helicopter operations began in December 1961 and quickly mounted in number. Between April and August 1962, the U.S. Marine helicopter squadron stationed at Soc Trang executed fifty combat assaults, flew 4,439 sorties, and made approximately one hundred thirty different landings against Vietcong opposition. The 93rd U.S. Army Helicopter Company, stationed at Da Nang, flew more than a hundred missions a week on transport service to and from mountain outposts in the northern provinces.

Helicopters dropped Special Forces teams deep into enemy-held territory, set radio masts into normally inaccessible paddies, carried sentry dogs on intelligence missions, and returned valuable para-chutes to repacking stations. During Operation Morning Star in October, Americans flying UH-1A helicopters armed with jury-rigged .30-caliber machine guns and 2.75-inch rockets made the first helicopter gunship attack of the war. Within months a new "Huey," the UH-1B, was in the air over Vietnam armed with four M60 machine guns and forty-seven rockets, more firepower, noted one chopper commander, than a battalion of artillery.

"We are being overrun"

Fearsome as they were to the terrified Vietcong, the American helicopters were not invulnerable. As early as April there were already regular reports of helicopters returning from patrols nicked by guerrilla gunfire. In July one of the ships of the 93rd Division was shot down near the Laotian border with three Americans killed. But by then, though it generated few headlines back in the states, Americans were dying all over Vietnam.

In a jungle clearing outside the village of An Chau during the first week of April, four Americans led by Staff Sergeant Wayne E. Marchand of Platsmouth, Nebraska, and Specialist 5th Class James Gabriel of Honolulu, Hawaii, had bivouacked for the night with thirty-one Vietnamese volunteers they were training in guard techniques and patrolling. Across a narrow river the long grass rustled in the darkness. What sounded like a dog's bark echoed in the night and,

The Three Wars

American military advisers in Vietnam quickly discovered that there was no such thing as *the* Vietnam War. There were, instead, at least three wars underway in the South Vietnamese countryside, each with its own terrain, its own set of adversaries, and its own tactical imperatives.

Most alien of all to the Americans, perhaps, was the watery world of the Mekong Delta, a flat expanse of rice fields crisscrossed by irrigation canals and the tributaries of the Mekong River. Most of the people of the delta lived in villages clustered along the sides of the canals. Travel was almost wholly by river boat and sampan, making rapid movement difficult if not impossible for the ARVN 7th Division, which spearheaded government operations in the area.

Lack of mobility was not the only problem. During the French Indochina War the delta had been a stronghold of the Vietminh, and even after 1954 the region—including the jungles of the Ca Mau Peninsula—had remained under Vietminh influence. Saigon had never been able to overcome the guerrillas' de facto control of many areas or win a majority of the peasants to the government cause.

By late 1961 the Vietcong were estimated to have seven to eight thousand regular force soldiers in the delta, an equal number of regional troops, plus a large number of part-time guerrillas. Operating out of bases located in all but impenetrable mangrove swamps, in isolated forests, and in uninhabited sections of the coast, the VC were able to move around the delta almost at will. Hunting them down or even locating them was, in the words of one American observer, "like trying to identify tears in a bucket of water."

North of Saigon, in the mountain plateau of the central highlands, a different sort of war was underway. "To seize and control the highlands," observed Vietminh General Vo Nguyen Giap dur-

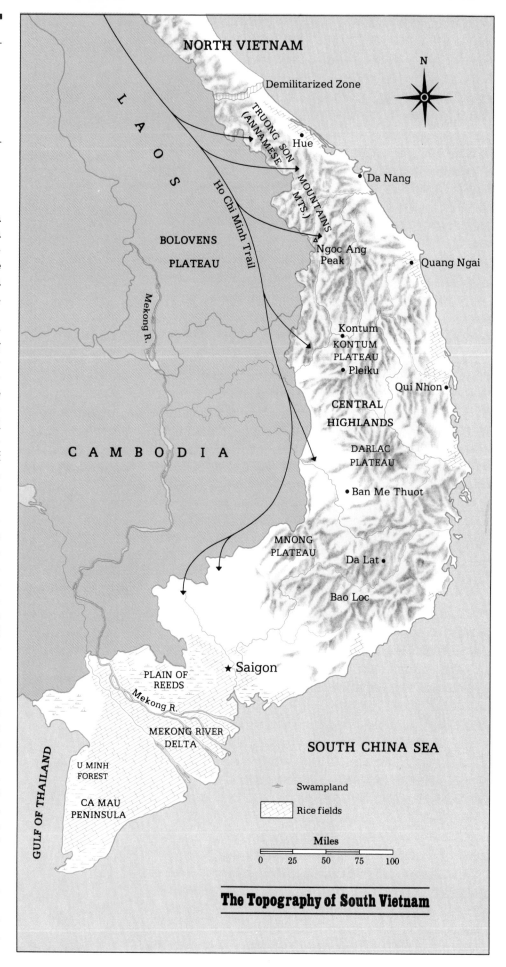

The Topography of South Vietnam

from a different direction, a rooster crowed. Then, at the sound of a bamboo tocsin, Vietcong rifle fire split the darkness. Gabriel's men repulsed the first attack, but shortly after daybreak the guerrillas rushed their position in force. Cradling a Tommy gun in one hand, "phoning and shooting and changing clips all at the same time," as a Vietnamese remembered afterwards, Gabriel radioed desperately for help: "Emergency, emergency . . . we are under attack . . . we are encircled." The first wave of VC broke through the outer defense perimeter; the second wiped out the seven-man flanking squad. Wounded twice but still firing, Gabriel managed a final message: "Completely encircled by enemy . . . ammunition expended . . . we are being overrun."

Two of the Americans were captured by the guerrillas and held for three weeks before being released. Gabriel and Marchand were not as lucky. Wounded during the attack, they were carried two miles and then each killed by a bullet in the face. During 1962 thirty-one Americans died in hostile action.

What distressed many Americans in Vietnam as much as the slowly mounting casualties was the special brutality of the war in which they were engaged: Vietcong prisoners summarily executed; torture employed as a commonplace device of interrogation; women and children burned to death by napalm; villages put to the torch for no other reason than their location in guerrilla territory; and increasing numbers of "suspects" routinely rounded up and sent to Diem's infamous "reeducation" camps. On the Vietcong side, the kidnappings of village officials and the assassination of villagers inclined toward the Saigon regime continued at a rate of nearly 200 a month, a reign of terror denounced by President Kennedy for its "deliberate savagery" and "wanton violence."

Saigon's year

These were but small shadows, however, in what seemed an otherwise bright picture of progress. The average weekly number of operations mounted by each of the eight ARVN divisions had increased during the year from one to four. In Washington the Defense Department reported that casualties were running at the rate of five Communists to every three GVN soldiers killed or wounded. Stepped-up training was supplying the ARVN with more officers and NCOs, while the troops themselves had benefited from the antiguerrilla instruction provided by the American advisers. Where once most Vietcong village intrusions had been accepted passively, now in some areas there was real resistance.

Success on the battlefield also strengthened Saigon's determination to resist a political settlement with the insurgents. The neutralization of Laos and the institution of a coalition government during the summer of 1962 had encouraged Vietcong interest in a similar settlement. On July 20, the eighth anniversary of the signing of the Geneva accords, the insur-

ing the French war, "is to solve the whole problem of South Vietnam." Varying in elevation from about six hundred to over three thousand feet, the highlands stretched two hundred miles from Bao Loc in the south to the Ngoc Ang Peak on the Laotian border, averaging about one hundred miles in width.

Largely by-passed by the Vietnamese in their long drive south during the eighteenth and nineteenth centuries, the extensive mountain forests and flat farm land of the highlands had remained sparsely populated by some thirty tribes of primitive mountain people called montagnards by the French, among them the Rhade, the Jarai, and the Sedang. No outside military force could operate safely in the highlands without the cooperation of the tribes, and the Vietcong had shown themselves adept at recruiting the montagnards to their cause.

By the spring of 1962 seven Vietcong battalions were reported to be operating in the highland region. Against them stood the four divisions of the ARVN II Corps, intent on driving the insurgents back into the mountains and away from the populated lowlands. The key to the government's success would be prying the montagnards loose from Vietcong influence. Although resettlement efforts had begun, the issue remained very much in doubt.

From Da Nang north to the DMZ, the central plateau gave way to the rugged peaks of the Truong Son Mountains. In a steep wilderness of dense rain forest, plunging rivers, and tortuous ridges, soldiers of the ARVN I Corps had the almost impossible task of interdicting the increasing flow of men and arms from the North. Along the Laotian border the Vietcong carved out a growing number of "combatant villages," complete with dou-

ble-walled huts and tunnels extending hundreds of yards into the surrounding jungle. From these secure bases the guerrillas shielded the nearby Ho Chi Minh Trail, dominated the local Katu tribe, and threatened to establish a "liberated area" in the coastal rice fields of Quang Ngai Province.

With few roads on which trucks or artillery might move, and little in the way of air reconnaissance, the government contested Vietcong control over the region with scarcely more than a series of military outposts. Dug in among peaks rising to eight thousand feet, these isolated garrisons sent out daily patrols on reconnaissance and ambush missions. It was a deadly game of hide-and-seek, and the guerrillas—better adapted to the brutal terrain than the ARVN conscripts—steadily wore down the government forces.

In a war that knew no bystanders, a GVN soldier removes the charred corpse of a small child from the remains of a hut destroyed in a fire fight with insurgents.

gents called for the establishment of a government made up of representatives of "parties, sects, and groups belonging to all political tendencies, social strata and classes, religions and nationalities existing in South Vietnam," and the formation of a "neutral zone" comprising South Vietnam, Cambodia, and Laos. Backed by the United States, which wanted nothing to do with a similar plan put forth by Cambodian Prince Norodom Sihanouk, Diem refused to consider the insurgent proposals.

Even those sympathetic to the Vietcong, such as the Australian journalist Wilfred Burchett, admitted that "1962 must be largely credited to Saigon." The new mobility of the government troops, the establishment of the strategic hamlets, the extension of a government presence in regions previously under the undisputed control of the NLF, the influx of American advisers—all created grave and unexpected problems for the VC. "In terms of territory and population," concludes Burchett, "Diem made a considerable comeback in 1962." The Vietcong defection rate was up, its recruitment rate down. So severe did the pressure become that the NLF leadership came close to abandoning its bases in the delta and withdrawing to the mountains.

In a year-end review, the *Atlantic Monthly* magazine concluded that the Vietnamese armed forces could look to 1963 with "far more confidence than seemed likely a year ago." So decisive had been the impact of helicopters and armored troop carriers in the delta that the rebels could no longer take the risk of concentrating their forces for a sizable attack. In the central highlands the efforts of the American Special Forces teams had started a "chain reaction of resistance." ARVN operations had begun to push the Vietcong out of the lowlands and into the dwindling security of ever more remote bases. The Strategic Hamlet Program was "producing some excellent results," while joint Vietnamese–American operations like that in Phu Yen Province had all but destroyed the NLF's "firm political base among the mass of the people."

Official Washington was hardly less enthusiastic. As early as July Secretary of Defense McNamara told the American public that U.S. aid to South Vietnam had begun to tip the balance against the guerrillas. "Every quantitative measurement we have," asserted the secretary, "shows we're winning this war." General Maxwell Taylor, the newly designated chairman of the Joint Chiefs of Staff, echoed McNamara's assessment during his inspection trip to South Vietnam in August, and in September, Roger Hilsman claimed that American assistance had given the South Vietnamese the "new confidence" necessary for victory.

Some American military men in Vietnam were more circumspect. "We are now doing a little better than holding our own," was the cautious assessment of Harkins's deputy, Major General Charles Timmes. But Harkins himself was convinced that the Vietnamese had seized the initiative, a belief shared by one well-traveled adviser who saw the balance "beginning to swing in the government's favor."

Equally hopeful was Lieutenant Colonel Frank B. Clay, the son of General Lucius D. Clay of Berlin airlift fame, who in late 1962 was the American adviser to Colonel Huynh Van Cao's 7th ARVN Division. As the first rains of the winter monsoon began their regular afternoon downpour over his My Tho headquarters, Clay talked with an American reporter about the prospects for the months ahead.

"Mobility remains the key to improvement, of course, and with better maps and any kind of visibility the helicopters will still be able to operate part of the time during the rainy months down here," said the American adviser. "We've got some new plastic boats that are unsinkable and some armored personnel carriers on tracks that can get around in this terrain." Clay could visualize "all sorts of delightful operations," like a mobile water force supported and resupplied by helicopters conducting extended sweeps through the swamps. Yes, it ought to be a lot different in 1963. "I'm going home in a month," Clay added, almost wistfully, "but I almost wish I were starting my year of duty in Vietnam right now."

The bodies of Vietcong guerrillas litter the ground while their comrades huddle at the feet of their American and ARVN captors after a successful GVN operation.

Choppers

In the beginning they were a symbol of President Kennedy's commitment to the government of South Vietnam. In the end they became the symbol of the Vietnam War itself. Among all the new instruments of technological warfare introduced by the Americans in Vietnam, none proved so adaptable or so effective as the helicopter.

First brought to Vietnam in 1961, dual-rotor, banana-shaped CH-21s were designed to serve primarily as cargo and personnel carriers, a means of avoiding the frequently soggy roads and sabotaged canals that hindered travel throughout the country. Piloted almost exclusively by Americans, they hauled equipment and supplies, transported ARVN troops into battle, and taxied government officials into and out of even the most remote regions of the Mekong Delta and central highlands. They served other purposes as well.

Throughout the war helicopters would save countless lives in rescue and "medevac"—medical evacuation—missions. Their rapid mobility enabled them to pick up downed pilots quickly and to whisk wounded soldiers from battlefield to medical tent in minutes.

Left. U.S. pilots plot a course for combat. American helicopters manned by American crews ferried ARVN troops to battle zones at the outset of U.S. involvement. Later, the troops would be American too.

CH-21 helicopters, flown by American pilots and protected by American gunners, transport South Vietnamese troops on a mission against a Vietcong force near the Cambodian border in 1964.

Left. An American ground crew readies a UH–1A for action. Developments in weaponry transformed helicopters from transport vehicles into mobile assault systems—flying tanks, as it were.

Right. A helicopter crewman surveys the landscape of the Mekong Delta for signs of enemy movement. The helicopter crew's role was a perilous one: Before the commitment of regular U.S. combat troops in 1965, helicopter crewmen suffered the majority of U.S. casualties.

UH–1B "Hueys" lift off after depositing South Vietnamese troops in swampy terrain for an Eagle Flight operation in the Mekong Delta. Helicopter assaults against areas of suspected enemy activity became a principal allied tactic.

Right. South Vietnamese soldiers hurry a wounded comrade to a waiting "medevac" helicopter.

U.S. Marines and ARVN troops unload supplies from a helicopter under enemy fire.

It was not until the arrival of the first in a series of UH-1 helicopters, or "Hueys" as they came to be called, that other, more directly tactical applications were made. In spite of their reduced load capacity, the turbine-powered, single-rotor "choppers" were both faster and more maneuverable than the large, lumbering CH-21s. Equipped with sixteen rocket mounts and four machine-gun brackets, they could be used as assault weapons in support of ground troops and as escorts for the more vulnerable troop carriers. Their relatively slow cruising speed, compared with fixed-wing aircraft, made them ideal for certain types of reconnaissance operations and allowed their crews to identify targets more easily in dense jungle terrain.

Despite their multiple advantages, helicopters were not without drawbacks as combat machines. With two open doors and virtually no protective armor, the Hueys left their passengers exposed to ground fire as they descended from the "safe" altitude of three thousand feet. The awkward CH-21s were even more vulnerable to attack. Both were also prone to mechanical failure, particularly during the early stages of the war when overuse and hot tropical air strained the limited horsepower of their engines. As the war progressed, so too did American technology and tactics. Bigger, faster, more powerful helicopters, like the CH-37 "Jolly Green Giant" and the CH-47 "Chinook," joined the ever-growing fleet. Capabilities varied, but from start to finish helicopters remained a principal weapon in the vast arsenal of the American military in Vietnam.

Even with improvements in speed and weaponry, helicopters continued to be vulnerable to hostile ground fire. Here a CH-46 plummets to earth in flames during Operation Hastings in July 1966.

Nation Within a Nation

He wasn't much to look at. Small, slight, wearing the same black pajamas as the peasants, on his feet a pair of crude sandals made from rubber tires. He fought mostly in small bands, with old rifles left from the war against the French or with homemade guns fashioned in jungle arsenals. He could live in a maze of tunnels or conceal his body with leaves and branches if he had to. He could hide in an irrigation canal for hours, breathing air through a bamboo tube, or march for days through the mountain jungles of the central highlands. He could turn a piece of metal pipe into a mortar, or an American howitzer shell into a mine. He had fought the Japanese and defeated the French, he had battled the ARVN and was willing to take on the Americans. He wasn't much to look at. But the small man in the black pajamas, the one they called Vietcong, turned out to be a difficult enemy to subdue.

The reasons for his durability lay partly in his own resilience and dedication, partly in a rigor-

ous military training and discipline, even more in the web of organizations and ideology that supported him. He was not just a guerrilla, after all, but a soldier of the People's Liberation Army, the military arm of the National Front for the Liberation of South Vietnam—the NLF.

By 1962 the front exercised some measure of control over most of the South Vietnamese countryside. In the "liberated areas" under complete NLF domination the front operated its own government, collected its own taxes, ran its own schools, trained its own army, and indoctrinated its own people with the precepts of a new Vietnam. Beyond his own toughness and experience, his capacity for killing, and his ability to endure, it was the strength of this nation within a nation that made the guerrilla so much more formidable than his appearance would suggest, and so much more dangerous to those who would stand in his way.

The front

The National Liberation Front emerged out of remnants of the Vietminh remaining in the South after the 1954 Geneva accords. Formed by Ho Chi Minh in 1941, the Vietminh had originally been a wartime coalition of Communist and nationalist groups that fought the Japanese, seized control of northern Vietnam in 1945, then waged an eight-year struggle against the French. Under the Geneva agreements, Vietminh forces operating south of the seventeenth parallel were to return to the North pending reunification elections scheduled for 1956. Most of them did so, but some of the native southerners regrouped into several former Vietminh base areas.

When Diem refused to let the elections take place, and instead began a systematic repression of all groups that had taken part in the Vietminh during the war, veteran Vietminh cadres initiated a new resistance movement and pressed Hanoi for support. In May 1959 the Central Committee of the North Vietnamese Communist party called for the overthrow of the Diem regime and the expulsion of the United States from Vietnam. Wide-scale fighting broke out in the South later that year, and in December 1960 a Cambodian radio broadcast announced the formation of the NLF.

One of the remarkable things about the NLF was its organizational sophistication. Between the outbreak of rebellion in late 1959 and the creation of the front in late 1960, an elaborate structure had been rebuilt on the earlier Vietminh organizational foundation. The ultimate governing body was the Central Committee, some of whose members composed an executive presidium responsible for military operations and foreign affairs, while others made up a secretariat in charge of domestic and political matters. The NLF divided South Vietnam into three interzones (plus a special Saigon-area zone), each of which was administered by an executive committee. Below the interzone commands were the zone, province, district, and village committees. Within the village framework there was also a variety of family, hamlet, and occupational associations (see chart, page 37).

During the twelve months of intense organizational activity preceding the formation of the NLF, the Vietminh veterans had drawn into their ranks elements of the Cao Dai and Hoa Hao religious sects, remnants of the Binh Xuyen gangsters, members of small nationalist and Socialist parties, as well as refugees from Diem's repression—disaffected peasants and dissenting intellectuals. At the first NLF Congress in February 1962, three political parties declared their affiliation with the front: the Democratic party, a middle-class Socialist group; the Radical Socialist party, a small collection of urban intellectuals; and the People's Revolutionary party, an avowedly Marxist-Leninist organization. It was at the February Congress also that the leadership of the NLF was first publicly announced.

The central individuals of the NLF during its early years were respectable middle-class intellectual and professional figures. Neither the president of the front, Nguyen Huu Tho, nor Secretary-General Nguyen Van Hien was a member of the Lao Dong (Communist) party apparatus. Of the five vice presidents on the Central Committee, one was a Communist and held his seat as such, Vo Chi Cong, the representative of the People's Revolutionary party. But the Central Committee was designed to reflect the diversity of classes, nationalities, religions, and organizations that had enlisted under the NLF banner and included among its ranks several Buddhist bonzes, Cao Daist leaders, a Catholic priest, and the chief of the Rhade montagnards.

References to "American imperialists" and American "monopolies" did give the NLF's ten-point program a somewhat Marxist cast, but the manifesto was principally concerned with the overthrow of the Diem government and the establishment of a neutralist regime in the South, the enactment of a broad range of social and economic reforms, a general amnesty for political prisoners, and the ousting of U.S. military advisers from Vietnam. The front's program envisioned the eventual reunification of the country, but in a "gradual" and "peaceful" fashion through "negotiations and discussions" and "on the basis of the aspirations and interests of all sections of the people of South Vietnam as well as the people of North Vietnam."

The party

It would be a mistake, then, to see the early NLF as nothing more than a Communist front, wholly directed by the North for its own interests. Its leadership was southern, its program reflected southern concerns, and these would not soon disappear. It is also true, however, that the Communists very quickly

came to dominate the NLF. The vehicle of that domination was the People's Revolutionary party.

The PRP was founded on January 15, 1962, as the successor to the southern branch of the Lao Dong party, a founding member of the NLF. The new party made no attempt to conceal its Communist identity or its objectives: independence, reunification, and social reorganization along "Socialist-Communist principles." Neither did it pretend to be merely an equal partner with other NLF organizations. The party referred to itself as the "vanguard" and "steel frame" of the NLF and quickly assumed a decisive role in its affairs.

The PRP operated much the same as the Communist parties of China or the Soviet Union, providing political education and leadership at every social and administrative level. Douglas Pike, the leading American authority on the NLF, describes the front as a "broad-based pyramid with the villages at the bottom and the Central Committee at the top," and the PRP as a "thinner and

NLF President Nguyen Huu Tho, at the microphone, leads a salute at a front convention. During the French Indochina War, Tho (also shown above) had been imprisoned for demonstrating against the U.S. supplying of the French.

harder core pyramid within, but also rising from base to apex."

In the villages, party cadres operating out of three-man cells and hamlet branch groups created and directed a variety of administrative and liberation associations. In the military units and at district and provincial headquarters of the NLF, they coordinated military and administrative machinery toward the accomplishment of the political goals established by the front. The use of overlapping committee membership—the Central Committee at each level composed in part of top-ranking leaders from the level just below—insured a high degree of party integration. The "single contact member," a party cadre placed covertly by the interzone Central Committee at all party levels from zone to hamlet branch, assured continuing intraparty surveillance. Taking the leading role in front administration at every organizational level, maintaining at the same time a tight organizational network of its own, with ultimate authority over all military and political activities, the PRP was, in short, the hidden government of the NLF.

The United States cited the existence of the People's Revolutionary party as proof of Hanoi's direct control of the National Liberation Front. For its part the PRP denied that it had any official relationship with the North other than the "fraternal ties of communism"; and publicly, Hanoi treated the PRP as a purely indigenous southern political organization. In fact, the relationship between the northern Communists and the PRP was very close.

When an attempted coup d'état against the Saigon government in 1960 suggested widespread disaffection within the South Vietnamese army, Hanoi ordered the creation of the NLF in hopes of capitalizing on the expected collapse of the Diem regime. A year later Hanoi replaced the old Lao Dong party of the South with the PRP, in part to insulate itself from charges of control over the front. But Lao Dong members assumed leadership positions in the new party, and a Lao Dong document described the creation of the PRP as "a necessary strategy required within the party and to deceive the enemy. The new party must maintain the outward appearance of separation from the Lao Dong."

The PRP remained subordinate to the Central Office of South Vietnam (COSVN), established in October 1961 as the successor to the Nambo Regional Committee, which had directed Communist affairs in the South since the early 1950s. Led by members of the Lao Dong party of North Vietnam, COSVN was linked directly to the North Vietnamese Politburo through the National Reunification Department of the Lao Dong party. In 1963 Hanoi created the Committee for the Supervision of the South, which took over responsibility for the administration of the PRP.

The relationship between the NLF and North Vietnam, however, was more complex and ambiguous than these developments suggest, especially during the early years of the front's existence. Hanoi considered what was happening in the South to be part of the larger Vietnamese revolution, which had been going on since the end of World War II. According to Ho Chi Minh the revolutionary task in the North was to transform the Socialist state into a Communist order. The situation in the South was not as far advanced, however, and the revolutionary task there was different. Between the Vietnamese of the North and South there could be moral support and unity of purpose, but each region had its own task to accomplish and should not look to the other to do its work for it.

When the American-supported ARVN offensives of 1962 resulted in significant leadership losses among NLF cadres, Hanoi did provide some trained northern replacements to take up the slack and continued to funnel regrouped Vietminh veterans back into the South—approximately thirteen thousand five hundred in the period 1961-63. But material aid from the North prior to 1964 was minimal. Hanoi was concerned during these years to build up a self-sufficient southern movement, leaving Communist influence over the front in the hands of the largely southern PRP.

Over the years the PRP provided the NLF with a notable degree of internal cohesion. The credit for this accomplishment can be divided equally between the party's impressive organization and the quality of its membership. The thirty-five thousand cadres who composed the party in 1962 were held to high standards of dedication, militance, and activity. Usually a native of the village where he worked, a party cadre was assigned full time to either an administrative committee or a liberation association, but the enormous range of his responsibilities is suggested by a partial list of the topics considered at one district cadre meeting:

Consolidate the intelligence network. ... Provide leadership for the guerrillas in the armed struggle and train them in combating airborne helicopter tactics. ... Work with youth groups. ... Instigate greater sabotage efforts. ... Hold meetings to discuss shortcomings and errors of members of the struggle movement. . . . Improve party relations with the front organizations. . . . Motivate the peasants and solve all their personal problems. . . . Encourage young men to increase agricultural production. . . . Gain the support of religious groups. . . . Start new indoctrination sessions for party members.

The burden of the revolution rested more heavily upon the shoulders of the party cadres than on anyone else, and NLF documents were filled with complaints of "lack of leadership capacity" among the cadres, "wrong ideology" and "wrong concepts about lines of action and policies," inability to plan organizational action, and even illiteracy. The impressive thing is not that so many fell short of the superhuman standards that were set for them, but that during the early years of the war so many of them continued to persevere.

Backed by the moral and technical support of the North, provided with the mass political organization of the NLF, able to call upon thousands of dedicated and committed party workers, the PRP set out to undermine the Saigon government and to effect the social revolution of the countryside. The key to the accomplishment of both tasks was neither guns nor manifestoes, but the conceptually sophisticated, ideologically refined mechanism of propaganda.

Political struggle

"Good or bad results in our Revolution," read an early PRP cadre directive, "depend on whether agitprop activity to educate and change the thinking of the masses is good or bad." The task of ideological indoctrination—what the NLF called agitprop (agitation-propaganda)—was not merely a part of the process of revolution, it was at the center of revolutionary activity.

The front was not interested in mouthing tired slogans in front of bored peasants, a frequent American complaint with the Saigon government's propaganda operation. They wanted commitment to the cause, and that could come only through intense education

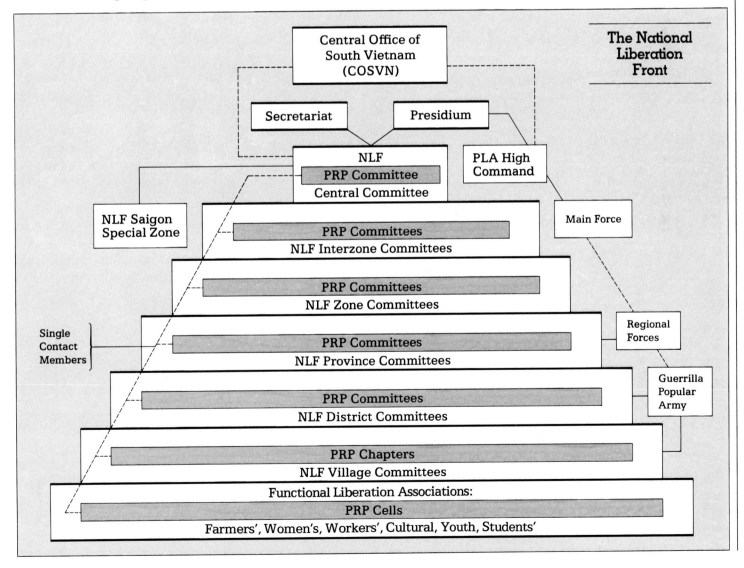

and indoctrination. NLF cadres looked first to individual contact as the principal medium of both covert and overt propaganda, but recognizing the power of ritual and social pressure, agitprop cadres also placed great reliance on such mass psychological techniques as rallies, demonstrations, parades, group criticism, neighborhood gatherings, and work meetings. The visit of an agitprop team to a Vietnamese village—with its speeches, singing, group meetings, question periods, and dramatic skits on revolutionary themes—was a meticulously conceived and carefully executed vehicle of social persuasion.

The mass of the peasantry could not be expected to understand the Marxist-Leninist analysis, but they could be imbued with the "proper spirit" of hatred for the enemy, sympathy with the purpose and method of the revolution, and confidence in the capabilities of the NLF. Most important, according to front directives, it was "necessary to change the attitude of the masses from a passive one to a desire to struggle strongly, to take part more and more violently to win their rights for survival."

The ultimate goal of agitprop work—indeed of all NLF activity—was to so develop the revolutionary consciousness of the Vietnamese masses that at one great moment they would spontaneously emerge from their villages to seize power under the banner of the National Liberation Front. This was the great myth of the front during the early years, the belief in *Khoi Nghia*, the General Uprising. The road to the General Uprising lay not through compliant acceptance of NLF doctrine, however, but through direct action against the South Vietnamese government.

There were several forms such action could take. The most important during the early days of the war was "political struggle." For the NLF, the revolution was not primarily a contest of arms but a contest of political allegiance. Actions that would throw into sharper relief the failures of the government, lower the morale of local government administrators, and mobilize civilian opposition to the GVN were at least as valuable as ambushing a government patrol or capturing a government outpost. Political struggle could be as simple as a village "misery-telling meeting," during which peasants had the opportunity to complain to each other about corrupt officials, or as large as a demonstration of ten thousand people at the provincial capital. The front organized rallies at country crossroads, held petition campaigns, staged celebrations of NLF victories, and provoked demonstrations at government offices and military bases.

Front cadres looked for any opportunity to initiate a local struggle movement. The theft of chickens by patrolling government soldiers might start a petition drive to end ARVN harassment. The body of a peasant woman killed by government shelling might be brought to a district marketplace in hopes of sparking a spontaneous demonstration. Neither the Diem regime nor its successors were able to come up with a coherent response to the struggle movement, leaving local officials to cope with the demonstrations as best they could. But few village headmen or district chiefs had the experience or capacity to turn such well-organized hatred to the government's benefit. Poor in arms but rich in the grievances of a beleaguered people, the NLF waged an unremitting political struggle against the Saigon government hoping to achieve through such "creative disorder" what they could not yet accomplish by military means: the destruction and collapse of the Diem regime.

The violence program

It wasn't Vietcong political agitation that most Americans were reading about during 1962 and 1963, however, but Vietcong terror. Yet to the NLF, violence was useful only to the extent that it supported the political struggle. In general the NLF leadership put a relatively low priority on the violence program, employed terror selectively, clothed it in legalistic forms, and claimed to exercise a strict economy of force.

There can be no denying, however, that political terrorism was a fundamental ingredient of NLF strategy. It has been estimated that in 1959 one government official or government supporter was killed every other day. By 1962 there were nine thousand kidnappings and seventeen hundred assassinations per year. In 1963 the rate of kidnappings decreased somewhat, but assassinations climbed to more than three a day.

Nor was the use of terror as selective or restrained as NLF propaganda declared. Vietcong terror squads infiltrated major cities to bomb markets and movie theaters. They hurled grenades into crowded cafés and other public places, leaving behind other bombs to kill medical personnel rushing to the aid of the victims. Outside urban areas violence fed by the desire for revenge, by the need to intimidate, and by the personal excesses of individual cadres helped transform the South Vietnamese countryside into a landscape of fear.

• The VC stop a Catholic priest at a roadblock near Kon-

In wet lowland areas like the Mekong Delta, rivers and canals often provided the guerrillas their only means of transport and attack.

Below. The image of revolutionary camaraderie was vigorously promoted by the NLF. The front was aware that it was not merely ideological conviction but also carefully nurtured esprit de corps *that* sustained the young peasants making up the ranks of the Vietcong.

Seemingly harmless paths often harbored lethal surprises. Here two young NLF followers ready a log studded with bamboo spikes, connected to a trip wire running across a well-worn trail.

tum, drag him from his car, drive bamboo spears through his body, then shoot him through the head.

• The chief of a village in Vinh Long Province protests the visits of a VC agitprop team. His son is kidnapped, the old man is executed.

• A hamlet chief in a delta village has been collecting taxes and registering young men for the draft. One night the Vietcong arrive, tie him to a stake in the center of the marketplace, and force his pregnant wife and his child to watch with other villagers as the VC slowly disembowel her husband. The child is then decapitated, the widow tied to the same stake and disemboweled.

Violence, according to front directives, was used to "destroy collaborators, villains, secret police agents, and spies," to intimidate recalcitrant villagers, and to suppress representatives of the traditional culture such as teachers and priests. But the primary use of terror was to destroy the government's administrative infrastructure. Directing their attacks against the very best and the very worst officials, they systematically wiped out an entire class of Vietnamese villagers.

By 1964 the rate of political violence had de-creased sharply as fewer and fewer local officials offered active resistance. By then, too, the NLF's confidence in a purely "political" victory had waned, and Vietcong assassination squads gave way to the much greater violence of the front's regular military force, the People's Liberation Army.

The armed struggle

The fighting forces of the PLA were divided into three categories. At the hamlet and village level was the paramilitary Guerrilla Popular Army, the part-time guerrillas who would plow their fields by day and blow up a bridge at night. Operating at the squad and platoon level (twelve to forty-eight men), these local units maintained village self-defense, set small ambushes, sabotaged roads, and provided supplies and intelligence to the regular guerrilla forces.

Serving at the district and province level, Regional Force companies (seventy-five to one hundred and fifty men) were better trained and armed and more mobile than the village soldiers. Regional units were expected to have "more political and class awareness" than the Popular Army guerrillas and to take part in the armed struggle at a higher level of violence: attacking strategic hamlets and small convoys on their own, or acting as a screening force for regular unit operations.

The Main Force battalions (two hundred and fifty to five hundred men) were the elite military units of the Vietcong. Highly trained, thoroughly indoctrinated, able to handle a variety of weapons, Main Force soldiers provided the NLF with the military strength to engage the regular units of the Saigon government. While accurate estimates are difficult to obtain, by mid-1963 there were perhaps ten to fifteen thousand Main Force and Regional Force soldiers and twenty to thirty thousand Popular Army guerrillas fighting in South Vietnam.

The People's Liberation Army—both regular and local forces—had two distinguishing characteristics. It was a guerrilla army engaged in revolutionary war, and it was an ideological army engaged in political struggle. Revolutionary war was a doctrine developed by Mao Tse-tung, Vo Nguyen Giap, and others that began with the assumption that at the beginning of such a war the revolutionary forces are weaker than the enemy. To achieve victory they must survive long enough for the reactionary forces to be worn down. During the early phases of revolutionary war,

the only operational mode that made sense was the guerrilla warfare of surprise and harassment, ambush and sabotage.

At the same time, the PLA was a highly politicized fighting force. The NLF regarded the military effort primarily in terms of support for the political struggle and insisted that military operations be subordinated to political activities. Even Main Force battalions spent only a few days a month on military missions. Much of the remainder of their time was devoted to indoctrination sessions, agitprop activity, and general propaganda work among the civilian population.

Each PLA unit received operational instructions from the appropriate political committee to which it was responsible (see chart, page 37). To insure a close integration of military and political efforts, PLA representatives sat at all committee levels, while the PRP-supervised Political Bureau assigned political commissars to all Main Force and Regional Force units. To guarantee the authority of the political arm, the political commissar of each unit simultaneously held the rank of chairman of the next highest political committee, thus outranking his military counterpart.

Like the PRP, the PLA received its ultimate instructions from North Vietnam. The senior military officers of COSVN were members of the North Vietnamese

A bullet-torn picture of President Diem and casualties of a battle with the VC litter a village in the Ca Mau Peninsula. The price for Saigon's determination to regain the long-held insurgent area was paid in blood by isolated ARVN garrisons and the frightened inhabitants of government hamlets.

army's high command. Several high-ranking North Vietnamese generals occupied leadership roles, including Major General Tran Van Tra, a member of the Central Executive Committee of the Lao Dong party, who was sent south in the early 1960s as deputy commander of COSVN, and General Tran Do, a veteran political commissar of many North Vietnamese units.

It was Mao Tse-tung who first insisted on close party supervision over every element of revolutionary war, and it was Mao who described for the guerrilla warrior the essence of his task: "When engaging a stronger enemy ... withdraw when he advances; harass him when he stops; strike him when he is weary; pursue him when he withdraws." It was on the basis of this Maoist dictum that the military forces of the NLF conducted their armed struggle during the early years of the Vietnam War.

Their primary tactic was the ambush. Carefully rehearsed, sometimes for weeks in advance, the Vietcong set elaborate traps often involving as many as four separate detachments: one pinning down the quarry, the second moving up for hand-to-hand combat, a third unit set to ambush reinforcements, and a fourth covering the retreat of the others. Ambushes were classic hit-and-run operations, useful also for their psychological effect. Attacks on strategic hamlets or government outposts were often staged solely to lure a relieving column into a trap. After one or two such experiences, most ARVN or Civil Guard detachments became much more timid in responding to calls for help.

The guerrillas engaged in other types of operations with primarily psychological value, such as mounting harassing fire on strategic hamlets or seizing and holding a village or military installation on the anniversary of a prominent front victory. But the NLF was also interested in more tangible returns for its military efforts: It launched military assaults on ARVN posts to capture weapons or supplies or dynamited railroad trains to destroy military cargo and disrupt the transportation network.

As their numbers grew and they began to substitute captured machine guns and other automatic weapons for old French rifles and homemade grenades, the VC adjusted the scope of their operations. By early 1964 the PLA was mounting multibattalion assaults against government units and installations, displaying a new level of firepower and a new willingness to stand and fight. But they would never abandon the guerrilla tactics that had won them their

first victories nor soon forget the central teaching of their Chinese master: "Without a political goal, guerrilla warfare must fail," wrote Mao, "as it must if its political objectives do not coincide with the aspirations of the people. The moment this war disassociates itself from the masses of the people is the precise moment that it disassociates itself from the hopes of ultimate victory."

The landscape of liberation

What the Americans called the Vietcong was not merely a political organization—the National Liberation Front; or a group of guerrillas—the People's Liberation Army. What the Americans called the Vietcong was also the attempt to bring a social revolution to the Vietnamese countryside.

Vietnam begins with the village, and the village begins with the land. The NLF seized upon the issue of land before all else and turned every social and political question back to the land: The GVN represented the rich landlords; the strategic hamlet was a device to cheat the farmers out of what land they had; U.S. military bases had been built on land confiscated from the peasants. Much more important, they followed up on earlier Vietminh land redistribution with a three-point land policy of their own.

Once a village had fallen under VC control, front cadres moved swiftly to confiscate the land of rich landlords, purchase land from well-to-do peasants, and distribute it to poor peasants at no cost. Previous titles of absentee landlords were swept aside, their properties ceremoniously parceled out to the tenants who worked the land themselves. Even in areas where the Diem land distribution program had taken effect, most of the peasants welcomed the front's efforts. Ngo Thi Meo, a sixty-seven-year-old resident of a Mekong Delta village, described what happened in her hamlet when the NLF arrived:

They went from house to house, telling people to hand over the land certificates they had received from the government. These were burned. Then the cadres explained, "The land belongs to the front, not to Diem. Now people can continue farming and owning the land without the permission of the Saigon lackeys." Some of the people were worried, but most were in favor of the cadres because there were four more years of payments to be made on the land.

The NLF did not challenge the idea of individual ownership of land, arguing internally that the

Vietcong equipment was often ingeniously simple, like these perfume bottle lamps shaded by leaves that light the guerrillas' paths during night attacks.

long-time slogan "Land for the tillers" must be ful-filled "in accordance with existing circumstances and requirements of the revolution." The front was not yet prepared to risk alienating the better off peasants. At the same time, it remained committed to the goal of collectivization. If existing conditions did not permit the organization of the peasants "or the collective mode of doing business on a large scale and under perfect forms," this did not mean that cadres could not organize "new modes of doing business that bear a collective character."

One of the keys to the success of the front's early efforts to reshape the social landscape of the villages was the long tradition of communal life in rural Viet-nam. For centuries the Vietnamese village had been a largely autonomous political and social unit, collec-tively responsible for the behavior and well-being of its members. Life within the village revolved around such communal activities as the maintenance of dikes and canals, collective religious observances, and a variety of village associations for mutual assistance. One hundred years of French colonial rule had un-dermined the communal social bonds that had held the villages together, and the Diem regime had little success in reversing this pattern of social disruption. By offering the peasants a set of communal arrange-ments in tune with time-honored village values, the NLF was able to win their support as it superimposed a new ideological framework on the traditional col-lectivism of the Vietnamese countryside.

The new collective mode was apparent in the re-constituted village councils, in the voluntary labor brigades, and especially in the liberation associ-ations. Of the six liberation associations—farmers', women's, youth, workers', students', and cultural—the first three were the most prominent, and the Farmers' Liberation Association by far the most important.

Claiming 1.8 million members in 1963, the FLA was simultaneously an engine of revolution, a forum for political indoctrination, and an exercise in collective leadership. The NLF looked to make the Vietnamese farmer the "master of the countryside" through the development of his "revolutionary struggle capability." Members of the FLA did propaganda work among other villagers and took part in struggle movements. They also engaged in a number of cooperative endeavors: organizing the collective work of maintaining irrigation ditches, distributing labor at harvest times, arbitrating land disputes among their members, and distributing the burden of the front's tax on rice.

The Women's Liberation Association, because it broke with traditional Asian attitudes about the secondary place of women in society, also proved a potent political instrument for the front. WLA members issued appeals and manifestoes, participated actively in the political struggle movement, and made a serious effort to develop class consciousness among village women. But the long-range significance of the Women's Liberation Association was its ideology of female equality. "If women do not participate in the Revolution," declared one NLF document, "it will fail.

Three Weeks with the Vietcong

by Georges Penchenier

En route to China on February 13, 1964, the French journalist Georges Penchenier made a detour to a Vietnamese rubber plantation in Phuoc Tuy Province. But before he reached the plantation, he was captured by the Vietcong. The following is Penchenier's description of his three-week captivity.

I was a prisoner, but once I reached the Vietcong camp, it was deluxe captivity. They had to decide whether I was a spy or a French journalist. If the latter were true, I would be an honored guest; if the former, I would have been killed.

The worst part of my ordeal was reaching the main camp. From noon on Thursday until 1:00 A.M. the following Tuesday, my captors forced me through exhausting marches and countermarches seemingly in no set direction. Sometimes they walked in circles to make me completely lose my bearings. We marched for five hours at midday, through the suffocating clamminess of the forest, and for five hours at night. In between we rested. We slept in cloth hammocks. My guards ate paddy rice without salt along with dried fish, which was so salty I couldn't get it down. I became so tired that I no longer bothered to take off my boots before crossing small streams and my feet were rubbed raw.

The Vietcong were perfectly adapted to the bush. Their sandals were made of old tires, enabling the men to cross running water without taking their shoes off and without having their feet blistered by wet socks. They wore no uniforms: only long, full-cut pants, shirts of any color, often a simple jersey. They used their indispensable scarf to mop themselves and as a protection against twigs and the ticks that continually rained from the tree tops: I killed twenty-seven ticks on my arms in one morning.

Their backpack was simple but practical: a deep sack with shoulder straps made of two tightly twisted scarfs. Inside the pack was everything necessary to provision a team on the move, which is to say nothing more than rice and dried fish. There were three other essentials: a hammock, a light blanket, and a piece of nylon. When the nylon was suspended between two trees, it kept off the rain and allowed the Vietcong to defy the tropical insects.

Another essential piece of equipment was the American cloth belt. From it hung, besides cartridge clips and pouches, a surgical dressing case, a lantern, a good old 1945-issue American canteen, one or two grenades, and finally, a long multipurpose machete.

When the Vietcong marched at night the forest seemed alive with fireflies. Each man held before him a lantern made of a plain pharmacy bottle, filled with gas and a wick, mounted on a spring, fed through the socket. A leaf placed in the palm of the hand prevented burns and at the same time acted as a reflector. Thus one saw them, like will-o'-the-wisps, a long procession of lights dancing through the trees, floating by without a sound, toward an unknown destination.

So equipped, not to mention their rifles and other arms, they could march for ten hours with fifty kilos (110 pounds) on their backs, keeping a rapid pace. Their mobility and autonomy were the primary reasons for the ease with which they escaped enemy attacks and encirclements. By carrying everything they needed for several days it was very simple for them to split up, to cross enemy lines like shadows, and then to regroup at distant, previously arranged locations.

I saw them operate only in the forest, the most perfect of hideaways. However, their methods of attack and withdrawal in the paddies must have been more or less the same. They hardly disturb a thing when they enter a village. The *canhas* (peasant huts) are normally built on six poles, three on one side and three on another. This allows them to hang their hammocks two by two, one above the other, so that they can sleep six to a *canha* without bothering the peasants, who, in the interim, sleep on the floor.

By contrast, when American or Saigon troops undertake a mopping-up operation, they can be seen from afar coming

... Further, a society cannot progress if female members are retarded."

The NLF did not always practice the equality it preached. The front employed women in such traditional female roles as nurses and cooks, and while many bore arms, many more carried ammunition or cultivated food for the soldiers. At the same time, the front maintained a strong prowoman stance in the male-dominated society of the Vietnamese village. Committed to liberating women from the "life of the water buffalo," the NLF channeled an untapped reservoir of energy into politically useful directions and set in motion a social idea as potentially revolutionary as the idea of the class struggle.

More militant than the FLA, more disciplined than the WLA, the Youth Liberation Association was doctrinally more hard-nosed and practically more demanding than the adult organizations. If older Vietnamese peasants could be induced to practice "new modes of doing business that bear a collective character," it was to the young men and women of rural Vietnam that the NLF looked for a wholesale repudiation of the social status quo. The only liberation association whose bylaws mentioned the Communist party by name, it was more concerned with revolutionary discipline than democratic rights. And while members of the YLA were expected to participate in propaganda work and political struggle, they were

across the dikes. They advance slowly, burdened by their equipment, and upon arrival throw the peasants out of their homes, a practice that further complicates their relations. Should there be insurgents in the area, they would have plenty of time to escape across the paddies, lightly equipped and rapid as ever.

In the forest the Vietcong followed their own special paths rather than using routes that their enemy might possibly take. An ingenious defense system protected them from surprise. There were lethal traps ranging from poisoned bamboo lances driven into the ground at a sixty-degree angle to impale parachuters, down to small, sharp-edged points hidden under leaves, capable of piercing the thickest boot sole. There were also dugout animal traps and snares which, when tripped, catapulted and held their prey upside down, ten or twenty meters above the ground.

In a small, semicleared area of the forest stood a Vietcong training camp, consisting of several huts rendered invisible by the trees and a large barracks where the young guerrillas gathered to learn revolutionary songs and to finish their political and military instruction. The clearing measured about one hundred square meters. I lived within its limits for about twelve days. I was warned: "Beyond, there are traps for the indiscreet; and guns go off quickly. It would be regrettable, but. ..." With a few exceptions the weapons at the camp were quite rudimentary—a craftsman made wooden rifle butts from barrels found God only knows where. Munitions were precious.

From time to time, aircraft would fly over. On each occasion the same scenario was repeated: All fires were immediately extinguished, and the Vietcong hid anything that would stand out. At night the first to hear an airplane motor signalled to the others with a short cry, upon which lamps, cigarettes, and even the smallest fires were extinguished. Once the plane passed everything was relighted.

All this was done without a sound, each person knowing exactly what he was responsible for. They had really gotten into the habit of being silent. Their daily exercises were done silently, and even when I sneezed my guard's gestures told me that I might be heard. But by whom? And what harm could it do? Those kids did everything by self-discipline, without orders: I never heard one of them yell.

The vastness of the forest allowed the Vietcong to live almost in a closed circle. Rice was provided "by the taxpayers," which is to say by peasants in the open "liberated" areas. The Vietcong themselves rediscovered the agricultural methods of the mountain people, cultivating cassava, papayas, bananas, and tobacco in small clearings. Sometimes they caught stags and wild boars in their traps. There were even stories of elephants brought down in the deep pits.

They left the forest only when they had to, for it was their greatest protection. The forests of Vietnam are man-eaters. Nobody goes there for fun. It took a war for the Vietcong to take refuge there and to learn out of necessity the old methods of survival of the primitive tribes who had lived there before them in the remote past.

You would never know that the forest where I spent my three weeks is right next to the highway connecting Saigon to Cap St. Jacques. Regular troops hardly ever adventured in. The last sizable attack, according to the local NLF political secretary, had been undertaken in January 1963 by two thousand men supported by aviation. The government troops had been held at the forest edge for two days. When they finally crossed the forest, they lost fifty men. Eleven months later ARVN forces undertook a new operation but were repulsed without penetrating the forest.

Penchenier was released on March 7, after his captors confirmed that he was, in fact, a journalist. In his diary, he recounted his mixed emotions: "In honor of my departure, we feasted on Vietnamese chicken and rice, a sticky rice cake, and cassava. My escort of four led me away from the camp at nightfall, in order to keep me from getting my bearings. We walked in circles again, as we had when we came into the camp.

"After a three-day march I found my car again and it is in one piece. I stop over at the plantation: scotch and cigarettes, it is divine. It's the end of the adventure; but it's the beginning of another. Now I'm going to fall into the hands of the Saigon police, which is no joke either."

A former correspondent for the French newspaper Le Monde, *M. Penchenier reported on the Vietnam War for French television.*

specifically directed to the education of younger children and the advancement of guerrilla activities.

The message of revolution was further reinforced through compulsory political indoctrination and through a formal education program heavily larded with Marxist doctrine and revolutionary morality. By 1963 the NLF claimed fifteen hundred elementary and adult classes disseminating the front's political message. In the reading course, for instance, instructors were directed to teach words "that relate to daily work and our present revolutionary task, such as 'unity,' 'production,' 'struggle,' and so forth." Mathematics lessons "should be related to production, the economy, mutual assistance, and the contribution to the Revolution." And typical writing assignments included such themes as: "You participate in a successful struggle movement against a U.S.-Diem outpost. Describe and give your impressions. . . . Describe a May Day celebration in your village. . . . The barbarous U.S.-Diem have shot to death one of your compatriots. Subsequently you went to the victim's funeral. Describe your feelings. . . ."

Children of the people

The NLF began by giving the Vietnamese peasant what he wanted most—land. And in accepting the land the peasant accepted the sociopolitical framework the front imposed. He supported liberation associations because they too offered benefits that had not previously existed—economic improvement, equal rights, a sense of purpose, a bond of commonalty. And in accepting the liberation association he became further enmeshed in the world of the front.

Not every peasant was won to the blandishments of the Vietcong, however, nor did every recruit remain a committed partisan. Many who cooperated with the front did so out of fear, and many who willingly joined the military arm of the NLF came to resent the privations, the regimentation, and the failure of the NLF to deliver on its often extravagant promises of democracy, equality, and material well-being. Although it elicited considerable popular enthusiasm during the first years of the insurgency, the temporary setbacks of 1962 and the increasing demands the front was forced to make on the villages as American military intervention intensified eventually led to bitterness, anger, and disillusionment among the peasants.

At the same time, the positive appeal of the NLF was authentic and powerful. It extended beyond the twin inducements of patriotism and self-interest, beyond the heroic memories of the resistance against the French and the promise of a better life. As important as anything else was the capacity of the front to connect its new social world with a new emotional order.

With all the difficulties that the NLF faced in mobilizing the peasants in the service of the revolution, the greatest obstacle was psychological. Brought up in a society that demanded a high degree of emotional self-control and acquiescence to authority, the Vietnamese peasant had no effective way of dealing with oppression. "The masses think their lot is determined by fate," lamented one early PRP directive:

They do not see that they have been deprived of their rights. . . . They swallow their hatred and resentment or resign themselves to enduring oppression and terror, or, if they do struggle, they do so in a weak and sporadic manner.

The solution was a systematic encouragement of hatred. "To guide the masses toward the Revolution," declared a Central Committee directive, "the agitprop arm must make the masses hate the enemy." The promotion of hatred must be "permanent, continuous, and as directly related to the struggle movement as a man is to his shadow." Hatred would enable the peasants to overcome the chains of dependency that bound them to the government, to the landlords, to the westerners. Hatred would unify the village against the enemy. Hatred would release pent-up aggression for political purposes.

It was a daring experiment. For in conjuring up the genie of hatred the front ran considerable risks. The free expression of rage overturned the basis of the traditional patriarchal society and threatened a flood of anger difficult to contain. One means of control was to restructure social and economic relations in a more equitable fashion. Another was the device of political indoctrination. But hatred could finally be transformed into a creative political force only by the disciplined expression of mutual respect between the villagers and the cadres.

That many villagers came to trust the authority of the front more readily than the authority of the government was a continual source of mystery to most Americans in Vietnam. Yet, when asked why this was so, villagers consistently gave the same answer:

The Liberation cadres were nice to us . . . they behaved politely and nicely to the people . . . they talk to us in a friendly manner . . . they do not thunder at the people like the government soldiers. . . . The things that the people don't like about the government officials is their behavior . . . the Vietcong treat us well.

To peasants who rarely even saw government officials, who feared their arrogance and felt their disdain, the behavior of the front cadres was a revolution in itself. The oft-repeated NLF injunction to "live together, eat together, and work together" with the people was a recognition of necessity. Unlike GVN officials who believed that the peasants needed them, the NLF *knew* it could survive only with the active support of the people.

At the very beginning of their relationship, the Vietcong made it clear to the peasants that the guerrillas depended on the villagers for their survival. Once they had established their authority in the village, they regularly subjected themselves to the criticism of the people. By including the villagers in their circle of trust, the Vietcong encouraged the peasants to return that trust in kind. By accepting the criticism of the vil-

lagers, the Vietcong acknowledged that commitment to the front did not mean an unconditional surrender to authority.

During the years to come this new relationship would be severely tested. As regimentation and economic appropriation increased, as demands for ideological conformity became more insistent, as a generation of young men and women disappeared into the seemingly endless war, the peasants would grow weary of the new tyranny. But when the Americans first encountered him in the swamps of the Mekong Delta or the jungles of the central highlands, the pajama-clad soldier they called "VC" remained a figure of unexpected strength: strong in political organization, strong in ideological purpose, and strong in the support of the people. "The soldiers came from the people," remembered one cadre of those early years. "They were the children of the villagers. The villagers loved them, protected them, fed them. They were the people's soldiers. If the soldiers love the people, the people will love the soldiers in return."

Prior to 1963 Vietcong recruiters relied primarily on appeals to nationalism and youthful idealism, as these captured NLF propaganda pictures suggest. After 1963 they were forced to depend increasingly on conscription, abduction, and forcible indoctrination.

Into the Long Tunnel

In late December 1962, intelligence reports began coming into ARVN 7th Division headquarters
of heavy Vietcong concentrations in western
Dinh Tuong Province. Some two hundred men of
the Vietcong 514th Battalion, reinforced by local
guerrillas and equipped with three machine guns
and a dozen Browning automatic rifles, had
been located on the edge of the Plain of Reeds.
For the division's new commander, Colonel Bui
Dinh Dam, this would be the first opportunity to
send the 7th into battle under his direction. The
operation was scheduled for January 2. The
target area was just west of a small village
called Ap Bac.

No one was more pleased at the prospect of the
coming action than the division's senior American adviser, Lieutenant Colonel John Paul Vann.
For more than a year the continuing elusiveness
of the Vietcong had been a source of mounting
frustration to the U.S. military command. Ap Bac
would be the place for a traditional set-piece

A UH-1A helicopter salvages the remains of a sister ship downed by the VC during the battle of Ap Bac. Fourteen of fifteen helicopters taking part in the operation were hit by guerrilla gunfire.

battle in which government forces could bring to bear their vastly superior firepower. Ap Bac would certify the vaunted new aggressiveness of the South Vietnamese army. Ap Bac was the golden opportunity that everyone had been waiting for.

Shooting ducks

The plan of operation was straightforward and apparently sound. Infantry and Civil Guard battalions would advance on Ap Bac from the north and south. A company of M113 armored personnel carriers would attack from the west, with reserve forces available to back them up. The open rice fields to the east could be left unguarded. If the Vietcong tried to run,

Preceding page. An American crewman flees a helicopter downed by the Vietcong during action on the Ca Mau Peninsula. Disabled helicopters were routinely destroyed to prevent them from falling into enemy hands.

they would be easy targets for aircraft and artillery. Caught neatly inside the government's claw, the Vietcong moved from the village into a nearby tree line and dug in.

With the trap sprung, Vann and Colonel Dam decided to land the reserve force between the APCs and the tree line (see map, page 52). The first three helicopter lifts disembarked without incident, but as the fourth approached the landing site the guerrillas opened up with everything they had. Virtually motionless, the banana-shaped CH-21 troop carriers were helpless targets. Five went down, nine others were riddled with bullets.

"When those poor Vietnamese came out of the choppers, it was like shooting ducks for the Vietcong," said one American observer. Pinned down under a hail of fire, the soldiers burrowed into the mud of the paddies, refusing to continue the assault. Trying to rally the ARVN for a counterattack, Captain Kenneth Good, a West Pointer from Hawaii, was cut down in a burst of machine-gun fire. The soldiers stayed put.

Government forces shelled the tree line with artillery, and Vietnamese air force planes pummeled the guerrillas from the sky. Still the Vietcong held their positions. Colonel Dam ordered the company of M113s forward, but the commander of the mechanized unit, a Diem appointee, first refused to move, then spent four hours negotiating the one-mile stretch to the tree line. When the M113s finally arrived, they proved singularly inept. Cowering behind the downed helicopters, the gunners never raised their heads, their .50-caliber machine guns firing wildly into the sky. Instead of mounting a concerted assault, the APCs made only sporadic stabs at the tree line, allowing the Vietcong to concentrate their fire on one vehicle after another.

With his infantry pinned down and the APCs being picked off one by one, Colonel Dam ordered the two Civil Guard battalions to come up the tree line from the south. They should have been able to outflank the 514th and drive them from the safety of the trees. But the province chief, Major Lam Quant Tho, a political appointee with personal influence at the presidential palace, wouldn't allow them to budge. Three times during the day Dam ordered Tho to attack. Three times Tho refused.

The only hope now was to bring in an airborne battalion from Saigon. Knowing that the Vietcong would try to escape during the night, Dam and the Americans wanted the airborne troops to block the gap to the east. With that force in place, the combination of flares and artillery bombardment might keep the Vietcong bottled up until morning.

But IV Corps commander General Huynh Van Cao, who had already suffered more casualties than he had bargained for, ordered the airborne battalion deployed to the west, behind the reserve force. As Vann said later of Cao's decision: "They chose to reinforce defeat rather than to try for victory." Ironically, when the airborne unit landed at dusk it became engaged in a fire fight with the remnants of the reserve force.

During the night the Vietcong escaped, but the nightmare hadn't ended. When ARVN troops advanced into Ap Bac the next morning, Major Tho began firing artillery toward the village. By the time the barrage ended, five government soldiers had been killed and fourteen wounded. Meanwhile the Vietcong continued to flee south. Civil Guardsmen sent to block the escape route disappeared. Desperate to

"Victory at Ap Bac" proclaims this NLF postage stamp commemorating a Vietcong triumph, the worst GVN defeat since the introduction of American advisers and equipment in late 1961.

salvage something from the wreckage, Colonel Vann commandeered every American in the vicinity—advisers, maintenance personnel, cooks, communications men, even a water purification specialist—and with his motley force of irregulars rounded up thirty-two prisoners.

It was the only positive result of the whole sorry affair. The golden opportunity at Ap Bac had turned to ashes in a battle that revealed all the small and large failings of the South Vietnamese army obscured by the renewed military activity of 1962, a battle that displayed the vulnerability of the American equipment the ARVN had come to rely upon so heavily, a battle that demonstrated as well the growing gap between the official optimism of MACV in Saigon and the grim reality of the war on the ground.

Two hundred Vietcong guerrillas armed with a few machine guns and automatic weapons had soundly thrashed two thousand government soldiers backed by artillery, APCs, and air power, killing sixty-eight and wounding one hundred more. Among the dead were three Americans. Vietcong losses were estimated at no more than twelve. Yet the U.S. military command in Saigon refused to admit the dimensions of defeat—refused even to admit defeat. "We've got them in a trap," General Harkins reported after the Vietcong had escaped, "and we're going to spring it in half an hour."

Out in the field, the U.S. verdict was much more savage. "A miserable damn performance, just like it always is," Vann fumed. Under tremendous pressure the guerrillas had maintained battlefield discipline and continued to fire with deadly accuracy. "The

Vietcong were brave men," one American pilot said. "My God, we got a fix on one machine-gun position and made fifteen aerial runs at it, and every time we thought we had him, and every time that gunner came right back up firing." The government soldiers, by contrast, had panicked. They showed little inclination toward aggressive action, and, as a result, suffered far heavier casualties than they would have from an all-out assault. Concluded one American officer: "They moved in slowly and gave the Vietcong a chance to piecemeal them to death."

Catalogue of failure

What bedeviled the South Vietnamese at Ap Bac was a catalogue of operational failures that had begun to emerge over the previous six months. The rapid deployment of American men and equipment had caught the Vietcong off guard, and during the first half of 1962 the VC took a beating. But the ARVN had not taken advantage of the enemy's temporary vulnerability. There were too many units led by political appointees who avoided combat whenever possible, too many generals in a top-heavy senior staff who had little idea of how to maneuver small mobile battle groups in the jungle and rice fields, too much reliance on American-supplied firepower as a substitute for aggressive action. There was too little coordination between provincial forces and regular units, too little cooperation between province chiefs and army commanders.

The flashy ARVN operations of 1962—Morning Star, Boondodge, and the rest—were themselves a major part of the problem. American advisers argued vainly against large-scale sweeps that involved too many men over too great an area to have any reasonable hope of success, and afterward left the contested areas no more secure than before. They objected to the prolonged artillery barrages to "soften up" enemy positions, which succeeded only in

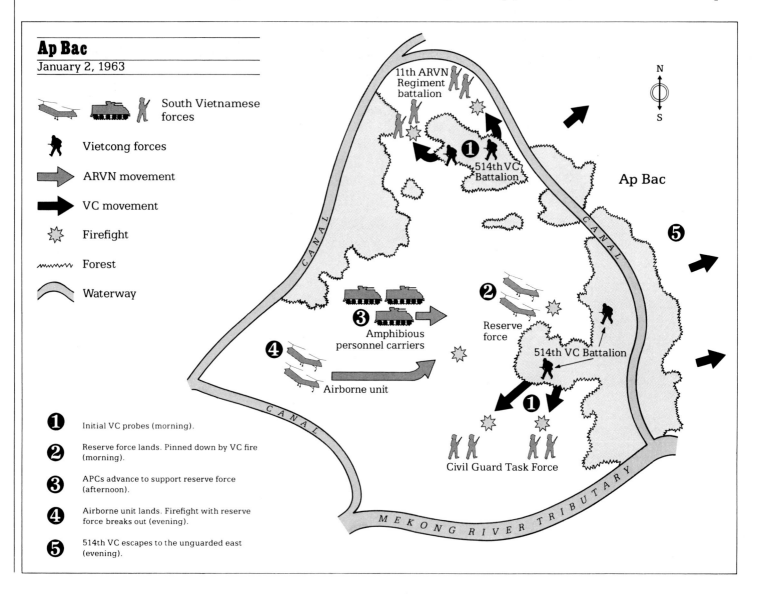

Ap Bac

January 2, 1963

South Vietnamese forces

Vietcong forces

ARVN movement

VC movement

Firefight

Forest

Waterway

11th ARVN Regiment battalion

514th VC Battalion

Ap Bac

❶

❷ Reserve force

❸ Amphibious personnel carriers

❹ Airborne unit

514th VC Battalion

❶

Civil Guard Task Force

❺

CANAL

CANAL

CANAL

MEKONG RIVER TRIBUTARY

N / S

❶ Initial VC probes (morning).

❷ Reserve force lands. Pinned down by VC fire (morning).

❸ APCs advance to support reserve force (afternoon).

❹ Airborne unit lands. Firefight with reserve force breaks out (evening).

❺ 514th VC escapes to the unguarded east (evening).

ARVN soldiers, exhausted after chasing a group of Vietcong guerrillas through swamplands south of Saigon, try to get some sleep in a navy troop carrier.

removing any element of surprise. They deplored the practice of leaving escape routes open for the Vietcong to flee. Americans fresh from training camps in the United States were surprised to find that the tactics employed in the counterguerrilla war were highly orthodox. Vietnamese officers themselves complained about "the American-type war we train for, and the Indochina-type war we have to fight." There was little fighting at night, little emphasis on patrols, mobile defense, or ambushes, little attempt to turn guerrilla tricks against the VC themselves. With all the talk of counterinsurgency and antiguerrilla operations, the war was fought mostly on the Vietcong's terms, when they wanted, and where they chose.

Tactical deficiencies were exacerbated by interference from the presidential palace. No major troop movement, no officer promotion could proceed without Diem's approval. At the same time, the Ngos operated outside of any overall strategy: They could and did act unilaterally as the whim struck them. Units were moved about by order of the palace without the knowledge of superior commanders, while general reserve troops were dispatched on hastily organized operations based on sketchy intelligence, without coordination with ongoing military operations. In situations demanding speed and flexibility, the palace's tight control of the army killed initiative and made rapid response almost impossible. When a Vietcong ambush wiped out a convoy forty miles north of Saigon one morning, it took hours before presidential consent could be obtained to send reserve forces in pursuit. By the time U.S. helicopters put them down on the ambush site it was early evening. The guerrillas, despite their heavy load of captured weapons and ammunition, were long gone.

Nor had other problems been solved during 1962. The Diem regime insisted on maintaining isolated outposts that the Americans began calling "Vietcong PXs," because they were so regularly looted for weapons and supplies. The futility of the outposts was matched by the government's reluctance to arm the Self Defense Corps, for fear that the weapons would fall into Vietcong hands. Since without weapons the SDC could not protect the multiplying strategic hamlets, it never really became possible for the ARVN to free itself from static defensive duties. But because government soldiers locked themselves into district towns at nightfall, they provided no real protection for the hamlets either.

Nowhere had the bright promise of 1962 fallen so far short as the Strategic Hamlet Program. The spectacular statistics of hamlet construction, the glowing accounts in the *Times of Vietnam*, the "model" hamlets through which American VIPs were ferried, obscured for most observers what life was really like behind the moats and fortifications.

Rejecting Sir Robert Thompson's recommendation to begin in secure areas and proceed slowly, the Diem government wanted strategic hamlets everywhere, even in regions where they had little chance for survival. Hamlet construction was slipshod, defenses shoddy. Peasants were herded into the fortified villages against their will or driven there by random bombing in the "open zones" surrounding each hamlet. Forced to construct the villages with their own labor, usually without compensation, they rarely received the social services or the protection they had been promised. Meanwhile, hamlet officials prospered on the distribution of patronage, and district chiefs grew rich siphoning off U.S.-supplied cash and construction materials. Diem had promised the peasants a social revolution. What he gave them was imposed authority, rigorous taxation, political indoctrination, and a constant demand for affirmations of loyalty to the central government.

It was not loyalty the hamlets created, however, but massive resentment. Instead of centers of resistance they became easy targets for Vietcong subversion and attack. Yet, the alienation of the peasants within the strategic hamlets was only part of a much larger estrangement of the population from the government. In the wake of the February 1962 bombing of the presidential palace by two disgruntled air force officers, Diem had arrested hundreds of non-Communist liberals with no connection to the plot, clamped even tighter censorship over books and newspapers, and passed a public meetings law so restrictive that even weddings and funerals needed government permission. Unrestricted journals of opposition opinion, independent opposition political parties, or membership in the government for non-Communist opposition figures was out of the question. "You open a window to let in light and air,

not bullets," explained Madame Nhu, Diem's sister-in-law. "We want freedom, but we don't want to be exploited by it."

Meanwhile, whether from fear of the Vietcong or suspicion of Saigon, the countryside of South Vietnam continued to be a hostile place for government forces ostensibly sent to protect the rural population. Soldiers on patrol were not welcomed but shunned. As the troops approached, everyone would flee except a few old men and children. No one in the deserted villages offered information, no one hurried to put out flags. By early 1963 the government had come no closer to solving its most intractable problem—commanding the support of the mass of the people. Without it there could be no hope of victory.

"A state of total insecurity"

Instead, throughout 1963 the Vietcong transformed the government's military deficiencies into victories of their own. In the wake of Ap Bac the guerrillas overran three government outposts in the Mekong Delta, killing over a hundred defenders and making off with sampans full of American rifles, machine guns, and mortars. By March the fighting was clearly running in their favor. In a week of attacks south of Saigon, including a ferocious daylight ambush of two companies of Civil Guards, the guerrillas captured enough weapons to arm two companies. In April the insurgents seized two strategic hamlets in An Xuyen Province, then mauled the two companies of South Vietnamese troops sent to the rescue.

If the government was able to make headway along the central coast, and the American Special Forces were able to stabilize the situation in the central highlands, the heavily populated, agriculturally vital Mekong Delta was rapidly falling into Vietcong hands. The situation was most serious in the Ca Mau Peninsula, a long-time insurgent stronghold. Despite warnings by American advisers that it would be impossible to defend them adequately, the government continued to build isolated outposts throughout the area, which were just as regularly overrun by the Vietcong.

The situation was scarcely better in the district capitals. ARVN commanders, fearful of incurring the wrath of the guerrillas, restricted patrols and made little effort to gather intelligence, while their men, as one American said, "sit there waiting for the executioner." Meanwhile, the ARVN 7th Division avoided combat, leaving the VC to steadily extend their con-

The government policy of wholesale destruction of Vietcong areas turned thousands of Vietnamese into refugees and further alienated an already embittered population.

trol over the important central delta provinces of Long An and Dinh Tuong. According to an American working in the delta, by September both provinces were in "a state of total insecurity."

The Vietcong casualty rate was rising, but so was their hard-core strength, now estimated at more than twenty-five thousand. They were losing many old rifles and obsolete devices, but capturing modern American automatic weapons and mortars. Even more ominous, they no longer needed to husband ammunition so stringently. Between what they captured and what they received in supplies from the North, they appeared to have enough to stand and fight it out with ARVN firepower.

Government forces did continue to mount major assaults against Vietcong strongholds during the first half of 1963. Rarely, however, did these full-scale offensives engage the enemy, although in the delta in July elements of the ARVN 7th Division got some measure of revenge on the Vietcong 514th Battalion. Once again the well-armed, well-entrenched guerrillas came up against far larger government forces supported by air strikes and armored personnel carriers. But this time, said one American adviser, "I think we gave a bit better than we took." In one bitter assault on guerrilla positions a government company suffered more than 25 percent casualties but managed to drive the Vietcong back.

The government's task was made easier by the introduction of the UH-1B ("Huey") helicopter. Originally designed as a utility aircraft and personnel carrier, the speedy, heavily armed chopper turned out to be the ideal support for the larger, more vulnerable CH-21 troop carrier. Before the arrival of the UH-1Bs, guerrilla ground fire had begun to jeopardize helicopter airlift operations, the government's single most effective offensive tactic. With their maneuverability the small Hueys could slide back and forth just a few feet above the rice fields, sorting out targets like a cowboy sorting steers. With their rockets and their .50-caliber machine guns, the new helicopters packed an enormous wallop, subjecting landing zones to intense clearing fire only seconds before the troop carriers dropped off their loads. After their arrival on the battle front in late 1962, the UH-1Bs helped cut the number of hits on troop-carrying helicopters by 25 percent. "The Hueys," said General Harkins, "are the most essential unit in my command."

The Serong report

Yet neither sporadic government victories nor the deployment of new American equipment could overcome the manifold problems of the South Vietnamese armed forces. In a secret report to General Harkins in October 1962, the Australian counterguerrilla expert Colonel F. P. Serong described an army beset by structural flaws, tactical deficiencies, and a deteriorating relationship with the rural population.

Serong found an officer corps poorly trained, fearful of making mistakes, and constantly shifting initiative and responsibility to ever-higher levels of authority. He discovered that private soldiers were neglected by their officers, inadequately paid, and provided with a ration allowance "no higher than that for a dog." Serong bemoaned the ARVN's inadequate inspection procedures, haphazard weapons training, and failure to promote battle-tested NCOs.

This was all the more unfortunate, the Australian insisted, because the enemy was not ten feet tall. Despite his relative success he was plagued by problems of his own. "His personnel, other than cadres, are weak, his logistics are bad, and his communications worse. He is in trouble." But the ARVN had failed signally to take advantage of Vietcong weaknesses. No serious attempt had been made to disrupt the flow of men and equipment along the border areas, no attempt even to formulate a unified policy toward border defense. And the fundamental rule of

counterguerrilla warfare—that once contact with the enemy is made he must be pursued until he can be destroyed—was seldom observed. There should be "no question of stopping at a province boundary, or the nearest outpost, or because you have other orders or because you may be ambushed, or you haven't the equipment to stay out overnight," complained Serong, yet such hesitation continued to be the usual state of affairs.

Serong was equally critical of the government's efforts at rural pacification. While the disintegration of security procedures in the strategic hamlets laid them open to VC attack and subversion, the village medic program—"the keystone of our civic action work, and our intelligence net"—was grinding to a halt. Meanwhile, indiscriminate bombing and the needlessly cruel behavior of ARVN troops toward rural villagers jeopardized whatever military gains had been made.

The colonel also cast a cool eye on the American advisory mission. He pointed in particular to the lack of mutual confidence between the American advisers and their Vietnamese counterparts, the unwillingness of ARVN commanders to accept advisers on operations below battalion level, and the sometimes exaggerated reluctance on the part of the Americans to take the initiative in presenting operational plans.

Although compared to the situation in early spring there had been some improvements, the continuing deficiencies could not be ignored. Given several years it should be possible to win the war, but "it is possible to lose it," Serong concluded, "quite quickly."

Despite the Serong report, and despite the disturbing example of Ap Bac, officials in Washington continued to express confidence in the military situation. "The spear point of aggression has been blunted in Vietnam," proclaimed President Kennedy in his State of the Union address on January 14, 1963. In March, Secretary of State Dean Rusk declared that Saigon's forces "clearly have the initiative in most areas of the country." He thought the Strategic Hamlet Program was producing "excellent results," that "morale in the countryside has begun to rise," and that to the peasants, the Vietcong looked "less and less like winners." There was no question, announced Secretary of Defense McNamara in May, that "the corner has definitely been turned toward victory."

Official optimism was not a deliberate attempt to mislead. It was compounded in part out of a natural desire to see things as positively as possible, in part out of the assessments Washington was receiving

Sweeping low across a suspected Vietcong position, an American instructor in a T-28 fighter-bomber watches a Vietnamese napalm strike.

from Saigon. It was the result, as well, of the press of other events. Beset by the continuing tension in East-West relations symbolized by the Cuban missile crisis of October 1962, arguing with French President Charles de Gaulle over the American role in Europe, seeking to move forward on an "Alliance for Progress" with Latin America and a nuclear test-ban treaty with the Russians, Kennedy and his advisers were easily distracted from what appeared to be the relatively minor crisis in Southeast Asia.

"Kill ratios" and "body counts"

As management of the Vietnamese situation passed to the men in the field, Washington became increasingly dependent on the evaluations of American civilian and military officials in Saigon. The U.S. ambassador to South Vietnam, Frederick Nolting, continued to express confidence in the Diem government. Meanwhile impressive statistics, such as "kill ratios," "body counts," "weapons lost/weapons captured ratios," and "incident counts" flowed from MACV via the Pentagon with reassuring regularity. So confident were the reports that in May 1963, at Kennedy's direction, the Defense Department began work on a plan for the total removal of American advisers from South Vietnam by the end of 1965.

Unfortunately, both the embassy and MACV based their judgments on information provided mainly by the Vietnamese government. Reports filtering up the military and administrative hierarchies, subject at every level to revision by political appointees intent on pleasing the presidential palace, were often taken as fact. GVN figures on casualties, on areas of control, on strategic hamlet construction, on the political loyalties of the peasants—most of which the U.S. Mission accepted—were questionable at best. And if it was understandable to rely on an ally for reasonable information on a situation of joint concern, it was harder to explain why the reports from Americans in the field—often presenting a far bleaker picture—were so routinely ignored.

The advisers complained that military operations were constantly hobbled by political considerations and accused ARVN commanders of sacrificing innocent civilians by indiscriminate use of napalm and artillery. They wondered whether the Vietnamese were really interested in listening to American advice and complained that too much of the burden of the relationship had been placed on them to "get along." The Americans scoffed at exaggerated claims of government victories and inflated casualty counts, and they resented the overly optimistic reports the U.S. military command was sending back to Washington.

They resented most of all the Catch-22 attitude of the Diem government. In order to defeat the Vietcong,

ARVN commanders had to become more aggressive, and an aggressive pursuit of the enemy inevitably meant more casualties in the short run. But fearful that military victories might catapult an ambitious officer into a political rival, and equally concerned lest casualties turn the people against him, Diem made career advancement a function of optimistic reports and a minimum of government bloodshed. Junior and even senior U.S. officers tried to convince their superiors that the war was not going well. But neither the army, nor the politicians, seemed to be listening.

The war against the press

The only Americans paying attention to what U.S. field advisers had to say were the members of the Saigon press corps. But when they reported that things weren't going well they distressed the U.S. Mission, infuriated the GVN, and inaugurated their own war with the Diem regime.

When David Halberstam arrived in Saigon in August 1962 as correspondent for the *New York Times*, he was ecstatic. "Vietnam was a reporter's dream. It had everything: a war, a highly dramatic and emotional story, great food, a beautiful setting, and lovely women." The man he was replacing, Pulitzer Prize-winning reporter Homer Bigart, was "sick of it"—sick of the restrictions and harassment imposed on reporters by Diem and what seemed to him the indifference of American officials to the reporters' plight.

The Diem government regarded the journalists as "scabby sheep," and treated them accordingly. There was almost nothing in the way of working press facilities and only a single official spokesman, an obscure Lieutenant Bang who was seldom available. The daily communiqué of military action was regularly three or four days behind the news and constantly played down unpleasant developments. The government made it difficult for newsmen to get

---

Voices of Dissent

Officially, the war in Vietnam was being won as 1962 ended. But underneath the optimistic rhetoric of the top command, a few respected civilian and military officials were already beginning to raise serious questions about the progress of the war. Two of the most determined voices of dissent belonged to Mike Mansfield, the new Senate Majority Leader, and Lieutenant Colonel John Paul Vann, a U.S. military adviser to the South Vietnamese armed forces.

*   *   *

Mike Mansfield, the laconic senator from Montana whose nonpartisan independence of thought and personal integrity won him the respect of Democrats and

Republicans alike, had proven before to be a man of insight into Asian affairs. In 1944 as a young congressman and former professor of Far Eastern history, he had been dispatched by President Roosevelt on a fact-finding mission to China. His report that Communist strength was impressive, and not limited to revolutionary ideologues, raised eyebrows in Washington but proved prophetic.

Eighteen years later Mansfield again packed his bags for the Far East at a president's request, but this time his destination was Vietnam. An early supporter of the Diem regime, but skeptical and independent minded, Mansfield was determined to find out for himself what was going on in the American-financed war. The senator declined several official briefings and met instead with American reporters to hear their misgivings about the military and political situation. Upon leaving the country he discarded the farewell statement prepared by the U.S. Embassy and delivered one of his own, markedly more reserved on the progress of the war.

If Mansfield was chilly in Saigon, he was icy in Washington. His report to Congress took alarming note of the fact that after seven years and $2 billion Vietnam appeared less stable and its government less popular than in 1955. To pursue the present course, he warned his colleagues,

could involve an expenditure of American lives and resources on a scale which would bear little relationship to the interests of the United States or, indeed, to the interests of the people of Vietnam.

The struggle for Vietnamese independence was fast becoming an "American war," raising serious questions about the nature of U.S. involvement in Southeast Asia.

Mansfield's private report to the president was more specific, and even more pessimistic. The senator told Kennedy that American programs in South Vietnam—both military and nonmilitary—had been "ill conceived and badly administered" and that South Vietnam was "far more dependent on us for its existence than it was five years ago."

Indeed, it was distressing on this visit to hear the situation described in much the same terms as on my last visit [in 1957].... Vietnam, outside the cities, is still an insecure place which is run at least at night largely by the Vietcong. The government in Saigon is still seeking acceptance by the ordinary people in large areas of the countryside. Out of fear or indifference or hostility the peasants still withhold acquiescence, let alone approval of that government.

Mansfield praised Diem but condemned the "handful of paid retainers and sycophants" surrounding and controlling him and doubted the ability of the South

to battle areas and held up "offensive" dispatches for twenty-four hours or more. Military commanders who offered realistic appraisals of the war in their area were ordered not to talk to American reporters and, if they continued to do so, were relieved of their commands or even jailed.

As Diem's difficulties grew, and the reports became more critical, correspondents were tailed and their telephones tapped. Vietnamese civilians who provided information to reporters were threatened or picked up for questioning. If all else failed, the government ordered journalists out of the country. A *Newsweek* article in September 1962 called into question the progress of the war and commented unfavorably on Madame Nhu's paramilitary girls. The government was incensed, and the author of the offending article, the veteran reporter and seventeen-year resident of Indochina, François Sully, was expelled from Vietnam.

The departure of Bigart and Sully left much of the day-to-day coverage of the war to a handful of young, intense, often brave, sometimes emotional correspondents. Malcolm Browne, thirty-two, an ex-chemist who kept the withered hand of a corpse tacked to his cubbyhole to serve as a reminder for people trying to ignore the war, was the oldest. Neil Sheehan, a twenty-six-year-old Harvard graduate living in a windowless room next to his UPI office, was the youngest. Halberstam, another Harvard graduate and the recipient of the Newspaper Guild's Page One Award for his dispatches from the Congo, was twenty-nine. Peter Arnett, a "tough little Associated Press correspondent" from New Zealand, was twenty-seven.

Priding themselves on the value of their independent judgment, the reporters assumed the responsibility for telling the people back home what was going on in Vietnam. They soon discovered that Diem and the Nhus simply would not tolerate an independent press. They believed—or affected to believe—that

---

Vietnamese armed forces to counter any serious aggression from North Vietnam. "In short," Mansfield concluded, "it would be well to face the fact that we are once again at the beginning of the beginning." With prospects for success growing daily less likely, the only answer was to begin to retreat from the costly dimensions of American involvement.

An angry President Kennedy attacked Mansfield's report as defeatist. "For us to withdraw," Kennedy told reporters, "would mean a collapse not only of South Vietnam but Southeast Asia. So we are going to stay there." But from that time on Mansfield would persistently challenge succeeding administrations to find a way to extricate the United States from what he saw to be a foreign policy gone awry.

      ★   ★   ★

Lieutenant Colonel John Paul Vann shared many of Mansfield's misgivings but not his doubts about the necessity of American intervention in Southeast Asia. An ardent anti-Communist who had volunteered for active duty in Vietnam, Vann believed that U.S. military aid and know-how were essential to maintaining a free South Vietnam.

A poor boy from Virginia who enlisted in the army at eighteen, Vann rose rapidly through the ranks, a dedicated soldier of great drive and curiosity. General William

Westmoreland, who condemned Vann for "sounding off" to the press, nevertheless described his military record in Vietnam as "almost legendary" and later wrote that no one better understood the Vietnamese than John Vann.

Vann was assigned as a senior adviser to the ARVN 7th Division, the spearhead of the government's pacification efforts in the southern delta, and quickly learned the depressing facts of life in the war against the Vietcong. Despite their greater numbers, the government forces were barely holding their own. Fearing Diem's wrath, and hoping to avoid the loss of their commands, senior officers refused to act on intelligence reports pinpointing areas of VC concentration and avoided combat whenever possible. In his year as adviser only fifty of the fourteen thousand 7th Division troops had been killed—not because they were fighting well, but because they weren't fighting at all.

A business statistician by trade, Vann documented the failure of the ARVN to bear the brunt of battle in the delta, leaving most of the fighting to the ill-trained and ill-equipped Civil Guard. He proved that commanders got troops not on the basis of military necessity but on the basis of political loyalty to Diem. None of this won him many friends in Saigon. And when Vann called the battle of Ap Bac

what it was—a defeat, and a bad one—General Harkins threatened to fire him.

In April 1963 Vann completed his tour and returned to the United States determined to make the army see what was really happening in Vietnam. But his report, while favorably received by many in the Pentagon, was removed at the last minute from the agenda of the Joint Chiefs of Staff by JCS Chairman General Maxwell Taylor. Vann retired from the service soon after, still claiming that the American military command in Vietnam had been encouraged by Washington to provide overly optimistic assessments of progress, that the political machinations of the Diem regime had profoundly disturbed the war effort in the countryside, and that the South Vietnamese government had no real interest in defeating the Vietcong.

Like others who had once been there, however, Vann found he couldn't keep away from Vietnam. Returning to Saigon in 1965 as a low-ranking USAID official, the former lieutenant colonel worked his way up to become a senior civilian adviser, considered by many the most knowledgeable American in Vietnam. He died in a helicopter crash in the central highlands in 1972, still trying to fight a battle he believed in, the way he thought it should be done.

---

the U.S. government controlled American reporters, just as the Saigon government controlled Vietnamese journalists, and blamed the U.S. Mission for the critical stories. The Mission, in turn, blamed the reporters for insensitivity to the need to win Diem's confidence, and the reporters accused the Mission of deliberately misleading them to protect Diem. The fact that Ambassador Nolting and his staff appeared to accept the optimistic South Vietnamese government reports at face value, and supported those claims against the pessimistic accounts of journalists who had gone out in the field to see for themselves, intensified the atmosphere of mutual hostility.

Immediately after the battle of Ap Bac, Arnett, Halberstam, and Sheehan arrived at the scene and talked with American advisers who admitted the enemy had slipped away. Sheehan was talking with Brigadier General Robert York when Major Tho's artillery barrage sent them diving for cover. When Halberstam and Arnett returned to the command post to question the military authorities, General Harkins told the reporters that the Vietcong were about to be rounded up. Halberstam and Arnett were incredulous. "As on so many other occasions in Vietnam," Halberstam wrote, "we never knew whether Harkins believed what he was saying, or whether he felt that it should be said."

The friendlies

The embassy was enraged by the stories on Ap Bac and accused the correspondents of harming American interests in Vietnam by sensational reporting. Recalled Saigon USIS Chief John Mecklin: "A man from Mars admitted to official inner circles in both Vietnam and Washington could have been excused if he got the impression that the newsmen, as well as the Vietcong, were the enemy."

The reporters in Vietnam were tenacious, professional, and not without courage. They could also be self-righteous, humorless, and needlessly abrasive. They issued ultimatums to government officials and persistently refused to see the humor in some of the absurdities they so regularly denounced. They had few thanks for the U.S. officials who took their complaints to the presidential palace—and who on at least one occasion succeeded in getting a banished reporter back into the country—and were apt to vent their frustrations on those caught in the middle. They hounded Lieutenant Colonel James G. Smith, Harkins's public information officer, unmercifully. One

An early victim of Diem's efforts to muzzle the press, François Sully of Newsweek *was expelled from Vietnam in September 1962 for articles offending the ruling family. Later readmitted, he died in a helicopter crash in 1971.*

night he received fourteen phone calls from newsmen between midnight and 7 A.M., none of them polite. Smith took to calling the reporters "the friendlies."

But while the American correspondents assigned to Saigon may have from time to time allowed their distaste with the ruling family and their anger at U.S. officials to color their reporting, there can be little doubt that in the main their accounts were accurate, their pessimism warranted. If they were critical, it was not of the American commitment: No more than the administration did they doubt that U.S. involvement in Vietnam was a necessary free world policy. What they objected to was the unwillingness of the Vietnamese government to prosecute the war effectively and the unwillingness of American officials to admit what was going on. Most of all, they objected to the indifference and hostility of the Diem regime toward the people of South Vietnam.

In Washington, too, there was growing exasperation with the Diem government. The Kennedy administration's decision to send American advisers and combat support units to South Vietnam had been predicated on the establishment of a "limited partnership" with the Saigon government. The United

Aggressive young American correspondents like New York Times reporter David Halberstam, Malcolm Browne of the AP, and Neil Sheehan of UPI (left to right) drew fire not only from the enemy in the field, but from the Diem regime and the U.S. Mission as well.

States would provide military expertise and equipment to defend South Vietnam against Communist insurrection in exchange for military, political, and economic reforms Washington believed necessary to defeat the Vietcong. Diem did make a number of marginal changes—higher pay and benefits for the armed forces, creation of a powerless National Economic Council, the establishment of an equally impotent National Security Council—but would not undertake any significant political liberalization or social reform.

A marriage of inconvenience

Throughout 1962 and 1963 there were a growing number of additional disputes between Washington and Saigon. They argued over American aid: whether U.S. food, blankets, medicine, barbed wire, cement, and other assistance would be funneled directly to local officials to avoid bureaucratic delay and diversion (Diem refused); and whether Saigon would be freed from its obligation, under the U.S. aid program, to buy American goods (the Kennedy administration withheld the waiver). They argued over

political policy and pacification: whether to hold elections for the National Assembly in which independent candidates would be allowed to run (the elections were put off); whether the Diem government would initiate a general amnesty to encourage Vietcong defections (Diem delayed for more than twelve months before putting the *Chieu Hoi*—Open Arms—program into effect in the spring of 1963); and whether the disastrous Strategic Hamlet Program in the Ca Mau Peninsula would be reassessed (instead more hamlets were constructed). And they debated military strategy: whether an additional ARVN division would be deployed in the Mekong Delta in the face of growing VC military gains (only after months of prodding were elements of the 9th Division moved into the vital region). Meanwhile, the Saigon government continued to accept U.S. economic and military aid at the rate of $1.5 million per day, further shortening Washington's patience.

So contentious did relations become that in late April 1963 both Diem and Nhu expressed their reluctance to accept more American advisers. Two weeks later the brothers told a group of journalists they had begun to doubt the quality of American expertise. "I

The "Other" Enemy

By David Halberstam

The day I arrived in Saigon in mid-1962 there was a farewell party for François Sully of *Newsweek* who had just been expelled by the Ngo family for writing unfavorably about how the war effort was going. So the mood at Tan Son Nhut—a name that was to become part of the everyday American vocabulary—was already bitter. It was soon to get far worse, for there were, I soon learned, two wars, one against the Vietcong, and one against the tiny American press corps.

In those days there were only fifteen thousand Americans in Vietnam in advisory and support capacities. By then fewer than one hundred Americans had died; the helicopters were still the old rickety CH-21s, already ten years old. I have a clear memory of my colleague Mert Perry's wife Darlene trying tearfully one day to dissuade him from going on a heliborne mission, saying, "They're only put together with Elmer's glue."

It was a small, slow-motion war in a distant country that no one back in the U.S. seemed to care about. The Vietcong did not fight set-piece battles; rather it hit quickly in the night and faded away before daybreak. That struck the American generals, victors over the Germans and Japanese, as cowardly. Besides, the VC did not wear regular uniforms, only black pajamas. They were small, and they were yellow. There was more than a touch of racism in this war.

To the generals in Saigon the Vietcong were not a serious enemy though they were to the advisers in the field. The men in Saigon, of course, were primarily trying to please Washington by telling it what it wanted and expected to hear. By contrast, the officers in the field were respectful of the enemy and increasingly contemptuous of the ARVN. Lieutenant Colonel John Paul Vann, later to become a legendary figure in Vietnam and very early on an outspoken critic of the ARVN's unwillingness to fight, was once reprimanded by General Paul Harkins for being insufficiently sensitive to the Vietnamese need to save face. "I'm not here to save their face," he answered, "I'm here to save their ass."

It became quickly clear that despite the immense transfusion of American technology and manpower, the war was not being won. In truth it was not even being fought. Most South Vietnamese commanders owed their jobs not to battlefield valor but their loyalty to the presidential palace. They seemed more preoccupied with stopping coups than seeking out the VC. South Vietnam was in truth an army without a country, controlled by a government rotting from within. Thus the difference between the world of Saigon and the world of the rice field. Saigon was a boom town of self-conscious Yankee enthusiasm. ("The only two exports of South Vietnam," one journalist said, "are rice and American optimism.")

An incident comes to mind: A group of American reporters was invited down to My Tho in the delta for what was to be three days of impressive victories. Among the reporters were Homer Bigart, of the *New York Times*, a two-time Pulitzer Prize winner, and Neil Sheehan, then a twenty-five-year-old reporter with UPI. On the first day, with American helicopters and armored personnel carriers everywhere, there was a small victory of sorts; on the second day very little happened. On the third it became clear that ARVN commanders, to the chagrin of their American advisers, were deliberately operating where the VC were not. That night Bigart and Sheehan drove back to Saigon, with Sheehan, upset over the lack of results, muttering to himeslf.

"What's the matter, Mr. Sheehan?" Bigart asked.

Neil muttered something about three days wasted and very little in the way of a story.

"Ah, but there is a story, Mr. Sheehan," Bigart said. "It doesn't work. That's your story, Mr. Sheehan."

So it was that a handful of American reporters soon became the other enemy. If only the reporters would confirm the official optimism then everything would be all right. "Do you have any problems in Saigon?" Secretary McNamara asked General Harkins at a meeting in Honolulu in December 1962, a time when the VC were moving up from company to battalion strength operations. "Only with the American press," answered the general.

We were excellent targets—when things go wrong, reporters usually are. We were young; after Bigart left, our average age was twenty-seven. No one had an established reputation (although six Pulitzer Prizes were to go to members of that original group). We were criticized constantly by the embassy, by MACV, by the Pentagon, by the president. It was not just our accuracy that was assailed but our maturity, our patriotism, our ideology, even our manhood.

For all of that we loved it. We knew by instinct we were reporting a great story. The will power to defy our own government was easy to come by. After all we were going out in the field ourselves with ARVN units. The American advisers who went with them were our friends; to betray them, to report optimistically when they were increasingly embittered would have been to betray a trust. Besides, day by day events were confirming our earlier judgments. As that happened, more officials became disillusioned, and our sources became more numerous. Our reporting made the government furious. Threats were directed at us. When Sheehan and I took cabs from a taxi stand, we never took the first one on the theory that its driver might be a government plant.

When I left Saigon in early 1964 I sat down and wrote a memoir of that time and place. In the end we needed a title. What about, I suggested to my editor, *The Making of a Quagmire?* Little did I know.

David Halberstam's books include The Best and The Brightest, *a chronicle of the American involvement in Vietnam.*

don't think the Americans are able to advise us on subversive warfare," said Nhu. "I am afraid the Americans don't know as much as we do." President Kennedy assured reporters in Washington that "we would withdraw the troops, any number of troops, any time the Government of South Vietnam would suggest it," and the storm blew over. But the public squabble was sorry testimony to the deteriorating condition of the American-Vietnamese "partnership."

What could not blow over, what ultimately stood in the way of any effective relationship between the United States and the Saigon government, was the erratic temperament of Ngo Dinh Diem and the tolerance he maintained for the unchecked behavior of his rapacious family.

The last mandarins

"In our age of mass society," the French journalist Philippe Devillers has written, "where all history seems to be determined by forces so powerful as to negate the individual, the Vietnamese problem has the originality to remain dominated by individuals." No individuals provoked more controversy or indignation among both Vietnamese and Americans than the powerful, complex, even bizarre figures of the ruling family: Ngo Dinh Diem, his brothers Can, Luyen, Thuc, and Nhu, and his sister-in-law Madame Nhu.

Some Americans in Saigon called him "the Penguin," this short, broadly built man with the round face, black hair, and the funny open-toed gait one journalist described as "a duck walk which bordered on a bustle," this president of the republic, with his white sharkskin suits and his monotone French.

Yet Diem maintained in his personal habits the austerity of his younger days as a seminarian, working sixteen to eighteen hours a day, then leaving more work beside his narrow cot when he went to bed in case he woke up during the night. His labors were immense in part because of his obsessive supervision of virtually all governmental activity. The American journalist Robert Shaplen recalled that Diem's habit of wanting to do everything himself "gradually reached ridiculous extremes, and ultimately he insisted on doing such things as individually approving all exit visas for Vietnamese traveling abroad and determining the position of newly planted trees in public gardens."

The favorite pursuits of his youth—riding, hunting, tending flowers, taking photographs—he gave up in later years. But the man who had enjoyed these solitary pleasures continued to prefer his own company, and counsel, to anyone else's, lapsing more and more frequently into the legendary monologues that effectively stilled most outside advice. John Mecklin labeled a two-hour session with Diem a "quickie," and recalled the ashen face of an American correspondent emerging from a six-and-a-half hour marathon with the president—the last hour and a half spent in the doorway as the desperate reporter attempted to leave. By 1963 Diem had begun to talk so compulsively that many observers viewed it as a psychiatric problem. The Vietnamese had a different and more serious explanation. For them Diem's endless monologues were a sign that he could no longer exercise the self-control of a Confucian leader. As the American journalist Frances FitzGerald has suggested, Diem's open mouth became a way of insisting on an authority he no longer commanded.

The bond between Diem and his people had never been based on much more than the regard they had for that authority. Diem was not a popular leader, and he didn't think it was important to be one. He believed his mandarin birth and moral superiority gave him a mandate to rule South Vietnam and the wisdom to know what was best for his people. Although a respected, if remote, figure in his early days as president, Diem and his people eventually came to live in mutual suspicion, a suspicion that turned to active dislike as the regime's pattern of political repression grew more ferocious.

Yet despite his growing unpopularity and his somewhat ridiculous ways, Diem maintained an air of dignity. He took himself very seriously and expected others to do the same. Even his enemies allowed for a certain integrity in the man, reserving their more intense contempt for the other members of the family.

Rogues' gallery

No charge was made so regularly against the Ngos as the charge of corruption, and not without reason. Ngo Dinh Thuc, the president's oldest brother, transformed the archbishopric of Hue into a source of personal revenue. A genial, relaxed, worldly man interested in real estate as well as religion, Thuc used the leverage of his position to buy apartment buildings, rubber estates, and timber concessions. He participated in shady land deals in Vietnam and Australia, and he put soldiers to work cutting wood for him to

Madame Ngo Dinh Nhu alternately charms, berates, and cajoles her listeners at a press conference in Paris in October 1963. Her unbridled tongue incensed her fellow South Vietnamese and eventually hardened international opposition to the Ngos.

sell or constructing buildings for him to lease. When Thuc set his eyes on a piece of land he desired, other bidders mysteriously lost interest. His requests for donations, one Saigon merchant observed, "read like tax notices."

Thuc was certainly not alone in his avarice. Ngo Dinh Can, the second youngest brother, made his money operating a smuggling ring that shipped rice to North Vietnam and a drug ring that sold opium in Hue. Brother Luyen, the youngest, made a fortune in currency exchange manipulation from his post as ambassador to London.

The Nhus also used their position to salt away a tidy sum for the future. At one time or another Nhu was implicated in illegal lotteries, drug traffic, waterfront rackets, exchange manipulation, and the extor-

tion of Chinese business leaders. Perhaps it couldn't be helped, for Nhu had not only his own greed to satisfy but also the notoriously expensive tastes of Madame Nhu.

Her parents named her Le Tran Xuan, "Beautiful Spring," but the woman herself was neither so lovely nor so innocent. She fancied precious stones and tight *ao dais*, fitting into her dresses "like a dagger in its sheath." But although her delicate features struck everyone at first, on closer acquaintance her reliance on cosmetics and her manicured appearance revealed a somewhat shallow beauty.

More practical than Diem or Nhu, she had fewer intellectual pretensions and was a stronger figure because of it. "I shall never, never, never admit defeat," she told a journalist during the Buddhist crisis of the summer of 1963. It was this attitude that won her a political voice with Diem when she alone during the 1960 coup attempt advocated standing firm and fighting the paratroopers. "Up until then they had not taken me seriously," she claimed. "But then they began to notice me, and began to worry when I said things."

She was obsessed with power, once confiding to Republican party leaders in the United States: "I'm not exactly afraid of death. I love power and in the next life I have a chance to be even more powerful than I am." She used her position to push through the National Assembly a series of laws making divorce virtually impossible, giving women heightened social and economic rights, outlawing prostitution, and forbidding dancing "anywhere at all." To disgruntled Americans in Saigon she was a woman with a "fixation against other people having a good time." But to many Vietnamese, her high visibility and pro-woman positions were dangerously disrupting the foundations of traditional society.

Equally damaging, she became an early target of those on the hunt for evidence of wrongdoing among the ruling family. When the mistress of ex-Premier Nguyen Van Tam was put on trial for corruption in 1955, she caused a sensation by accusing Madame Nhu of similar practices on a far grander scale. By 1957 rumors of illegal financial dealings by Madame Nhu had become so widespread that both she and her husband took out newspaper advertisements to deny the allegations. Needless to say, the denials only confirmed what many already believed.

Vanity and madness

Worse than the corruption, though, far worse, was the Ngo family's use of terror. Thuc and Luyen were venal, but Can could be truly dangerous. Considered the most primitive and severe of the brothers, he ruled central Vietnam as a virtual warlord. He spread fear through mass arrests, summary executions, and regular shakedowns of area businessmen. But he also created a devoted following that stuck with him because he established an unambiguous system of rewards and punishments. Those who did what he wanted were promoted or protected. Those who didn't were robbed or killed.

Nhu combined Can's ruthlessness with a particular cruelty and arrogance of his own. He was a striking man, the dark eyes and eyebrows against the pale complexion, the high cheekbones, and the thin lips.

He might have been called handsome, an American writer and one-time Diem supporter, Joseph Buttinger, remarked, but there was "something frightening in his face ... an air of Machiavellian mystery and cynical vanity, wicked intelligence and calculated malice. ... Dressed in a short-sleeved shirt made of local yellowish silk and black pants, he gave an impression of studied disdain and provocative arrogance."

All of the Ngos had a reputation for vanity and for scorn of those outside the family. But Nhu's pride was excessive even among the Ngos. It was that pride, and Diem's extravagant regard for Nhu's uncertain intellectual gifts, that enabled the younger brother to gain greater and greater sway over Diem during the last years.

Nhu had early sought to consolidate his own power through the semicovert Personalist Labor Revolutionary party—the infamous Can Lao. With its five-man cells scattered throughout the military and administrative hierarchies, the Can Lao became Nhu's private secret police force, keeping an eye on loyalists and eliminating bothersome opposition. Although Diem took an active hand in repressions of every sort during his nine years in office, it was Nhu—amid Communist denunciation campaigns, "reeducation centers," forced relocations, purges, and illegal arrests—who came to symbolize for the South Vietnamese the evil genius of the regime.

Nhu's megalomania eventually drove him further and further from reality. "We knew that Nhu was smoking opium in the last year and maybe taking heroin, too," recalled former Secretary of State Nguyen Dinh Thuan, "and that this helped create his moods of extremism. You could begin to see madness in his face, a sort of somnambulistic stare, always with the cold smile." For the Vietnamese, the first responsibility of a ruler was to mediate between his people and the world, to manifest in his own person the harmony and order of the universe. When madness destroyed that harmony, there could be no order, only chaos, darkness, and death.

By the summer of 1963 the Ngos had forfeited whatever regard the Vietnamese people may once have had for them. Backed by the political, military, and financial support of the United States, their intelligence, hard work, and ruthlessness had enabled them to dominate their country for nearly a decade. But their corruption, their arrogance, and eventually their madness undermined the basis of their authority and paved the way for their destruction.

NORTH
VIETNAM

Cape Vinh Son

GULF OF TONKIN

QUANG
BINH

Quang Khe
Chanh Hoa
Dong Hoi

Nong Khai

Udon Than (Udorn)   Nakhan Phanom   Thakhek

Xom Bang
Chap Le   Vinh Linh

VINH LINH
SPECIAL ZONE   Seventeenth Parallel (Demilitarized Zone)

Tchepone   QUANG TRI   Quang Tri

Savannakhet   Khe Sanh   Hue

THUA
THIEN   Hoa Phong

Muong Nong   Nam Dong   QUANG
NAM   Da Nang
Quang Nam

THAILAND   An Hoa

Saravane   QUANG TIN   Chu Lai

Muang Ubon   Chavane   My Lai
QUANG   Quang Ngai
NGAI   Nghia Han

Pak Se

Attopeu   KONTUM

Kontum   Dong Tre

Phu My
PLEIKU   BINH DINH

Khong   Pleiku   Qui Nhon

Plei Me

PHU BON   Phu Qui
PHU YEN   Tuy Hoa

Angkor   Stung Treng   Buon Brieng
Siem Reap   DARLAC

CAMBODIA   KHANH
HOA

Battambang   Tonle
Sap   Ban Me Thuot   Buon Enao

Nha Trang

Kompong Thom   QUANG DUC   TUYEN DUC   NINH
THUAN
Da Lat

Kompong
Chhnang   LAM DONG   Go Den
Kompong
Cham   BINH   PHUOC   Phan Rang
LONG   LONG
Mekong River   BINH THUAN
An Loc
Phnom Penh   TAY   HIGHWAY ONE
NINH   LONG
KHANH   BINH
Svay Rieng   Go   BINH   TUY
Dau Ha   DUONG
Ben Cat
Parrot's   Bien Hoa
Beak   HAU   BIEN   Long Thanh
NGHIA   HOA
KIEN   Saigon   PHUOC
Kompong Som   TUONG   GIA   TUY
LONG   DINH
CHAU DOC   AN   Ap Bac   Vung Tau
Ha Tien   KIEN   My   GO CONG   (Cap St. Jacques)
PHONG   AN   Tho   SOUTH
KIEN GIANG   GIANG   DINH   My
SA   THONG
DEC   Ben Tre   CHINA SEA
GULF OF THAILAND   Sa Dec   KIEN HOA
Village   VINH
LONG
Can Tho   VINH
Town   PHONG   BINH
DINH
City   CHUONG   Dai Ngai
THIEN   Soc Trang
Kien Long   BA XUYEN   0   25   50   75   100 miles
Road
BAC
LIEU   Bac Lieu (Vinh Loi)
Province boundary
South Vietnam
QUANG TRI Province name
AN XUYEN
(Poulo Condore)
Con Son

66

The Soldiers of South Vietnam

Like these men struggling in the pervasive mud of the Mekong Delta, ARVN soldiers displayed a remarkable stoicism in the face of hardship and death.

The soldiers of the Army of the Republic of Vietnam were overwhelmingly rural people of peasant background. Usually in their late twenties or early thirties, many of them were veterans of the French war a decade earlier. They were enrolled for three-year hitches, but most would serve for the duration or until they were no longer able to fight. Generally ill-led by an inadequately trained and class-conscious officer corps, given little idea of what they were fighting for, the ARVN soldier responded with a courage and endurance that won the respect of the American officers sent to teach him. Short, wiry, and tough, he shouldered weapons made for much larger men through miles of swamps or across the back-breaking ridges of the Truong Son Mountains. When asked what had been his most lasting impression of his tour in Vietnam, one U.S. adviser responded: "I think it would be the almost limitless ability of the Vietnamese soldier to bear suffering and pain without complaint. I've never heard a wounded Vietnamese cry, never heard a tired one complain."

For the ordinary enlisted man military service wasn't an easy life. He was usually assigned to a unit far from his own province; his leaves were infrequent and rarely long enough to permit a visit to his village. Some wives were able to follow their husbands and settle near ARVN camps, but many soldiers saw their families no more than once a year. Without formal education, and therefore with little chance for promotion, most survived on pay of about twelve hundred piasters (ten dollars) a month, with an additional thirty piasters for a married man and sixty piasters for each child. Their diet consisted of rice and dried fish, flavored with *nuoc nam* (fish sauce) and a simple vegetable soup. For amusement there was an occasional rice brandy and once in a while a movie, a lottery ticket, or perhaps a girl.

Left. The lack of education of most ARVN recruits hampered training in the use of modern weapons, such as this U.S.-made M114 155MM howitzer. Their willingness to learn, however, coupled with improved instruction, could bring excellent results.

Left. A soldier stationed in Binh Duong Province enjoys a visit with his wife and baby son. Military authorities welcomed those few wives who could afford to leave their villages and follow their husbands, hoping the proximity of his family would make a man less inclined to desert.

Far from home, ARVN soldiers on leave in the market of Vin Kim.

They could be sentimental, given to writing poems and listening to songs of lost love. Americans in the field found them gentle and generous men, ready to share their meager rations whenever necessary. For their part, ARVN soldiers admired American bravery and prized individual Americans as an endless source of cigarettes. Between them grew a special bond: The Vietnamese knew that if there were Americans around they were more likely to get decent treatment; the Americans recognized that the ARVN's worst sins were those visited on the enlisted men by their own officers. "These people may not be the world's greatest fighters," observed one long-time American adviser, "but they're good people, and they can win a war if someone shows them how."

Right. An American adviser and ARVN soldier exchange notes during a break on patrol. Although tension often marked the relations between U.S. advisers and ARVN officers, South Vietnamese enlisted men generally liked the Americans and admired them as soldiers.

ARVN reinforcements hurry to the rescue of soldiers caught in a VC attack just west of Da Nang.

Caught in a burst of automatic fire, a wounded soldier is helped by a comrade. If an ARVN soldier died, his wife was supposed to get a payment of about one hundred and sixty dollars in compensation.

Season of Fire

"*Na Mo A Di Da Phat . . . Na Mo A Di Da Phat.*" In the warm, humid morning air of June 11, 1963, the traditional Buddhist prayer rose above the small pagoda off Saigon's Pham Dinh Phung Street. Incense curling away from the ceremonial braziers, lips moving to the hypnotic rhythm of the chant, eyes fixed and staring into an inward vision of religious fervor, hundreds of Buddhist monks and nuns intoned the ancient supplication.

At precisely 9:00 A.M. the chanting stopped. Unfurling banners in Vietnamese and English, the monks and nuns formed a procession that began to move slowly from the pagoda. At the front of the line a gray sedan led the way. About a half block ahead a white police car cleared the street.

As the gray car rolled to a halt at the intersection of Le Van Duyet Street, one of Saigon's major boulevards, the marchers formed a circle around it. From the trunk of the car one of the monks took a five-gallon gasoline can. Another

Buddhists pray in Saigon's Xa Loi Pagoda, which along with other Buddhist temples became a center of political protest.

placed a small brown cushion on the pavement. Calmly seating himself on the cushion in the traditional lotus position, a seventy-three-year-old monk, the Venerable (Thich) Quang Duc, fingered a string of holy oak beads. Two of the monks brought the gasoline can to the center of the circle, poured most of its contents over the head and shoulders of the aging monk, then stepped back among the onlookers. Murmuring the sacred words "*nam mo amita Bud-*

dha" ("return to eternal Buddha"), the old priest struck a match and set himself ablaze.

"Oh my God," cried a westerner who watched from the crowd, "oh my God." As flames engulfed Thich Quang Duc's body, some of the attendant monks and nuns prostrated themselves, while others, many with tears streaming down their faces, forced back the white-clad policemen who tried to rush to the rescue.

For ten minutes, as the flames roared and the air filled with the sickly sweet stench of burning human flesh, Thich Quang Duc sat motionless, without a cry of pain, his hands folded in his lap. Into a loud-speaker a monk repeated over and over again, first

Preceding page. Shocking symbols of religious fervor and political protest, the fiery suicides of Buddhist monks stunned the world and marked the beginning of the end for the Diem regime.

in Vietnamese and then in English, "A Buddhist priest burns himself to death. A Buddhist priest becomes a martyr."

Finally, the monk fell backward, his fire-blackened legs kicking convulsively for several minutes. Then he was still. The flames slowly subsided.

David Halberstam, who was on the scene, noted tersely that "human beings burn surprisingly quickly." For Ngo Dinh Diem, however, the fire of Buddhist fervor would burn on and on until it consumed him, his family, and his regime in an inferno of retribution.

The first spark

The immolation of Thich Quang Duc elicited global horror and indignation and turned world opinion squarely against President Diem's regime. It seriously undermined U.S. relations with Diem and marked the beginning of the end of his nine-year rule. Yet the South Vietnamese president might well have avoided the incident and the entire outburst of Buddhist protest from which it emerged.

The crisis had erupted five weeks earlier on May 8 in the former imperial capital of Hue. Diem had prohibited the monks from flying their religious flags on the celebration of the birthday of Gautama Buddha. The Buddhists marched to the city radio station in protest. When they refused to disperse, government troops under the command of Major Dang Sy opened fire on the demonstrators, killing eight people, including one child, and wounding scores more.

The government quickly issued a statement absolving Major Sy of any wrongdoing, charging that the incident had been provoked by "liars, foreigners, and the Vietcong." On the next day, ten thousand peaceful demonstrators gathered outside the province chief's home in Hue to protest the army attack. When the authorities responded by prohibiting further demonstrations, Buddhist leaders demanded that Diem lift the ban on religious flags, recompense the families of the victims of May 8, punish those responsible, and admit the government's responsibility.

The Buddhist's dispute with the Diem government was not merely over whether they could fly religious banners or whether the government should be held accountable for the violence in Hue. For South Vietnam's 10.5 million Buddhists these were but symbols of a pattern of discrimination and hostility that Buddhists had endured for nearly one hundred years.

When the French gained control over Vietnam in the late nineteenth century, they gave Catholicism a special place in their new colonial society. The social, economic, and political distinctions of French Indochina were left largely intact by the Catholic president, Ngo Dinh Diem, who looked to his fellow Catholics—most of them anti-Communist refugees from the North—as his firmest base of political power.

Buddhists complained that under the Diem regime Catholics received the best civil service jobs, preferential treatment in army promotions, exemption from the forced labor necessary to construct strategic hamlets, and the choicest land redistributed by the government. They objected to restrictions on their right to own property, to ambitious functionaries who curried favor with the ruling regime by harassing Buddhist groups with government red tape, and to the morality crusade of Madame Nhu, which many Buddhists regarded as an attempt to make Catholi-

A monk cradles the charred heart of Thich Quang Duc. Later, his heart was placed on display inside Xa Loi Pagoda where thousands of the faithful came to venerate the memory of a Buddhist saint.

Buddhists protesting the Diem government's policies tear barehanded at a barbed wire barricade surrounding a Saigon pagoda manned by Diem's security police.

cism the state religion. There were darker charges, too, of harassment, intimidation, and murder of Buddhist activists by Nhu's secret police. Most western observers agreed that there was considerable favoritism toward South Vietnam's 1.5 million Catholics, if not outright persecution of the Buddhist majority.

On May 28, Thich Tinh Khiet, the head of the Buddhist hierarchy in Vietnam, issued a pastoral letter calling for a hunger strike to protest the government's intransigence. In Hue, almost a thousand monks and nuns responded to his call, and for the first time the demonstrations spread to Saigon where several hundred Buddhists assembled for a silent protest outside the National Assembly. What had been an isolated though serious incident was fast becoming a national movement.

Then on June 2 the Buddhist crisis for the second time took a violent turn. Using attack dogs and tear-gas grenades, police dispersed a student demonstration in Hue, sending sixty-seven people to the hospital with chemical burns. Diem immediately clamped a dusk-to-dawn curfew on Hue, ordering riot police and APCs to patrol the city streets. In an attempt to head off further violent confrontations he dismissed three officials responsible for the May 8 incident, including Major Sy, apologized for their "lack of sensitivity," and announced the appointment of an interministerial committee to meet with the Buddhists to discuss their grievances.

But the situation was rapidly getting beyond his control. While the initial discussions between the new government committee and Buddhist leaders were taking place, Thich Quang Duc made his awesome protest.

If the religious significance of Quang Duc's self-immolation was the triumph of spirituality over the limitations of the flesh, its political intent was to contrast the superior virtue of the Buddhist priest with the corrupt government that would persecute him. That this was the general lesson taken from Quang Duc's suicide there can be little doubt. One previously apolitical Buddhist told his western employer: "I have always believed in President Diem. But now this has happened. This proves that the president is bad."

Diem responded with a campaign of malicious rumor concerning the suicide. Blaming Quang Duc's "tragic death" on "certain minds poisoned by seditious propaganda," he accused the Buddhists of drugging the priest and charged that it was they who struck the fatal match. Madame Nhu labeled the Buddhists Communist dupes and concluded that "all the Buddhists have done for this country is to barbecue a monk."

Such outrageous statements only further alienated Vietnamese and world opinion, leaving Diem little choice but to make some sort of peace with his antagonists. On June 16 the interministerial committee and the Buddhist delegation issued a joint communiqué in which the committee acceded to most of the Buddhist demands, although the government still refused to accept responsibility for the incident.

But the Buddhists remained wary, particularly the new generation of politically sophisticated young priests determined to resist Diem's authoritarian rule. "The government has deceived us before," remarked one of them, "and we won't be fully satisfied until all our grievances are met."

The politics of religion

It was the young priests who would have the most decisive influence on the shape of the renascent Buddhist movement. Many of them had taken part in the resistance during the French Indochina War, gaining political experience and learning the strength of mass organization. They also had come to understand the power of the printed word. When the young monks took their tales of oppression and lists of grievances to western reporters, they found in the international press corps a sympathetic audience.

Already contemptuous of the Diem regime, American newsmen seized upon the Buddhist protest as an opportunity to paint in glaring colors the actual, and in some cases exaggerated, tyrannies of the Saigon government. The media gave Buddhists an indispensable channel not only to the rest of the world but also to the rest of Vietnam. Diem could not censor Voice of America radio broadcasts, nor could he easily halt the flood of American newspaper reprints that began to appear on city streets.

The transformation of the Buddhist movement into a full-fledged political struggle signaled the passing of the old leadership and the ascension of the new. When the Monk Superior Thich Tinh Khiet expressed his "firm conviction that the joint communiqué will inaugurate a new era and that no misunderstanding, no erroneous action from whatever quarter will occur again," he represented a rapidly dwindling minority within the Buddhist hierarchy. Thich Duc Nghiep, who acted as a liaison between the young monks and the western correspondents, spoke for a larger and more skeptical generation. "When I tell some of the other priests what has been signed," he lamented to several reporters on hearing of the June 16 agreement, "they will be very angry."

The young priests had reason for caution. Diem had signed the June 16 communiqué only reluctantly and against the vociferous opposition of his brother and sister-in-law. The day after the communiqué was announced, the Nhu-financed *Times of Vietnam* denounced the Buddhist "extortion" in a front-page article. Contrary to official promises, a number of Buddhist leaders remained under arrest, and Nhu made plans to suppress Buddhist organizations "once the present storm has subsided."

Throughout the month of July the government's schizophrenic pattern of repression and conciliation continued. The imprisonment of Buddhist priests, the removal of barricades around the pagodas, government tolerance of peaceful demonstrations, savage police attacks, mass arrests of protesters, the wholesale release of prisoners from jail—one followed upon the other in a bewildering syncopation. By the end of the month some observers had begun to wonder openly about the mental stability of the ruling family. Watching the Saigon authorities during those four months, David Halberstam would later recall, "was like watching a government trying to commit suicide."

The tension between the U.S. and President Diem is mirrored on the faces of Diem's brother Ngo Dinh Nhu, the moving spirit of the Saigon government, and Frederick Nolting, U.S. ambassador to South Vietnam. Nolting's failure to convince Diem to remove Nhu proved the end of effective American influence over the Diem regime.

Ridiculed by Madame Nhu as "barbecues," Buddhist martyrdoms helped bring down the government of Ngo Dinh Diem. This suicide occurred in late October 1963.

Getting tough

Indeed, one of the most disturbing aspects of all that took place during the summer of 1963 was the inability of the United States to prevent the Diem regime from plunging a knife into its own heart.

American officials had been quick to recognize the explosive potential of a Buddhist upheaval. On May 18 Ambassador Nolting met with Diem, urging the president to accept responsibility for what had happened at Hue, compensate the families of the victims, and reaffirm religious equality and nondiscrimination. Diem was frustratingly noncommital.

Nolting's inability to influence Diem at this critical juncture betrayed a glaring weakness in the relationship that the U.S. had established with the GVN. For nine years U.S. ambassadors had alternated "tough" and "soft" approaches toward Diem with equally little success. The problem was one of leverage. In their haste to assure Diem that he had the full commitment of the U.S. in his struggle against the Communist-supported insurgency, American officials had neutralized their own bargaining power.

When rebellion first flared in South Vietnam in 1959, Nolting's predecessor as American ambassador, Elbridge Durbrow, had pressured Diem to implement the programs the U.S. thought necessary to win the war. But under Durbrow's constant prodding, Diem turned sullen and uncommunicative. Meanwhile, the military situation grew more desperate.

Hoping to regain Diem's confidence, Nolting spent two years patiently cultivating the South Vietnamese president. But the basic American policy—that there was no alternative to Diem—remained the same. Realizing this, Diem continued to disregard whatever American advice did not accord with what he believed to be the interests of his family, secure in the knowledge that the U.S. would not abandon him.

Now in the spring of 1963, with Nolting on vacation and Diem continuing to favor repression over conciliation, Washington once again decided on a "get tough" approach. After the demonstrations in Hue on June 2, American Chargé d'Affaires William Trueheart warned Diem that, if the South Vietnamese government continued its repression of the Buddhists, the United States would publicly "disassociate" itself from the regime's policies. After the suicide of Thich Quang Duc, Trueheart repeated his threat and began to apply relentless pressure on Diem to abide by the June 16 agreement. Through the end of June and into early July, Trueheart had almost daily meetings with the South Vietnamese president and made innumerable visits and telephone calls to lesser officials. It was a "get tough" approach, recalled one member of the U.S. Mission, "such as the United States had seldom before attempted with a sovereign, friendly government."

In the end, it accomplished nothing. Deeply insulted by the "disassociation" threat, Diem stopped listening to the embassy altogether. At the same time the new American tactics provoked a serious split within the U.S. Mission between those who thought the threat of public rupture would encourage Diem to intensify his government's repression of the Buddhists and those who believed that only the shock of such a threat might avert impending catastrophe.

In Washington, meanwhile, concern over the progress of the war had been supplanted by discussions of how Nhu and Madame Nhu might be removed and of the likelihood of a military coup d'état. Nolting, whose vacation had been interrupted for high-level meetings at the White House, warned President Kennedy that a coup would produce a civil war. The only hope, thought the ambassador, was to try to regain Diem's confidence. Kennedy had already announced the appointment of Henry Cabot Lodge as the new U.S. ambassador to South Vietnam, signaling a more aggressive American stance toward Saigon. But the president decided to let Nolting have one more try at convincing Diem to settle the crisis peacefully.

The ambassador returned to Saigon on July 11, telling reporters he had come back to try to convince Diem to "change his image." Hoping to draw on the good will he had established over the preceding two years, Nolting met with the South Vietnamese president and convinced him to make a nationwide radio address announcing concessions to the Buddhists.

Diem's "concession" speech on July 19 lasted all of two minutes. Speaking in cold, grudging tones, he made a minor compromise on the question of flying religious flags, told the people to respect him, and announced the formation of another government commission to investigate Buddhist complaints. Even as Diem spoke, army troops were sealing off the pagodas with barbed wire.

A season of fire

With their leaders in jail or in hiding, their government refusing to compromise, the Buddhists visited upon their country a season of fire.

On August 5, in the small fishing port of Phan Thiet, a twenty-one-year-old Buddhist monk named Nguyen Huong poured gasoline over his robes, lit a match, and exploded into flames. On the thirteenth a seventeen-year-old novice priest from Hue wrapped himself in a kerosene-soaked Buddhist flag and

As the tide of popular protest against Diem rose during the summer of 1963, isolated acts of defiance gave way to mass demonstrations.

An injured student is led away by the police following a Saigon demonstration against Diem. Initially uncommitted, students soon swelled the ranks of anti-government protesters.

burned himself to death. In the village of Ninh Hoa, a young Buddhist nun sat down in a Catholic school playground and set herself on fire. Less than twenty-four hours later a seventy-one-year-old monk announced over the loud-speaker at Hue's Tu Dam Pagoda that he was going to kill himself, then burned to death in the courtyard of the pagoda.

The government responded by putting the Buddhist strongholds of Hue and Nha Trang under virtual martial law. But the loyalty of the army itself was increasingly uncertain. Leaflets containing western press accounts of the crisis were distributed at army bases, and soldiers began wearing saffron arm patches in support of the Buddhist clergy.

On August 20, ten senior army generals asked Diem for a declaration of martial law to enable them to return monks from outside Saigon to their own pagodas. The decree went into effect at midnight. And at midnight—unbeknownst to the generals—Ngo Dinh Nhu put into action his own plan for ending the crisis.

The pagoda raids

Out of the darkness the great gong began clanging from the tower of Saigon's Xa Loi Pagoda. Moments later squads of heavily armed soldiers smashed down the pagoda's main gate, battered a path through a small guard of young monks, and raced through the temple. The crack of gunfire and the crump of exploding tear gas grenades mingled with the confused screams of monks and nuns as the soldiers dragged their captives from the pagoda and threw them into army trucks.

In Hue, soldiers firing M1 rifles overran Tu Dam Pagoda, smashed a statue of Buddha, and looted thirty thousand dollars from the temple treasury. Near Dieu De Pagoda, men, women, and children fought with troops and police for five hours until the soldiers finally cleared a way through the furious mob with armored cars. The defense of the pagoda left thirty townspeople dead, two hundred wounded, and ten truckloads hauled away to jail. All told some two thousand pagodas were raided during the early hours of August 21 and more than fourteen hundred Buddhists arrested. Estimates of the number killed ranged from fifty to several hundred.

At 6:00 A.M. Radio Saigon crackled to life with a statement by President Diem. Insisting that three months of negotiations had failed to solve the crisis, he announced that the nation was under a decree of martial law. Given blanket search-and-arrest powers, the army prohibited all public gatherings and clamped tight censorship on all outgoing news. In Saigon, soldiers dressed in full camouflage battle gear and carrying automatic weapons and rifles with fixed bayonets established guard posts at every major bridge and intersection, patrolling the streets in jeeps bearing .30-caliber machine guns.

The raids on the pagodas and the imposition of martial law proved to be the last straw. In turning unequivocally away from conciliation, the Diem regime had finally forfeited whatever popular support it might still have had. Saigon University students boycotted classes in favor of turbulent antigovernment rallies. Martial law posters were defaced and soldiers openly jeered on the streets. Protesting the government's action, Foreign Minister Vu Van Mau quit his post, shaved his head, and sought Diem's permission to travel to India on a religious pilgrimage. More devastating still, Tran Van Chuong, South Vietnam's ambassador to the United States and the father of Madame Nhu, resigned in despair, denouncing the Diem government for "copying the tactics of totalitarian regimes."

Using the declaration of martial law as a façade, Nhu had attempted to blame the raids on the regular army. Press reports contradicted this charge from the outset, and within a week it was clear that the destruction of the pagodas had been carried out by Special Forces troops under the command of Colonel Le Quant Tung, an old and reliable Ngo family loyalist. Once Nhu's role in the affair was established, world opinion turned decisively against the Diem government.

Most visibly shaken was Washington, which condemned Saigon's strong-arm tactics as "a direct violation by the Vietnamese government of assurances that it was pursuing a policy of reconciliation toward the Buddhists." But expressions of U.S. dismay had ceased to carry much weight with the Diem regime. On the day after the raids, no Americans were able to see high Vietnamese officials, and Americans arriving for work at the U.S. aid mission were turned away by Vietnamese police. Even more galling, ordinary Vietnamese refused to believe that the United States had nothing to do with the crackdown. "You Americans have trained this army well," complained one young Vietnamese officer bitterly. "Your country can take a lot of credit for what's going on now."

At 9:30 P.M. on August 22, the new American ambassador to South Vietnam arrived at Tan Son Nhut Airport. Driving through the hot tropical blackness into Saigon, the wet streets gleaming dully in the headlights of his police escort, Henry Cabot Lodge had the sharp impression of entering a city in a state of siege. The only human beings he saw were the soldiers guarding his route, their backs to the street, their rifles ready to fire. On the very next day Ambassador Lodge learned that a group of South Viet-

namese generals had informed American agents that they were prepared to undertake the overthrow of the Diem government.

Mis-coup

The generals who approached American CIA agent Lou Conein on August 23 were all veterans both of the war against the insurgents and the even more vicious political war with the Ngos. Duong Van "Big" Minh, former ARVN field commander, Tran Van Don, former commander of I Corps, and Le Van Kim, former commandant of the National Military Academy, had all been deprived of their duties by Diem and placed in figurehead positions. Minh, the leader of the cabal, was a burly, affable "soldier's soldier" with a reputation as a man of action. A product of the French colonial army who first came to prominence in 1955 when he crushed the Binh Xuyen crime lords, Minh was a man who "didn't believe in paper," according to an aide. "His style is to pick up the phone and say 'Let's go.'" Don, the liaison with the Americans, was an urbane Vietnamese aristocrat. Born and educated in France, he was regarded by his colleagues as a candid, thoughtful figure, as adept at administration as Minh was in the field. Kim, who was in charge of political planning for the successor government, was considered by many Americans the most intelligent of the generals. At the time of the coup he had fallen so far out of favor with the presidential palace that Diem had neglected to find him a position of any kind. Lacking real power of their own—they commanded between them a mere fifty soldiers—the three generals enlisted into their conspiracy Don's successor at I Corps, General Do Cao Tri, and II Corps Commander General Nguyen Khanh, as well as Don's executive officer, General Tran Thien Khiem.

In the new American ambassador the generals found a man receptive to their plans. A Massachusetts Republican who had lost a Senate seat to the young John Kennedy in 1952 and lost again to his fellow Bay Stater as the Republican vice presidential candidate in 1960, Lodge had served in the interim as U.S. ambassador to the United Nations where he gained a reputation as a penetrating debater and a vigorous foe of Communist expansion. Cool, reserved, polished, and articulate, Lodge was a man of "serene ruthlessness," seemingly indifferent to the opinion of his associates, yet shrewd, tough, and penetrating. If he alienated many Americans in Saigon with his patrician manner, he won their respect with his intelligence and devotion to duty.

Studying the State Department files on Vietnam before leaving Washington, Lodge had been appalled at the treatment American representatives were being accorded by the Diem regime, and he was determined to do something about it. After informing Diem and a few other top Vietnamese officials precisely what the United States desired, he made no further attempt to negotiate. In fact, he made no further attempt to call. "They have not done anything I asked," Lodge said. "They know what I want. Why should I keep asking? Let them come to me for something." In the aftermath of the pagoda raids he had little faith in the capacity of the Diem regime to escape the political turmoil which surrounded it. Convinced that no amount of pressure would turn Diem and Nhu around, he was more than willing to contemplate a change of government.

On Saturday, August 24, Lodge received a cable from the State Department acknowledging the central role of Nhu in the expanding repression against the Buddhists and starkly setting forth a new American policy:

U.S. Government cannot tolerate situation in which power lies in Nhu's hands. Diem must be given chance to rid himself of Nhu and his coterie and replace them with best military and political personalities available.

If, in spite of all your efforts, Diem remains obdurate and refuses, then we must face the possibility that Diem himself cannot be preserved.

Lodge was told to inform Diem that the United States would not accept further repressions and that active measures to redress the situation must be taken. The ambassador was to inform key military leaders privately that if Diem refused to remove Nhu the United States would give them direct support in any "interim period of breakdown [in the] central government mechanism."

The cable of instructions had been prepared by Roger Hilsman, George Ball, presidential adviser Michael Forrestal, and Undersecretary of State for Political Affairs Averell Harriman and cleared with the president. But by Monday Washington was having second thoughts. Maxwell Taylor complained that the anti-Diem group at the State Department had taken advantage of the absence of senior officials to stake out a confused and possibly untenable position, a view shared by McNamara and CIA Director John McCone. By the time the National Security Council

met that morning, President Kennedy had become annoyed at the disagreement among his senior advisers and may also have begun to feel that he was being pushed too hard and too fast. Robert Kennedy would later assert that the August 24 cable and the communication of American encouragement to the dissident South Vietnamese generals had compromised the country, badly split the government, and started the administration down a road it never really wished to travel.

There was dissension, too, in Saigon. Expressing confidence in the generals and arguing that "chances of success would be diminished by delay," Lodge strongly endorsed the new policy. Indeed, he went even further. Since the "chances of Diem's meeting our demands are virtually nil," Lodge proposed that he forego a futile approach to Diem in favor of throwing full American weight behind the coup. General Harkins, however, questioned whether the plotters had a clear-cut military advantage. He favored giving Diem one last chance. If the South Vietnamese president refused to remove the Nhus, there would still be time to support the generals. Confident that the coup could not take place until the U.S. gave the word, Harkins told Taylor on the twenty-seventh that in his opinion there wasn't "sufficient reason for a crash approval on our part at this time."

Despite the apparent momentum of events, the division of opinion among the men in the field disturbed President Kennedy and fueled the increasingly heated debate between those at the State Department who wanted to go ahead with the coup and those at Defense who favored one more try with Diem. After a National Security Council meeting on the twenty-ninth, Kennedy formally approved the coup operation, although the president reserved the right to change his mind at the last minute. For his part Lodge continued to insist that the planned coup was "essentially a Vietnamese operation," warning the president that if the "go signal" was given by the generals, Kennedy might have no way of stopping it.

In the event, the generals were far too unsure of themselves to proceed. On August 31 Minh met with Harkins to inform him that the coup had been called off. The generals' failure to win over General Ton That Dinh, commander of the key III Corps near Saigon, their continuing doubts about the firmness of American support, their anxiety that the close relationship between CIA Station Chief John Richardson and Nhu might have led to critical leaks, and a lack of cohesion within their own ranks all precluded ac-

Boston Brahmin meets Vietnamese mandarin. U.S. Ambassador Henry Cabot Lodge arrived in Saigon determined to "get tough" with South Vietnam's intractable president.

tion, leaving Lodge to complain somewhat bitterly that there was "neither the will nor the organization among the generals to accomplish anything."

Deeper questions

Even as Washington received news that the coup had been aborted, questions began to be raised about the whole nature of American involvement in South Vietnam. Paul Kattenburg, chairman of the Interdepartmental Working Group on Vietnam, told an NSC meeting on the thirty-first that there was no future for American support of the present regime. Kat-

tenburg conveyed Lodge's estimate that if Diem remained in power the United States would be driven out of South Vietnam within six months. The question the NSC should be considering, he declared, was the "decision to get out honorably." One week later, Attorney General Robert Kennedy brought the issue into even sharper focus. For Kennedy, as Roger Hilsman recalled, the fundamental question was what we were doing in Vietnam in the first place.

As he understood it we were there to help people resisting a Communist takeover. The first question was whether a Communist takeover could be successfully resisted with any government. If it could not, now was the time to get out of Vietnam entirely, rather than waiting.

For the first time the negative logic of American involvement in Vietnam was placed on the table for discussion. If the war could not be won with Diem, then his removal was a necessity. But if Diem's ouster would leave such political instability that military victory would be impossible, then he could not be removed. Kattenburg's and Kennedy's analyses suggested that already by the fall of 1963 only two alternatives remained: finding a way to disengage honorably from an irretrievable situation or assuming more direct responsibility for the prosecution of the war. Senior officials rejected the first alternative out of hand and would not be prepared to accept the latter for nearly a year and a half.

Washington was no more ready to consider French efforts toward a political settlement of the war. In the spring of 1963 the French ambassador to South Vietnam initiated secret discussions between Ho and Diem, using as an intermediary Mieczyslaw Maneli, the Polish member of the International Control Commission established in 1954 to supervise the Geneva agreements. For several months Maneli shuttled between Saigon and Hanoi seeking a common ground for negotiations. By July the North Vietnamese had agreed in principle to the establishment of a coalition government headed by Diem in a neutralized South Vietnam. They added that if the U.S. agreed to withdraw, they would not be opposed to American participation in the transition process.

According to William Bundy, assistant secretary of state for Far Eastern affairs, neither the pro–Diem faction at the Department of Defense nor the anti–Diem faction at the State Department was willing to take the reported negotiations seriously. Both were angry at what they regarded as French meddling, and neither considered neutralization to be anything more than a prelude to takeover by the North.

Meanwhile, neither Kattenburg's gloomy predictions nor Kennedy's trenchant analysis generated a searching reappraisal of U.S. policy. They prompted instead yet another fact-finding mission. On the same day as Kennedy's remarks to the NSC, Marine Corps Major General Victor Krulak and State Department official Joseph Mendenhall left for Saigon in search of new information.

After talking in the field with U.S. advisers and Vietnamese officers, Krulak reported to the president that the war was "going ahead at an impressive pace" and discounted the effect of the political crisis on the army. What dissatisfaction there was among the military was with Nhu, not Diem. The Diem government, concluded the general, could see the war through to victory.

Mendenhall had spent most of his time in Saigon, Hue, and Da Nang talking with old Vietnamese friends. He found disaffection with the Diem regime so great that a collapse of civil government had become likely, fratricidal religious conflict a real possibility. The war against the VC could not be won with the present regime. When Mendenhall had finished, President Kennedy looked at both men and asked, "You two did visit the same country, didn't you?"

Not sure how bad things were, divided over whether to press for a new government in Saigon, Washington decided to prod Diem into responsibility by threatening the source of his financial support. On September 17 the NSC instructed Lodge to press for Nhu's removal from the scene, using the aid program as his club. At the same meeting the National Security Council authorized still another fact-finding mission. This time, however, McNamara and Taylor would go themselves, unencumbered by State Department skeptics.

It's their war

Although the suggestion for the mission came from McNamara, it appears that it was Kennedy's idea to send the secretary of defense and the chairman of the Joint Chiefs of Staff to South Vietnam to see with their own eyes the negative effects of the protracted Buddhist crisis and the necessity of applying pressure on Diem. During a September 2 interview on CBS television, the president himself had questioned "whether that war can be won out there." Calling the repressions against the Buddhists "very unwise," he suggested that the Diem regime had "gotten out of touch with the people." Kennedy was not prepared to withdraw from Vietnam: That would be a "great mistake." And he believed that with "changes in policy and perhaps with personnel" the GVN could regain the allegiance of its people. The United States was still prepared to support the military struggle, but there were limits to what the Americans could do. "In the final analysis," observed the president, "it is their war. They are the ones who have to win it or lose it. We can help them, we can give them equipment, we can send our men out there as advisers, but they have to win it—the people of Vietnam."

McNamara returned from Saigon on October 2 convinced that the military campaign had made "great progress and continues to progress." On that basis he recommended the implementation of a plan, first proposed by Sir Robert Thompson in April, for the withdrawal of one thousand U.S. soldiers by the end of 1963 and the initiation of a program to train Vietnamese to replace Americans in all essential functions by 1965.

But McNamara also returned with an added appreciation of the dangers inherent in the confrontation between Diem and the Buddhists. The secretary had come to believe that while U.S. pressure on the Diem regime might in the end prove futile, there was no real alternative. To push Diem in the right direction, McNamara recommended a selective suspension of aid, the end of support for the Special Forces responsible for the pagoda raids, and a continuation of Lodge's studied aloofness from the Saigon government. And while he cautioned against any active encouragement of a coup, McNamara urged the embassy to identify and cultivate alternative leadership, "if and when it appears."

The recommendations received immediate approval by the NSC, and later that day McNamara announced to the press the one-thousand-man troop withdrawal. The aid suspensions—including suspension of the commodity import program and elimination of financial support for Colonel Tung's Special Forces—were handled more circumspectly. Most were communicated to the Saigon government without public announcement.

No going back

Instead of backing down, however, the Ngos met the suspension of aid with defiance. Banner headlines in the *Times of Vietnam* initiated a violent anti-American press campaign, while government surveillance and even harassment of Americans and their Vietnamese employees mounted. Arriving in the United States for a three-week speaking tour, Madame Nhu immediately launched into vituperative denunciations of American policy. At the same time, the GVN took a number of belt-tightening steps to contend with the loss of U.S. funds. Unmoved by American pressure, the Ngos were preparing for a long fight.

The generals had made it clear to U.S. agents in August that they would take a suspension of aid as a signal of American support. Now, in the face of Diem's intransigence and a worsening military situa-

tion, they reactivated their conspiracy. On October 5, three days after the McNamara-Taylor mission reported to the president, Minh told Lou Conein that the government's loss of popular favor was endangering the entire war effort. He and his colleagues were once more prepared to act.

Plans had been drawn up involving military action against Saigon units loyal to Diem and the assassination of Nhu and Can. Minh didn't expect any direct U.S. aid but had to know the American position with respect to a change of government. Lodge immediately recommended that the United States not stand in the generals' way. He suggested that U.S. agents be available to review any plans not involving assassinations and that U.S. aid be forthcoming for a successor government with a "good proportion of well-qualified civilian leaders in key positions."

Washington was willing, but nervous. Kennedy told Lodge that while the United States government did not wish "to stimulate a coup," it also didn't want to leave the impression that the U.S. would "thwart a change of government or deny economic and military assistance to a new regime." What worried Washington most was its position should the coup fail or if Americans became implicated with the plotters.

An American agent met with General Minh on October 10 and conveyed the U.S. position. Between the tenth and the twenty-eighth there were several more meetings during which the Americans learned which South Vietnamese units would take part in the coup. The generals refused to reveal further details for fear of security leaks but promised to turn over the operation plan for Lodge's "eyes only" two days before the coup took place. As the final week of October began, the generals' plans were in place.

It was the Americans who were having problems. The new policy of simultaneous pressure on Diem and covert support of the plotting generals had been left largely in Lodge's hands, creating strains within the official U.S. community. The ambassador ran the U.S. Mission as a one-man operation, insulating himself from the general embassy staff with a pair of special assistants, restricting the circulation of cable traffic to and from Washington, and monopolizing direct contact with top Vietnamese officials. Even high members of the Mission were uncertain about what was going on.

Lodge had to contend with Washington's concern that the United States avoid implication in the impending coup. He had to contend as well with the generals' suspicions of Harkins and the CIA. Years later in his memoirs Lodge defended himself by claiming that President Kennedy had asked him to keep their cables secret. Nevertheless, his lone pursuit of policy led to much bitterness within the Mission and made it impossible for agencies such as USIS and MACV to act in an informed manner.

Particularly damaging was the growing division between Lodge and General Harkins, who was kept largely in the dark about the generals' plans until a few days prior to the coup. Irate at having been excluded from information and consultation, Harkins fired off angry cables to Washington urging loyalty to Diem and casting doubt on the generals' chances of success. Lodge replied with his own cable disputing Harkins's judgment of the situation and stressing the irrevocability of American involvement.

The sharp disagreement between the ambassador and the chief U.S. military officer in Saigon, and a CIA evaluation that the generals might not have sufficient forces to act decisively, heightened Washington's anxieties as the coup drew nearer. Cables flew back and forth during the last week of October, Washington asking for reassurance, Lodge insisting that there was no turning back.

On the thirty-first the White House sent Lodge his final instructions. U.S. authorities were not to intervene directly on behalf of either side. If the outcome was indecisive they could take acts mutually agreeable to both sides but should avoid any appearance of favoritism. If the coup failed, the embassy could offer asylum to anyone at Lodge's discretion, but he should encourage people to go elsewhere. "But once a coup under responsible leadership has begun, and within these restrictions," concluded the cable, "it is in the interest of the U.S. government that it should succeed."

Four days earlier there had been one last opportunity to halt the onrush of events. After weeks of official harassment and anti-American rhetoric, Diem invited the U.S. ambassador to his villa in Da Lat. Lodge went to the meeting looking for any movement by the GVN on U.S. demands, but the discussion was frustrating in almost all respects. Diem offered evasions and complaints, justifications and excuses, but gave no indication that he was prepared to change his position on any matter of importance. Lodge recalled:

When it was evident that the conversation was practically over, I said: "Mr. President, every single specific suggestion which I have made, you have rejected. Isn't there some one thing you may think of that is within your capabilities to do and that would favorably impress U.S. opinion?" As on previous occasions when I asked him similar questions, he gave me a blank look and changed the subject.

Death of a mandarin

On the morning of November 1, Lodge and Admiral Harry D. Felt, the commander of U.S. Pacific forces, made a courtesy call on Diem. It was a strange meeting. During the small talk Diem told his visitors that the Americans should not be alarmed by new rumors of a coup. Everyone laughed. Then, just as Lodge was about to leave, Diem took him aside. He was ready to talk about what it was the United States wanted him to do. When could they get together? The ambassador would see.

But while Lodge and Felt said their good-byes to the president, rebel troops had already begun to deploy around Saigon. At a meeting of all senior officers called by General Don at the Joint General Staff headquarters, the insurgent generals told their colleagues that a coup had begun and "requested" their support. Several officers suspected of continuing loyalty to the regime were taken into custody. Conein was summoned, arriving with forty-two thousand dollars that the embassy had authorized some days earlier to procure food for the generals' soldiers and pay death benefits for those killed in the fighting. (The generals could not risk an attempt to raise the money themselves.) For most of the coup Conein stayed at JGS headquarters, providing information to the embassy by telephone.

As Saigon dozed languidly in the midday heat, marine, airborne, and army battalions, backed by nearly forty tanks, marched into the city. By three-thirty, fighting had erupted between rebel forces and the palace guard. Insurgent tanks raked the central avenues with bursts of machine-gun fire, as two rocket-firing T-28 fighter-bombers dived toward the palace, only to be driven off in a hail of 20 MM antiaircraft shells. Small-arms fire crackled around the center of the city and beyond, the deep thump of mortars reverberated in the humid air. At four-thirty, the generals went on the radio to announce the coup and demand the Ngos' capitulation.

As the generals took to the radio, Diem called Lodge to ask where he stood.

Diem: Some units have made a rebellion and I want to know what is the attitude of the U.S.

Lodge: I do not feel well enough informed to be able to tell you. I have heard the shooting but am not acquainted with all the facts. Also it is 4:30 A.M. in Washington, and the U.S. government cannot possibly have a view.

Diem: But you must have some general ideas. After all, I am a chief of state. I have tried to do my duty. I want to do now what duty and good sense require. I believe in duty above all.

Lodge: You have certainly done your duty. As I told you only this morning, I admire your courage and your great contributions to your country. No one can take away from you the credit for all you have done. Now I am worried about your physical safety. I have a report that those in charge of the current activity offer you and your brother safe conduct out of the country if you resign. Had you heard this?

Diem: No. (A pause) You have my telephone number.

Lodge: Yes. If I can do anything for your physical safety, please call me.

Diem: I am trying to reestablish order.

It was the last conversation that any American would have with Ngo Dinh Diem. No further instructions issued from Washington. Lodge, as was his custom, retired that night at about nine-thirty.

Meanwhile, Diem and Nhu had rejected the generals' repeated calls to surrender. The brothers, instead, made frantic attempts to rally loyal army commanders throughout the country. But no one came to the rescue. Sometime early in the evening, they escaped from the presidential palace through secret tunnels and made their way to the home of a friend in the neighboring Chinese section of Cholon.

Still believing the brothers were inside, rebel forces positioned tanks and armored personnel carriers in every street and alley offering a line of fire toward the presidential palace. At 4:00 A.M. they attacked. From virtually point-blank range .50-caliber machine guns and 75 MM tank guns pounded the palace defenders in a pandemonium of fire. Red tracers arched through the night as phosphorous parachute flares poured their eerie light over the besieged fortress. At 6:45 A.M. on November 2, Saigon radio announced that the palace had been overrun.

Only then did the generals learn that Diem and Nhu had fled to the house in Cholon. The brothers went from there to a nearby Catholic church, but with no hope of further escape Diem called General Don and offered to surrender unconditionally. The first man who leapt out of the armored personnel carrier sent to arrest them was Colonel Duong Ngoc Lam, the head of the Civil Guard and a trusted friend. Behind him was General Mai Huu Xuan, one of the original plotters, and a bitter enemy.

Their hands held behind them with metal wire, Diem and Nhu were driven in the back of the personnel carrier to JGS headquarters. They never made it alive. En route Diem was shot in the back of the head. Nhu was also shot, then repeatedly stabbed. According to one report, it was General Xuan who gave the orders for the brothers to be killed. According to another, the command came directly from General Minh.

In a gesture of humiliation and contempt, the death certificate described Diem not as the head of state but as "chief of province," a position he had held during the French colonial period. Nhu was listed as "chief of library service," one of his early posts. They were buried in unmarked graves somewhere near Saigon.

Jubilation and despair

Washington's reaction was somber but calm. Officials emphasized to reporters that the plot had been organized and executed by the Vietnamese and expressed regret that Diem and Nhu had not accepted the generals' offer of safe conduct. The State Department was principally concerned with avoiding any appearance of U.S. complicity. Rusk cabled Lodge to discourage the generals from "reporting in" at the U.S. Embassy and stressed the need to underscore publicly that "this was not so much a coup as an expression of national will."

When news of the killing of Diem and Nhu was given to President Kennedy during a high-level meeting in the Cabinet Room of the White House, he was visibly shaken. "Why did they do that?" he asked bitterly. The murders seemed a miserable finale to nine years of American-Vietnamese cooperation, a shabby conclusion as well to his own administration's efforts to deal successfully with the Diem regime. Whatever he had become, Diem had fought for his country for much of his life, Kennedy told one of his advisers. It shouldn't have ended like this.

If Diem's death brought consternation to Kennedy,

it brought jubilation to Saigon. Once the presidential palace had fallen, an American correspondent reported, crowds of people "delirious with excitement and joy, laughing, crying, shouting slogans, and waving banners" poured into the streets and climbed onto the rebel tanks to cheer the surprised but delighted soldiers. As newly released political prisoners began telling ugly stories of torture and beatings, mobs smashed the book shop of the dead president's brother, Archbishop Thuc, ransacked the offices of the *Times of Vietnam*, and tore down a statue modeled after Madame Nhu. Bar girls discarded the plain white smocks decreed by Madame Nhu, and Buddhists flocked to Xa Loi Pagoda to celebrate the release of their leaders with an emotional day-long service of thanksgiving.

Assassination in Saigon

by Robert Shaplen

The phone in my New York apartment rang at three o'clock in the morning of November 1, 1963. The call, from Hong Kong, was for Dang Duc Khoi, who was living with me. A former press aide of President Ngo Dinh Diem, Khoi had been engaged in some of the early plotting against Diem and his nefarious brother, Ngo Dinh Nhu. Khoi had fled Vietnam and come to New York several weeks before when he found out that Madame Nhu's brother was planning to assassinate him.

I awakened Khoi and stood by as he got the news from a Vietnamese friend that a coup against Diem and Nhu was taking place. Two days later, although I had returned from Saigon only a few weeks before, I was on my way back to find out as much as I could about the coup.

I found the city surprisingly placid. There was a certain air of relief, but also of trepidation and skepticism. The new twelve-man military junta, cumbersome as it was, appeared to be in control, though no one knew who was really in charge. Under Diem the war had been going badly. Would these new, politically inexperienced leaders be able to turn the tide, to get rid of corruption and nepotism? And how far would the Americans go in supporting them?

During the month prior to the coup, a small number of Americans on the scene in Saigon, notably CIA agent Lieutenant Colonel Lucien Conein, acting on behalf of Ambassador Henry Cabot Lodge, were apprised of and, to some extent, involved in its planning to a degree that qualified them to be described as coconspirators. As I learned later, while the Americans did not finance it as such, as friends of Diem charged and as the principal plotters vehemently denied, a certain amount of cash was funneled through the embassy and distributed through various channels to the coup leaders. Though the CIA admits to only a negligible amount—some forty-two thousand dollars—I was told the payments approximated six hundred thousand dollars. This money was used to "persuade" a number of key officers in III and IV Corps to go along with the coup passively, if not actively. IV Corps, in the delta, in particular, was dominated by pro-Diem commanders, and the men who mounted the coup, notably Generals Tran Van Don and Duong Van Minh, were concerned about "neutralizing" these officers so they wouldn't cause any trouble.

The coup makers had some funds at their disposal, but as the conniving with different military and civilian groups became more complicated, they ran short. It was at this juncture, especially in the final fortnight, my American sources told me, that Washington decided to help out. Thus, though they were not active participants in the coup, the approval if not encouragement given by top American officials, including President Kennedy, became a determinant factor.

Diem had always struck me as a paradoxical, anachronistic, and somewhat tragic figure. A short, broadly built man with a round face and shock of black hair, he walked and moved jerkily, as if on strings. His total self-absorption with the cause of the nation in his own image made it hard to interview him. Diem simply engaged in a series of monologues amounting to a mixture of self-justification and hortatory ideological lectures. Yet, in an odd sort of way, I liked him, or perhaps simply felt sorry for him.

Nhu, whom I had also met, and disliked, and his inordinately ambitious and scheming wife, had manipulated and brainwashed Diem away from his earlier nationalist aspirations, narrow and unrealistic as they may have been, and into pure dictatorship that led to the brutal suppression of the Buddhists in the summer of 1963. This more than anything else provoked the coup. I have always thought that if the U.S. had really wanted to support and protect Diem, as it professed until the end to do, if we had been more politically sophisticated and less purely militarily motivated, we would have done what we could to get rid of the Nhus as early as 1957. At the time, Diem, without the Nhus, was salvageable. By 1963 it was too late. He was the captive of his familial Svengalis.

The plotting to depose Diem and Nhu began as far back as mid-1962, pursuing a serpentine course of plots within plots, contests for loyalty, and countermoves by the ever-suspicious Nhu. By fall of 1962 Generals Don and "Big" Minh were the dominant plotters. On October 2, Don met Conein at Tan Son Nhut Airport in Saigon. Three days later Conein met with General Minh in Saigon. The purpose of these meetings was to obtain from Conein the promise of American moral and perhaps financial support for the coup. Conein simply relayed the requests of Don and Minh to Lodge and John Richardson, the CIA station chief. A number of other meetings took place between Don and Conein, one of them at a dentist's office in downtown Saigon, where they met "by accident."

Lodge, who had arrived in Vietnam

Americans were hailed wherever they went. Convinced that the U.S. had engineered the coup the usually reserved citizens of Saigon responded with smiles, waves, and applause for any American walking about among the celebrations. Lodge was regarded as a hero. More than one Vietnamese was heard to say that if an election for president were held that day, Lodge would win in a landslide.

On November 20, Lodge flew to Honolulu with General Harkins for a conference with Secretaries Rusk and McNamara and presidential adviser McGeorge Bundy. The new Saigon government had taken some positive steps to consolidate its support and reduce the authoritarianism of its predecessor, the ambassador reported. But the new leadership was inexperienced and fragile, and the military situ-

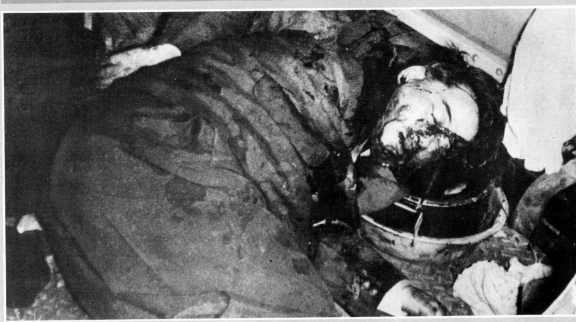

President Diem escaped the tanks ringing the presidential palace, but he could not escape a violent death at the hands of rebel officers.

shortly after the action against the Buddhists, worked closely with Conein thereafter and maintained constant contact with the State Department and the White House. Although there was considerable difference of opinion in Washington as to how far the U.S. should go in abandoning Diem, Lodge's argument for a change of leaders, supported by the State Department against a number of Defense Department officials, eventually won the passive, if not overt, backing of President Kennedy and the National Security Council.

Conein conveyed this decision to Don. As the plot approached a climax, the White House sent a cautious message inviting Lodge to "discourage" the coup if quick success appeared unlikely. Lodge cabled back that the United States was no longer able to "delay or discourage" any action. So, with American support assured, the planners moved swiftly.

After a number of last-minute hitches the plot went off smoothly. Assault forces gathered around the palace, and both Don and Minh called on Diem to surrender. Nguyen Dinh Thuan, the secretary of

state under Diem who had come to hate and fear Diem's brother Nhu, told me that the atmosphere around the palace toward the end was "like the last days of Hitler." Diem refused to give up and, bargaining for time, indicated he would negotiate. This Don rejected. Diem and Nhu then fled by a side entrance and escaped by car to Cholon, the Chinese part of the city. At 6:20 A.M., November 2, Diem telephoned Don and said he and Nhu would surrender but only with "military honors." Don rejected that too and told him they should simply give up and go peacefully into exile. Conein had previously arranged for a plane to take them to Manila, and it was standing by at the airport.

As things turned out, Diem and Nhu had sealed their fate by leaving the palace. From their initial hideout in the home of a Chinese businessman, they had made their way to a small Catholic church nearby. Five officers were assigned by Minh to fetch them. As Don later told the story, when the convoy returned to military headquarters, the bodies of Diem and Nhu were in one of the two vehicles. They had

been shot, on General Minh's secret orders, by two of the escorting officers, and Nhu's body had been mutilated.

I have always blamed the Americans in part for the failure of the November 1-2 coup d'état to be anything more than just that—it certainly did not lead to a legitimate revolution and it lacked any direction. The Americans had supported the violent change, but neither Washington nor the embassy had any sound ideas about fostering a strong new government that, in the time-worn phrase, would "capture the hearts and minds" of the people. The big war was still ahead, and the United States, having missed an opportunity after the fall of Diem either to get out of Vietnam or to help establish a firmer civilian political structure and a more broadly based economy, became more deeply embroiled in an unfolding tragedy.

Robert Shaplen, long a correspondent for the New Yorker *in Asia and elsewhere, has written six books about Vietnam.*

ation it faced was graver than anyone had realized.

In the weeks since the coup it had become apparent that the Diem government had systematically falsified military statistics. New information now pointed to a steady deterioration over the past six months including a substantial increase in guerrilla attacks and government weapons lost, and a significant decrease in Vietcong defections. With a marked upsurge in VC activity in the wake of the coup, the situation remained grim.

On the grounds of the presidential palace a happy soldier toasts the victory of insurgent government forces and the collapse of the Diem regime.

A divided legacy

John Kennedy had from the beginning of his administration approached the Vietnam problem with reluctant determination. Haunted by the French catastrophe of 1954, fearful that western military intervention would transform an anti-Communist struggle into a racial war, opposed on principle to the introduction of U.S. combat troops on the Asian

mainland, yet worried lest the collapse of South Vietnam pave the way for Communist domination of all Southeast Asia, Kennedy tried to strike a balance between American interests and American capabilities. If he felt that the Eisenhower administration had overcommitted the U.S. in Indochina, he was not prepared to simply retreat from that commitment. Encouraged by the apparent willingness of the Diem government to resist the insurgents, Kennedy sought to bolster South Vietnamese self-reliance without resorting to direct military intervention.

The president intended to keep the American role in the fighting as limited as possible, hoping to buy time for the Vietnamese without compromising his own government's ability to withdraw if necessary. Convinced that the key to victory lay not in military might but in winning the support of the peasantry through social and economic reforms, he placed his confidence in the doctrine of counterinsurgency and resisted constant pressure from his senior military advisers to introduce American combat forces.

But buoyed by the false optimism of 1962, Kennedy permitted Diem to delay and then ignore necessary reforms. Preoccupied with other matters, he delegated the formulation of American policy to men less concerned than he about maintaining a line between assistance and intervention. He left management of the American effort in Vietnam to individuals who either overemphasized military victory over the Vietcong or were all too willing to "save" the American position by becoming more deeply embroiled in Vietnamese politics. Worse, they consistently overestimated the possibility of resolving the Vietnamese problem without the participation of the NLF.

Kennedy had the self-confidence to permit a vigorous assertion of conflicting viewpoints within his administration on the Vietnam question. But he displayed little inclination to examine the assumptions on which those disagreements rested. Intent on maintaining his own room to maneuver, he tolerated a debilitating level of confusion and division over American objectives in Vietnam, allowing policy makers to devise an endless series of short-term solutions to chronic military and political crises. As a result, two years of intensified American effort, more than nine hundred million dollars of American aid, sixteen thousand American military advisers, and 108 American dead had done little to bring stability to the South Vietnamese government, diminish the insurgent threat, or guarantee either the security or well-being of the Vietnamese people.

Throughout 1963 Kennedy had betrayed in private a mounting apprehension about the direction of American policy. In January the president told Senator Mike Mansfield that the United States had overextended itself in Vietnam. "He felt we'd made a mistake, that he was going to begin pulling out the troops on the first of the next year," recalled Mansfield, "and he was very concerned and, I believe, mortified at how far we'd gone in." The inability of the Diem government to deal constructively with the Buddhist uprising and the administration's confused support of the dissident generals only aggravated Kennedy's nagging doubts about the whole nature of American involvement in Vietnam. He flatly rejected McNamara and Taylor's recommendation to affirm "the overriding objective of denying [South Vietnam] to communism," and in mid-November instructed White House Far Eastern affairs adviser Michael Forrestal to begin a "complete and very profound review of how we got into this country, what we thought we were doing, and what we now think we can do. . . . I even want to think about whether or not we should be there."

But the United States was in Vietnam, much deeper in Vietnam than it had been three years earlier. The American commitment that Kennedy had hoped to limit had grown, not only in men but also in the public's perception of the importance of South Vietnam. The room to maneuver he believed he had protected by refusing to introduce combat troops was far less for his successor than it had been for him. Whatever his private doubts about the American enterprise in South Vietnam, he had not conveyed them to the American people. Perhaps worst of all, he had perpetuated the idea that there could be an American solution to the Vietnamese problem. And now there would be no opportunity to retrieve the mistakes he had begun to regret. On November 22, 1963, John Kennedy met the same violent fate as Ngo Dinh Diem: shot in the head by an assassin's bullet.

Saigon, which had celebrated wildly the death of its own president, mourned the passing of the American leader. On the day of his funeral, thousands of students paid their respects at the U.S. Embassy, then marched silently through the rain down the city's streets in his honor. In the darkest of times John Kennedy had been a star of hope, declared the new English-language daily, the *Saigon Daily News*. Now we shall bury him said the journal, echoing the feelings of many Vietnamese, "with all the flowers of Vietnam and all the tears we can shed."

LBJ Takes Charge

Lyndon Baines Johnson waited in an examining room in Parkland Hospital, his wife Lady Bird at his side. Secret Service agent Rufus Youngblood, who had thrown himself across Johnson at the crack of gunfire ("as brave an act as I have ever seen," said Johnson), took up a post by the door. The Secret Service, not knowing if the shooting was the work of one man or several men, or if a conspiracy existed to kill the country's leaders, wanted to hurry the vice president out of the hospital to Air Force One and on to the security of the White House. He refused. He would not leave while President Kennedy lay on the operating table, his life in the balance. For an agonizing forty-five minutes, Johnson waited, in a whirl of thoughts and emotions. He knew that if Kennedy died—killed in Johnson's home state—he would assume an awesome burden.

At 1:20 P.M. central standard time, Kenneth O'Donnell, the president's appointments secretary, came to the examining room. "He's gone,"

he said. A few minutes later President Johnson left the hospital for the ten-minute ride to Love Field and the somber swearing-in ceremony aboard Air Force One.

In the stateroom afterward, en route to Washington, the new president reflected on the legacy he had suddenly and unwillingly inherited and—as he later remembered—made a solemn vow:

I would devote every hour of every day during the remainder of John Kennedy's unfulfilled term to achieving the goals he had set. That meant seeing things through in Vietnam as well as coping with the many other international and domestic problems he had faced. I made this promise not out of blind loyalty but because I was convinced that the broad lines of his policy, in Southeast Asia and elsewhere, had been right. They were consistent with the goals the United States had been trying to accomplish in the world since 1945.

Only two days later, on Sunday, November 24, Johnson met for a full dress briefing on Vietnam with Ambassador Henry Cabot Lodge, who had come to Washington to report to Kennedy. Joining them were CIA Director John McCone, Secretary of Defense Robert McNamara, Secretary of State Dean Rusk, Undersecretary of State George Ball, and National Security Adviser McGeorge Bundy. The ambassador expressed mild optimism, believing that General Minh was an improvement on Diem and that the South Vietnam military junta would enlarge the war effort. But McCone was much less encouraging. The Vietcong had stepped up activity since the Diem assassination, he said, and intelligence indicated that the enemy was preparing to exert even more serious pressure. Moreover, Diem's successors were encountering difficulties organizing the government and had won little cooperation from civilian leaders.

President Johnson accepted these conflicting reports with misgivings. He believed strongly that the failure to support Diem had been an error, but with Diem dead the United States must now help the new government to achieve stability and strength. To offer that help the U.S. Mission to South Vietnam must be unified. Internal dissension had hampered the embassy's effectiveness, and the president instructed Lodge to build a coherent team, one that worked together.

Preceding page. Above the roar of Air Force One's idling engines, Lyndon Baines Johnson takes the oath of office. Moments later, the new president issued his first order: "Let's get airborne."

Johnson also drew on reports of the Honolulu conference. The day before President Kennedy's departure for Texas, top foreign policy advisers had met with the Vietnam country team at Pearl Harbor. The one-day conference had produced a modestly encouraging assessment, including a confirmation that 1,000 of the 16,500 American servicemen in Vietnam would be withdrawn by the end of the year.

General Harkins had presented a sobering report on thirteen critical provinces. ("There were forty-four provinces in Vietnam," General Maxwell Taylor would later say. "There was not one war going on. There were forty-four wars going on.") The CIA's William Colby informed McNamara that putting covert Vietnamese teams into the North for intelligence gathering and sabotage simply wasn't working because of tight North Vietnamese security. He recommended that the missions cease and that emphasis be placed on psychological operations. McNamara had rejected his advice since he believed applying pressure on the North must remain a priority.

President Johnson and his advisers agreed to stress the continuity of policy in the new administration. Thus a National Security Action Memorandum, NSAM 273, was drafted for the president's signature: "It remains the central objective of the United States in South Vietnam to assist the people and government of that country to win their contest against the externally directed and supported Communist conspiracy." The memorandum restated the goals of ending the insurgency in I, II, and III Corps by December 1964 and in the Mekong Delta (IV Corps) by the close of 1965. In conclusion NSAM 273 called for further South Vietnamese clandestine operations against the North and up to fifty kilometers into Laos. To justify such measures, the State Department was directed to document a case demonstrating to the world "the degree to which the Vietcong is controlled, sustained, and supplied from Hanoi, through Laos and other channels."

The political Lyndon Johnson

Vietnam figured little in the public statements of Lyndon Johnson during the early months of his administration. His concerns were to restore confidence in the government and to take advantage of the outpouring of sympathy and respect for the deceased president to push civil rights and antipoverty bills through Congress. Johnson was preoccupied with a vision of social equality and economic opportunity for America's

Saigon's night life picked up considerably after General Duong Van "Big" Minh revoked Madame Nhu's morality laws. Dancing the "twist" was no longer a punishable offense.

disadvantaged. Yet from his first days in office, he stamped his imprint firmly upon America's involvement in Southeast Asia.

Johnson's concept of foreign policy began with Chamberlain's appeasement of Hitler at Munich and stretched to the Cold War, which he viewed as a permanent state of affairs. He also adhered to the domino theory. Yet as Senate minority leader, he had strongly opposed U.S. intervention in Indochina because America intended to act alone, without any support from her allies. Indeed, political consensus would prove to be a Johnson trademark. He would always hesitate to move until he had nearly unanimous backing from his advisers and political support from the Congress. In future debates over Vietnam, the master of Senate strong-arm politics, compromise, and flattery was out of his element: He would never be able to corner his adversary in a room and force him to come to reason.

His only direct experience in Vietnam policy making came from his 1961 visit to Vietnam and his participation in the 1963 meetings over the Buddhist and Diem crises. Now he had inherited both a policy and the men, whom Johnson urged to remain with the new administration, who had forged it. The Kennedy advisers took prosecution of the war for granted. As disappointments piled up, they would continue to recommend more of the same measures that had already failed, as they waited in vain for the elusive turning point—political stability in the South, a decline in the insurgency, and peace negotiations with Hanoi.

But America's options would continually decrease until the recommendations from frustrated advisers to an initially reluctant, but increasingly truculent, president would be to rescue a flawed policy by direct military intervention. "I did everything I could to avoid taking the steps that would escalate our commitment," Johnson would explain years later. "But I finally came to the conclusion that all of my advisers reached, namely that we had either to run or to put extra men in to protect [those already there]. I knew that if I ran out I'd be the first American president to ignore our commitments, turn tail and run, and leave our allies in the lurch."

The junta struggles

In Saigon General Duong Van "Big" Minh removed remnants of the Diem dictatorship by revoking Mad-

Wreathed in flowers, a former political prisoner celebrates his release after the overthrow of Diem.

ame Nhu's morality laws. Night life crept back into the ancient city; bar girls reappeared; and the clubs along Tu Do Street filled with students dancing to jazz and pop music. At the Saigon docks, political prisoners returned from their island solitude at Poulo Condore, the Alcatraz for Diem's political opposition. Political circles also re-formed, and students once again gathered to argue government policy, though exercising restraint.

The new freedoms quickly led, however, to more factionalism within political and religious parties. As the Socialists, Cao Daists, Buddhists, and Catholics gathered again, they quarrelled over a direction for the future. Most of the forty newspapers, serving a Saigon population of about 1.5 million, mounted a clamorous campaign of denunciation against the new regime.

The junta had a distinctly French flavor. Tran Van Don had been studying economics in Paris when war broke out in 1939. Le Van Kim began his career in film, working with René Clair, and Mai Huu Xuan had spent many years in the French police. In fact, Kim and Don were still French citizens. Each had returned to Vietnam to climb the military ladder. They strongly supported the French view that "neutralization"—a negotiated treaty with the North—would relieve the crisis in South Vietnam. Students took to the streets, however, to protest neutralization.

Presiding over the junta was General Minh, president and chairman of the Military Revolutionary Council. A popular military figure, Minh admitted he had no taste for politics. But at the urging of United States officials, he traveled to the countryside to rally "rice-roots" support for the war against the Communist guerrillas. Initially stiff and straight faced during one December visit to the provincial capital of Tay Ninh, he loosened up and by the end of his three-hour visit was shaking hands and engaging in political small talk.

By late November disturbing reports from the provinces filtered back to Saigon. Control over rural politics had all but disappeared after the coup as leadership positions passed from hand to hand. Thirty-five province chiefs had been replaced by the junta after the coup; nine of those provinces had a new leader monthly for three months, as one chief after another was sacked for incompetence or malfeasance. With entire areas left ungoverned, the NLF was rapidly gaining control of the countryside.

The NLF presses

One week after the coup, the National Liberation Front broadcast several demands over its clandestine radio: the cessation of American aggression, a halt to "raids and massacres" of the NLF's compatriots, and a call for "negotiations between various interested groups in South Vietnam, in order to arrive at a cease-fire and a solution to the great problems in the country."

But the call for negotiations contrasted with the

The Vietcong planned meticulously for every operation, often with scale models of their targets. Here a VC cadre drills guerrillas for an assault on a strategic hamlet.

NLF's military planning. VC attacks doubled in the weeks following the coup, to an average of 745 incidents weekly in November, as the NLF seized the initiative.

In September two generals from North Vietnam had convened a "military conference" at a guerrilla camp on Cambodian territory across the border from Darlac Province in the Vietnamese central highlands. NLF units were restructured and expanded. In October these battalions and companies were given special two–week training courses in "conventional and small military unit tactics" and antiaircraft defense. The northerners were teaching the front guerrillas to stand and fight.

In December the Central Committee of the North Vietnamese Lao Dong (Communist) party, meeting in Hanoi, issued a top-secret resolution ordering an offensive strategy for the southern insurgency and increased support from the North. In the committee's view the ideal moment had arrived to turn the guerrilla struggle into a military campaign large enough "to disintegrate the enemy's troops and government." Hanoi was calling for the NLF, with help from the North, to move into the ultimate stage of insurgency, the general counteroffensive.

The reporting turns bad

From December onward, the major concern for officials in Washington and Saigon was how rapidly the situation was deteriorating. Shortly after returning to Saigon from Washington, Ambassador Lodge for-

97

warded a report on Long An Province prepared by an American civilian provincial representative. Once considered a model of the Strategic Hamlet Program, the populous province, near Saigon, was in danger of being overrun by the Vietcong. The appraisals astonished Washington officials.

The hastily formed and poorly trained Self Defense Corps proved incapable of combating the aggressive Vietcong, and the ARVN 7th Division, chastened by its defeat at Ap Bac, had effectively ceded the Long An countryside to the enemy.

In September, Diem's province officials had puffed up the number of completed strategic hamlets in Long An Province to 219. But two months later new officials appointed by the military junta scaled that figure down to just 45. That Vietcong attacks had dropped markedly (from seventy-seven in June to twenty-seven in November) proved only that fewer hamlets merited attacking. Premier Nguyen Ngoc Tho, Diem's vice president who had been retained by the junta to run the postcoup government, believed only 1 strategic hamlet in 5 nationwide to be viable.

Vietcong ranged at will throughout Long An, controlling an estimated three-fourths of the province. Unlike earlier bands of lightly armed, quick-striking guerrillas, they had expanded their arsenal and now carried heavy Browning automatic rifles and machine guns. According to a *New York Times* dispatch, "Vietcong squads would come into a hamlet and make the villagers dismantle the barbed wire defenses. [They] would make villagers take the roofs off their huts as a sign of obedience."

Resisting hamlets had to withstand repeated attacks, without ARVN support, and faced the ultimate certainty that when the defense finally collapsed, its leaders would be executed. The hamlet of Thanh Tam had repelled three Vietcong attacks, despite the loss of many families that had fled back to their farms. For the local Self Defense Corps chief's obstinate courage, the Vietcong put a price on his head of 100,000 piasters, or $1,300, twenty times an average peasant's yearly income.

Provoked by these gloomy reports, Defense Secretary McNamara departed on a two-day inspection trip just before Christmas. He returned to report, "The situation has in fact been deteriorating in the countryside since July to a far greater extent than we realized because of undue dependence on distorted Vietnamese reporting. The Vietcong now control very high proportions of the people in certain key prov-

Fishermen listen to a lecture on how to combat the Vietcong. As the war damaged their livelihood, fishermen banded together to patrol trade routes and marketplaces.

After he seized power on January 30, 1964, the new South Vietnamese premier, General Nguyen Khanh (right), invited the popular if ineffective General Minh (left) to stay on as figurehead chief of state.

inces, particularly those south and west of Saigon." McNamara found the government of General Minh indecisive and drifting and faulted the American country team for continued bickering. Unless current trends were reversed within two or three months, they would "lead to neutralization at best and more likely to a Communist-controlled state."

The Khanh coup

General Nguyen Khanh, whom some American military figures considered, at age thirty-six, the ablest of South Vietnam's generals, doubted the war-making abilities of the junta. After the Diem coup, Khanh had sought a command in the war-torn delta, but a wary

General Minh had transferred him to the I Corps command, to keep him as far away from Saigon as possible.

Minh had acted with good reason. The corpulent Khanh, whose tiny goatee and easygoing manner belied a great ambition fueled by a fierce determination, had schemed against Diem at the height of the Buddhist crisis. Only the betrayal of his plot to Nhu forced Khanh to fade wisely into the background.

In his northern exile, Khanh bristled and convinced himself that the divisive junta was incapable of running the war. He pieced together a conspiracy composed of disaffected generals and colonels equally disgruntled at having been shunted to the sidelines.

Only the problem of timing remained. French President Charles de Gaulle provided a solution by recognizing China on January 27 and calling for neutralization of the former Indochina states. Many Vietnamese believed that de Gaulle had traded Chinese approval of his neutralist vision for French recognition. Neutralism would result in U.S. withdrawal and an isolated South Vietnam left to make what peace it could with the North.

Neutralization rumors had peaked with wild, and false, stories that French agents had arrived in Saigon laden with cash for the French sympathizers in the junta. Colonel Duong Van Duc, Khanh's confederate in the Joint General Staff, had already prepared documents purporting to show that the three French-bred junta members, Generals Kim, Don, and Xuan, had been paid off by the French.

On January 29, Khanh moved. Troops alerted by his coconspirators, Generals Tran Thien Khiem and Do Mau, took up positions around Saigon and surrounded the homes of the junta generals. General Khanh seized JGS headquarters at Tan Son Nhut Airport at four o'clock, and the junta members were arrested in their homes. By dawn the clockwork coup was accomplished. Not a shot had been fired.

Khanh invited the popular General Minh to remain as a titular, but powerless, chief of state, presiding over a fifty-three-man military junta with Khanh himself as premier. He removed the supposed neutralist generals to special custody until May when he ordered a trial at Da Lat. The government introduced no evidence to support charges they were promoting a neutralization policy, and the trial ended with a vague communiqué accusing the generals of lacking proper revolutionary views.

Although surprised by the coup, many Washington officials privately heaved sighs of relief. As military security had collapsed, Minh's committee government had proven ineffective, and American officials hoped that the one-man rule of Khanh might be more competent. Besides, Lodge and Johnson realized they had no choice but to support Khanh. Maintaining that the essential character of the government had not changed, the United States recognized the Khanh regime on February 8.

Khanh's move was but the opening of a coup season. In the next year five coups or attempted coups would occur, and South Vietnam would experience seven governments in 1964 alone. The reliance on coups as the means of change poisoned the national life, sowing suspicion in place of trust and cooperation. While American planners pleaded for political harmony as a prerequisite for prosecuting the war, the successive coups had only the opposite effect. Political instability would remain for more than a year. In the hope of discouraging plotters, President Johnson ordered a campaign of support for Khanh, calling him the "American boy." That support provided Khanh with a wide plane for maneuvering. Desperate for a strong Vietnamese leader who could turn around the war effort, the U.S. could do little but support General Khanh and hope he could rally his people.

NSAM 288

Early in 1964 Washington military planners developed contingency plans for applying pressure on the North, which many regarded as the source of the insurgency. Late in January General Maxwell Taylor cited NSAM 273 as authority to broaden the war to the North. In a lengthy memorandum to the secretary of defense, Taylor, passing on the recommendations of the Joint Chiefs of Staff, argued that NSAM 273 "makes clear the resolve of the president to insure victory over the externally directed and supported Communist insurgency. In order to achieve that victory . . . the United States must undertake bolder actions which may embody greater risks." Taylor reasoned that the war was being fought on the enemy's terms. Self-imposed restrictions kept the war in the South and prevented the interdiction of external aid to the insurgents. Taylor recommended among other actions an invasion of Laos to impede infiltration, bombing of North Vietnam, the commitment of U.S. combat forces to South Vietnam, and "as necessary, in direct actions against North Vietnam."

The Vietnam Working Group, a largely civilian in-

The "American boy." Premier Khanh, U.S. Chief of Staff Maxwell Taylor (left), and Defense Secretary Robert McNamara (right) demonstrate U.S.–South Vietnamese solidarity.

teragency task force, agreed with Taylor in its report on March 1. The United States could improve its negotiating position, the group believed, with a gradual campaign against the North, beginning with air reconnaissance and escalating to a blockade of Haiphong Harbor and the bombing of North Vietnamese infiltrator training camps and industrial complexes. Essentially an underdeveloped country, North Vietnam had built just enough of an industrial base to be vulnerable to bombing, the group believed. Apart from increasing their flow of aid, Chinese or Soviet intervention was unlikely. Bombing the North was, however, "no substitute for successful counter-insurgency in the South." The most to be expected was a reduction in North Vietnamese aid to the Vietcong, which could provide precious time.

Armed with this report, McNamara and Taylor embarked on yet another fact-finding trip to South Vietnam. Added to their tasks was an order from President Johnson for strong public support of Khanh as a deterrent to coup plotters. The president wanted Khanh to appear on the front pages of the world press with McNamara and Taylor raising his arms as

if he were a heavyweight champion.

The trio barnstormed the country, from the delta to Hue in the North, holding up Khanh's arms, with McNamara stiffly calling "Vietnam moun man" ("Vietnam a thousand years") to the throngs. (Because of mistaken pitch and pronunciation, what he intoned often sounded to Vietnamese ears like "Southern duck wants to lie down.") The resulting front-page coverage satisfied Johnson, though General Taylor thought it proved that Khanh was the "American boy" only for the time being.

In Saigon, McNamara and Taylor learned at briefings of the discouraging political and military situations. During these meetings, McNamara would take a seat at the head of the table and scribble left-handed on a yellow pad. As the briefing officers ran through their charts and shaded maps and figures, McNamara would occasionally interrupt his note taking to question their conclusions. The briefing ended, he would bombard the MACV officers with requests for statistics on barbed wire, petroleum, and weaponry—the supply side of the war. McNamara, in the eyes of one participant, "sought to assure himself that the massive supply of logistics and forces was having an effect on the course of the war by sheer weight of numbers." Another participant said, "I sat there amazed, and thought to myself, what in the world is this man thinking about? This is not a problem of logistics and, in any event, there are plenty of people here at MACV fully competent to handle the materiel side of the war. This is a war that needs discussion of strategic purpose and of strategy itself."

News from the briefing officers was grim. In the wake of political turbulence, the Vietcong actions had increased. Heavy weapons of Chinese origin—recoilless rifles, machine guns, and mortars—had been captured, proving that supplies were being sent from the North. ARVN desertions continued at a high rate, and public confidence in the military sank alarmingly. General Khanh, nonetheless, was reluctant to bomb the North until his political base was more firmly established.

On his return to Washington, Secretary McNamara submitted a long memorandum to the president, and the following day the National Security Council met to weigh the findings. With the domino theory as a premise, McNamara stated the United States's objective: "We seek an independent, non-Communist South Vietnam." To achieve that goal, the U.S. would support a program of national mobilization to put South Vietnam on a war footing, assist in adding fifty thousand men to its military, help to enlarge South Vietnam's Civil Administrative Corps for pacification work, and provide further economic and military aid.

To counter the military decline, the secretary outlined three possible options for escalation: improved control of the Cambodian and Laotian borders; retaliatory action against the North, including "tit-for-tat" bombing strikes by South Vietnam against northern infiltration routes and training camps in response to Vietcong attacks; and a gradually escalating bombing campaign against the North that would go beyond mere tit-for-tat reactions.

This last option McNamara rejected for the time being because of the risk of Communist escalation, the instability of the Khanh regime, and the delicate politics of justifying such action to the American public and foreign governments. In his final recommendations, however, he urged planning to begin immediately on a program of "graduated overt military pressure"—a euphemism for bombing the North—which could be initiated on thirty days' notice.

During the perfunctory National Security Council debate, only the Joint Chiefs expressed doubt. They wanted immediate offensive action against Hanoi. Disregarding his military advisers, President Johnson accepted McNamara's report and issued it as National Security Action Memorandum 288. The same day—March 17—the president cabled Ambassador Lodge instructions "to prepare contingency recommendations for specific tit-for-tat actions."

The limited bombing campaign had already been examined in war games held at the Pentagon. Top level military and civilian officials, using computers, systems analysis, and experience, had played out the gradually escalating campaign. In this exercise, when the U.S. increased its bombing, North Vietnam sent more soldiers down the trails to the South. With a change in targets to include industrial complexes, Hanoi removed its factories to remote areas and ordered the Vietcong to attack American bases, tying troops to defensive positions. The U.S. restrained itself by not attacking cities or irrigation dikes.

At one point, Marshall Green, a State Department representative with long Asian experience who was arguing Hanoi's view, said he would move women and children to an airstrip, announce their presence to the world, and dare the United States to bomb them. The war game exercise suggested that America was stymied and that North Vietnam did not appear vulnerable to limited bombing.

The war games widened the rift that had developed between the military men, who believed only a full-scale campaign with deep American commitment would bring results, and the civilians, who favored limited bombing aimed at inducing negotiations. As the focus shifted to action against North Vietnam, dissenting civilians in Washington were being weeded out of policy-making positions. William Trueheart, Lodge's deputy chief of mission, had angered the military by demanding more realistic reporting when MACV was accepting inflated statistics from Vietnamese field officials. Recalled from Saigon in December 1963, he was given a State Department assignment that excluded Vietnam.

Paul Kattenburg, head of the Interdepartmental Working Group on Vietnam, was another State Department doubter. He had returned from a trip to Vietnam in December 1963 appalled at the political decay and the state of the Vietnamese army. With

North Vietnam on the Eve of War

In the summer of 1961, a riddle circulated in Hanoi:

Q: The party has at last found the only long-term solution for our food problem. Do you know what it is?

A: Capture South Vietnam.

This stab at humor embodied the struggle for economic stability waged by North Vietnam after its 1954 victory at Dien Bien Phu. Not only for political reasons did the Democratic Republic of Vietnam desire reunification with the South: The Geneva accords that temporarily separated the country had deprived the North of its major food supply, rice from the fertile Mekong Delta. North Vietnam could not produce enough food for its 17 million people, and the result was chronic food shortages. Yet a decade after Dien Bien Phu, North Vietnam was not only making headway in feeding its people and providing jobs; through rapid postwar recovery and military mobilization, North Vietnam stood, however shakily, on the edge of war.

Discipline imposed by the Lao Dong party had been a major factor in the decade's journey. In a 1960 speech, aging President Ho Chi Minh declared, "Our party's immediate task is to lead the people to increase production and practice economy to build socialism in the North, in order to serve as a firm base for the struggle for national reunification."

With an extremely high birth rate of 3.5 percent (a half million more mouths to feed each year) and deprived of the southern food source, North Vietnam's Communist planners realized the only feasible route to economic recovery lay in industrialization with the help of foreign aid. In a six-year period, North Vietnam pumped nearly $1 billion solicited from Communist-bloc countries, especially China, into the import of rice and the rudiments of an industrial base.

In December 1961 Hanoi Polytechnical Institute graduated its first class of 633 engineers who joined their Soviet- and Chinese-trained counterparts in positions of responsibility in public works, military, and industrial projects, overseeing thousands of workers. Among the new projects were textile mills in Nam Dinh, a steel mill in Thai Nguyen, phosphate and cement factories in Haiphong, and chemical, paper, and sugar factories in Viet Tri.

Despite the new activity, life in North Vietnam remained for many a grim affair. Cities were almost entirely neglected as construction materials were diverted elsewhere. A generally shabby Hanoi had seen no improvements in a decade, and along the broad avenues, empty of cars, the old French shops were boarded up. Also, many able-bodied workers still had little to do. Members of farm cooperatives, for instance, worked one hundred days during the growing cycle and remained idle the rest of the year.

Military service provided a way out of economic hardship for many. The Vietnam People's Army recruited underemployed farm workers during the military mobilization of the early 1960s. An estimated two hundred thousand men flocked to the army, and an equal number joined paramilitary forces and local militia units (compared to two hundred fifty thousand troops and militia at arms in South Vietnam).

Housing, good food, and social status—more than most civilians could expect—rewarded those who joined North Vietnam's army. But the soldiers worked for their benefits as they trained to fight the Americans and South Vietnamese. Armed with Soviet automatic weapons and carrying full gear, they marched beneath the blazing tropical sun in cross-country maneuvers. They also instructed the local militia in the techniques of assaulting concrete bunkers. In addition, the troops labored in public works and construction projects, fulfilling the centralized planning of the Communist leaders. Commander in Chief General Vo Nguyen Giap had written:

"The People's Army is the instrument of the Communist party and the revolutionary state."

Military-like discipline spilled over into other aspects of life in North Vietnam. Children between the ages of six and eight donned the red scarf of Young Pioneers in their schools. Street and Inhabitant Protection Committees monitored individual behavior, instilling a sense of "civic duty." Production cell cadres on farms and in factories constantly exhorted citizens to work harder and to take an interest in village politics.

For all its discipline and new factories, North Vietnam's economy in 1964 could not support another war without a substantial increase in foreign aid. The need for immediate delivery of sophisticated military hardware, especially antiaircraft batteries, was paramount. The steadily escalating ground and air war in the South posed serious risks to the industrial development in the North, for the new factory complexes were nearly defenseless targets for superior American air power. Yet in obtaining that aid from its allies, China and the Soviet Union, the DRV strove to avoid becoming a client state of either, as South Vietnam had become dependent on the United States.

China, the leading supplier of economic aid, was experiencing the economic and political turmoil of the Cultural Revolution and was unable to increase its foreign aid. From the Soviet Union, North Vietnam received only modest aid in 1964 ($25 million). But the Soviet Union was capable of providing the more sophisticated military hardware, including AK47 assault rifles, that Hanoi required for the coming conflict, and Moscow recognized the opportunity to counter China's influence in Asia.

The means to bolster Ho Chi Minh's defenses and extend his war-making capabilities did not come quickly. His negotiations with Moscow came to fruition with Soviet Premier Aleksei Kosygin's presence in Hanoi during America's Flaming Dart air strikes in February 1965, when the Soviet leader vowed massive aid if North Vietnam were invaded. A year later, according to American intelligence estimates, Soviet aid to North Vietnam had increased eightfold over 1964 figures, to a total of more than $200 million a year.

The NLF arsenal contained more sophisticated weapons by late 1964. These Chinese-made 75 MM recoilless cannons and American .50-caliber machine guns were captured from a Vietcong battalion in a battle at Dai Ngai, a village in the Mekong Delta.

years of experience in Vietnamese affairs, he concluded that the war was already decided and the Vietcong were winning. The only alternative he saw for the U.S. was to send combat troops, in effect replacing the French, and Kattenburg wanted no part of such a decision. He requested reassignment and was transferred to Policy Planning in March 1964 to be readmitted to the East Asia bureau over a year later so long as he avoided the problems of Vietnam and concentrated on the Philippines.

The assistant secretary of state for Far Eastern affairs, Roger Hilsman, who had campaigned for patient counterinsurgency—as opposed to military escalation—also departed in March. In fact, firing Hilsman had been one of Lyndon Johnson's priorities as president. Not only had Hilsman been an author of the August 24 cable that led to the downfall of Diem, an act that Johnson deplored, but Hilsman had committed the ultimate Johnsonian sin—that of disloyalty. "I heard Hilsman all over town blaming the secretary of state, the president, and everybody else for what was happening in Vietnam," Johnson later recalled. "I was at a dinner party . . . and Hilsman was just outright disloyal . . . just an anarchist fouling his own nest. . . . It took three to four months, but [firing him] was one of the first things I did."

In a farewell memo, Hilsman, a World War II veteran of guerrilla fighting in the Burmese jungles, sounded one final time the theme of pacification and counterinsurgency and disputed the move against the North: "The way to fight a guerrilla is to adopt the tactics of a guerrilla. As to the question of operations against North Vietnam, I would suggest that such operations may at a certain stage be a useful *supplement* to an effective counterinsurgency program, but . . . not be an effective *substitute.*"

Pacification

The Strategic Hamlet Program had been effectively dismantled by the Vietcong. Strategic hamlets, wrote IV Corps Commander General Nguyen Huu Co early in 1964, had failed

to achieve the most important goal, that is people's confidence. . . . The Vietcong claim that we use U.S. barbed wire and iron stakes to confine the people in U.S. military bases. . . . They ask that the people call to each other to return to their old lands and farms and refuse all attempts to

Her guerrilla husband fled when the ARVN swept this Vietcong village. Succoring her children, the terrified wife knows not what to expect.

move their houses to hamlets. . . . With the loathing and hatred the people already have, when they hear the seemingly reasonable Vietcong propaganda, they turn to the side of the Vietcong and place their confidence in them.

Because strategic hamlets were associated with Diem, General Khanh renamed them "new life hamlets" as part of an ambitious countrywide "Victory" plan. Forced resettlement was abandoned. Stressing rural reconstruction and economic development and financed by an infusion of U.S. aid—$40 million—the New Life Hamlet Plan would operate on the "oil spot" expansion concept: Concentrate on the secure areas and expand outward through military operations followed by civil and economic programs. In NSAM 288 Secretary McNamara had commended this idea but noted, "It is necessary to push hard to get . . . unity of effort at all levels."

That unity of effort didn't materialize. Provincial administrators hesitated to implement the program, lest they be associated with the Diem regime. New province officials, unfamiliar with their tasks and deluged with paperwork, allowed materials to pile up in storehouses, from which they often disappeared. Ironically, economic gains accrued by the peasants provided more income for the Vietcong to tax.

Unsolved problems

Early in the year, the commander of the 21st ARVN Infantry Division, stationed in the Mekong Delta, initiated the pacification plan in his area by exhorting his subordinates to "Keep up the tempo, even at night. Stir up the countryside. Don't let the Vietcong get set or rest. Most importantly keep ARVN units on the move. Static security should be eliminated as a mission." But such zest was rare. A continuing lack of administrative coordination rendered military action ineffective, since problems of security remained after the military had moved through an area; the Vietcong simply filtered back.

In weekly reports for the month of May, a U.S. adviser continually listed the same administrative frustrations. His May 3 report stated "No authorization for equipment has been received for pacification groups although letters have been sent through MAAG . . . and GVN channels." Needed were radios, revolvers, flashlights, and training ammunition for Self Defense Corps platoons. The following week, the adviser wrote, "All problems reported on May 3 remain" and added requests for mobility pay for the SDC and helicopter support.

In the succeeding three weeks, the adviser commented in his reports:

18 May—All problems, except lack of helicopter support, reported on 3 and 10 May remain. . . .

24 May—All problems reported on 3, 10, and 18 May remain, except pay for hamlet action teams. . . .

31 May—None of the major problems listed in the 24 May report have been adequately solved.

Territorial defense was the responsibility of the Civil Guard and Self Defense Corps. Retitled Regional Forces in 1964, Civil Guards played an especially important role in provinces where few ARVN units were present. They were often barely mobile when concentrating on static defense of bridges, depots, and posts. The Self Defense Corps, composed of local recruits who trained for six weeks and returned to platoons near their homes, undertook defense of hamlets and villages. SDC forces were renamed Popular Forces in 1964. After the Diem coup, Popular Forces fell under the operational command of ARVN units in their area. Occasionally Popular Forces were transferred by army commanders and forced to leave their home villages undefended.

This three-tiered system of security—ARVN, Regional Forces, Popular Forces—should have proven that the Saigon government could protect and treat its citizens justly. At times, however, the forces acted above the law and treated the peasantry with arrogance. One adviser reported from Quang Tin Province in I Corps: "A high incident rate of stealing, robbing, raping, and obtaining free meals in the rural areas has not endeared the population towards ARVN or Regional Forces." Such excesses could also lead to greater atrocities.

To an official report applauding the bravery and efficiency of the local Popular Forces, an American AID civilian adviser in Tay Ninh Province added a gruesome note. In contrast to the Popular Forces' behavior, he wrote: "There are some reports of ARVN atrocities; for example, on February 19, [1965], a company leader killed a draft dodger in Ben Soi district town. He disemboweled the boy, took his heart and liver out, and had them cooked at a restaurant in Ben Soi. The heart and liver were eaten by a number of soldiers. . . . Many civilians witnessed this atrocity."

On both sides, as the war intensified, accelerating brutality was to afflict the people of Vietnam.

The Brutal War

In the Vietnam War, both the Saigon government and the Vietcong competed for the allegiance—"the hearts and minds"—of the people. But it was an especially brutal war and the peasants themselves, inured to years of fighting, were caught in the competition. The peasant was manipulated at night by the Vietcong and during the day by government forces. At night the VC collected taxes and strove to discredit the government and win the people to their side. They often executed a village chief, and sometimes his family, as punishment for his government collaboration and as a means of terrorizing the villagers. A favorite Vietcong tactic was to fire on government soldiers from a village and then flee, leaving the villagers to incur the soldiers' wrath and learn first hand of the "evils" of their government.

The Vietnamese army was often equally merciless. Entering a village by day, the ARVN would demand to know who the Vietcong were and where they had gone. To obtain the information ARVN soldiers resorted to torture of the people they were supposed to protect. Guerrillas captured in battle could expect to be tortured if they did not talk. Although the military maintained that any instance of government torture was an isolated event, many journalists knew that an ARVN unit that had taken heavy casualties would be bent on retaliation. By accompanying such a unit, they could witness torture. If an American adviser tried to intervene, he was usually ignored.

Preceding page. His face frozen in anger, an American medic evacuates the body of a Vietnamese girl, slain in a VC attack on her Mekong Delta village on November 6, 1963. Her father died manning the village's only machine gun. Her mother and infant brother were wounded.

Two favored methods of ARVN torture. (Left) Hands bound, a VC suspect is held under water by Rangers in a Mekong Delta village where the ARVN had lost ten men a month earlier. The man produced no valuable information. (Right) A muddy-faced guerrilla, beaten and tortured with water poured through a rag into his nose and mouth, defiantly refused to talk.

Following page. Capture by either side was not a pleasant fate. Vietcong prisoners, taken by U.S. Marines in November 1965, are roped together and led toward an interrogation camp.

Insurgency–
Counterinsurgency

In 1962, twenty-four-year-old Frank Scotton
found himself in Vietnam, half a globe away
from his Needham, Massachusetts, home. An
employee of the United States Information Service, the junior officer worked in field operations,
assisting the Vietnamese in psychological operations and political intelligence. From his base at
Qui Nhon, he traveled to military outposts in
northern South Vietnam, from Quang Ngai to
Pleiku to Kontum provinces. He filed regular reports but otherwise had little contact with his superiors in Saigon.

Fluent in Vietnamese, Scotton worked long
hours and scarcely thought about who was paying his salary. "My pay was deposited into the
bank," he said. "It was like working for Vietnam." Without discouragement from anyone, he
was free to involve himself more and more in political and paramilitary activities. In 1963, while
Scotton was reporting on the Buddhist crisis,

Diem's province chief expelled him from Binh Dinh Province, with the ambiguous comment that his safety could no longer be assured. Like many young Americans who came to Vietnam in the early 1960s, Scotton was beginning a passionate affair with the country and its people. He was "going native." "Vietnam was the most intense experience of my life," he would later say. He examined village life and questioned the relationship of the military to the villagers. He wondered why no community cohesion existed to repel the VC. Early in 1964, Scotton found answers to some of his questions.

Transferred to Long An Province in IV Corps to help in a major U.S. effort to improve security, Scotton surveyed thirty hamlets. His squad of six civilians, one armed with a machine gun, the others carrying concealed pistols, talked to every family in each hamlet so the Vietcong would not single out any family for retribution. The experience confirmed an impression Scotton had begun to form in central Vietnam: "In limited warfare you could establish ascendancy with a highly motivated, small unit that really wanted to operate. The government could think it had established a presence with schoolteachers, an agricultural team, a Self Defense Corps. But it hadn't. That survey proved to me that we could operate like the Vietcong, at night, and set them off balance. But the people would have to be motivated."

People's Special Forces

Returning to Quang Ngai Province, Scotton found an immediate opportunity to put his ideas into practice. An anti-National Liberation Front group led by a former Vietminh soldier came to the American seeking weapons; the men wanted to form their own village protection. From the U.S. Special Forces and the CIA, Scotton obtained four crates of Thompson submachine guns, two crates of M3 submachine guns, and a crate of .45-caliber pistols. With the help of a like-minded USAID representative and CIA funding, he organized a forty-man unit and designed a twelve-day training period that combined field work,

intelligence gathering, and so-called motivation exercises in anti-Communist propaganda.

Scotton appropriated elements of General Vo Nguyen Giap's and Mao Tse-tung's theories. The groups would practice the three "withs": eat, work, and live with the people. They would act as government agitation-propaganda (agitprop) agents. Called People's Special Forces, they learned how to remain in the field, patrol at night, and sleep during the day under cover and far enough apart to prevent the VC from happening upon an entire squad. They wore no uniforms. A promise of death benefits paid to the survivor's family was an important inducement to recruitment. "We did not see it as pacification," Scotton said, "but as a non-Communist instrument that established an effective, armed government presence."

The first group, operating in the Tu Nghia District, in the late spring of 1964, met with immediate success, killing numerous Vietcong and capturing others with their weapons (a rarity). Two months later Scotton was asked to form another group for the Nghia Han District, east of Tu Nghia.

A fundamental goal of the work was to separate the Vietcong from the peasantry, to deprive the guerrilla "fish" of the peasants' "water." The premise was that helping the villagers would persuade them to divulge what they knew of the local VC. By living with the villagers, the People's Special Forces developed intelligence on Vietcong activities and movement, allowing night ambushes to be set and cadres to be identified. Sometimes the cadre or Vietcong sympathizer could be neutralized by gifts, or simply by public association with the antiinsurgent forces.

One day Scotton returned from a Saigon trip with a carton of drawings of black eyes, resembling the CBS logo, printed on four-by-six-inch slips of paper. Soon the sinister black eyes appeared on the bodies of the ambushed Vietcong and were tacked at night to the doors of cadres or sympathizers. The black eyes were intended to imply the message: "We are watching you." Torn down in the morning by an alarmed Vietcong, the black eye would reappear during the night. This caused the cadres to begin moving about, never sleeping in the same bed two nights, a tactic government officials had long been forced to practice.

Scotton trained more teams. A suggestion of their effectiveness came in June when one team found a letter on the body of a VC courier killed in an ambush. Addressed to a district cadre, it read: "Most of the soldiers in these [People's Special Forces] units

Preceding page. "It is the Americans who have committed aggression in our country, it is they who have been killing our people with planes and bombs," cried Nguyen Van Troi shortly before his execution on October 18, 1964. He was convicted of trying to blow up a bridge over which Defense Secretary McNamara and Ambassador Lodge were to pass, an act that earned him heroic status with the NLF.

USIS officer Frank Scotton issues equipment to a newly trained People's Action Team in Nha Be District near Saigon.

are outstanding. ... The plan of operation is good. They usually launch an ambush right in our control zone with a small unit, based on information furnished by spies. ... If the situation is not corrected, our activity will be hurt." The People's Special Forces, meanwhile, suffered very slight losses.

People's Action Teams

The CIA, which provided the funding, began to absorb the growing operation and Scotton's role receded. A small training camp at Vung Tau Peninsula was expanded by August 1964 to hold five thousand trainees. The CIA's Vietnamese trainers expanded the drills to thirteen weeks with courses of political indoctrination against the evils of communism, and classes on handicrafts to use in aiding the villagers. Recruits returned to their home districts. The groups were renamed People's Action Teams, and the program, said CIA Station Chief Peer de Silva definitively, became "the most effective counterinsurgency tool devised during the period of our American involvement in Vietnam."

Compared to the usual battle achievement of South Vietnamese forces, the PATs' statistics were impressive because they patrolled at night in the darkness that had formerly been the exclusive domain of the enemy. Over a five-month period, three teams killed one hundred and fifty Vietcong and retrieved their weapons and captured more than two hundred of the enemy with their arms, while suffering six of their own men killed in action. Moreover, there were no desertions, a significant departure from the norm in ARVN and Regional and Popular Forces. MACV sector advisers voiced universal approval. They were the only effective force in the province, according to one U.S. adviser in Quang Ngai.

As the PAT program grew, the military came to covet both its success and its reservoir of eager volunteers. MACV was responsible for overseeing the draft of men into the armed forces, national police, Regional, and Popular Forces, and the South Vietnamese military worried about a diminishing pool of draftees if the PATs should continue to expand. Furthermore, the military viewed events through its own conventional prism and believed that full-fledged

U.S. Army Captains Philip Werbiski (left) and Jim MacGill demonstrate hand-to-hand combat to a unit of People's Action Team recruits.

military programs would be more effective than the paramilitary operations run by the CIA. Although the PAT men were highly successful, the military foresaw even greater success if they fell under the control of MACV and were transformed into soldiers.

Briefings to ranking military officers elicited questions about uniforms or special insignia to stimulate unit pride. One general said that the PAT men were soldiers and therefore should dress and act like soldiers. Another suggested that such a large program inevitably must pass from the CIA's control to that of the military, and that is what happened.

By the beginning of 1965, MACV was drawing up plans to absorb the People's Action Teams, although the final transfer did not occur until mid-1967, when the entire pacification effort passed from civilian to military hands. The teams would be completely militarized under the Civil Operations and Revolutionary Development Support (CORDS). To expedite training of the teams, increased in size from forty to fifty-nine men, the indoctrination courses of anti-Communist motivation and community organizing—the mainsprings of the program's resounding success—would be severely curtailed.

The record was to show that paramilitary programs like the People's Action Teams and Civilian Ir-

regular Defense Groups enjoyed their greatest success—to the extent they were successful at all—under the CIA and lost their effectiveness under the military. Under the CIA such programs benefited from a unique combination of flexibility and zeal. Yet the military ultimately won the inevitable bureaucratic tug of war for control and took over the unconventional programs. Fashioning them in its own conventional image, the military expanded the programs and broadened their mission, in the process diluting their success.

Stripped of its major animus, the Revolutionary Development Cadre program, which subsumed the former PATs, was destined to become little more than another district conventional military force, plagued by slipshod performance and desertions. Rapport between the teams and villagers evaporated, as did the flow of intelligence on Vietcong activities. The program continued until the early 1970s, but its earlier startling successes dwindled almost to nothing.

Counter-Terror Teams

Early in 1964, the CIA also provided arms and funding for another form of counterinsurgency—counterterror. Four- to six-man teams, adopting guerrilla tactics, gave the Vietcong doses of their own terrorist formula, particularly in "liberated" zones, such as the U Minh Forest in the delta and War Zone D.

The CIA and Vietnamese security agents recruited convicts and deserters, offering them a chance to redeem themselves by killing Vietcong. Dressed in black peasant pajamas and armed with folding-stock carbines hidden beneath their clothes, the Counter-Terror Teams slipped into the VC's own "secure" villages at night to kill the Vietcong cadres and tax collectors. The cadres were identified by rural secret agents in the pay of the CIA and South Vietnamese. Key Vietcong cadres began to die mysteriously, often in their own beds. The Counter-Terror Teams were soon arriving at their destinations only to find empty beds, as the cadres prudently kept on the move.

Results of the program varied, however. It proved difficult to forge the convicts and deserters into a motivated fighting force, and discipline was especially hard to enforce. Some teams, arrogant because of their elite mission, engaged in gangsterism in friendly villages, and other teams wound up serving as bodyguards for province chiefs. A spate of unfavorable coverage in the U.S. press, emphasizing terror and assassination carried out by "mercenaries,"

forced the CIA to reduce and reorganize the program. In 1967 Counter-Terror Teams would reappear as Provincial Reconnaissance Units (PRUs) under the banner of the Phoenix Program.

Lions against tigers

With the direction of North Vietnam's Lao Dong party, the NLF shifted to an offensive strategy in 1964. In the period following the Minh and Khanh coups, small-unit guerrilla actions increased. But company and battalion-sized attacks decreased, and self-criticism contained in captured documents suggested that many Vietcong units were caught off guard by the sudden change in the political climate. The Vietcong were not very flexible; their success came when operations were meticulously planned and rehearsed. Early in 1964 North Vietnamese General Nguyen Chi Thanh, equal in rank to Commander in Chief General Vo Nguyen Giap, was sent to the South to assume command of all Communist military forces there. The NLF was developing its ability to engage in conventional warfare.

In January two 400-man NLF battalions trapped 400 South Vietnamese Rangers on a river bank thirty-five miles northwest of Saigon. The Rangers'

Bui Dang Su, a People's Action Team instructor, conducts a training session for new recruits. Political indoctrination sharpened the PATs' willingness to fight the Communists.

American advisers were ecstatic: The NLF had finally engaged itself in a set-piece battle, and eight ARVN battalions lay within striking distance. While the Rangers traded fire with the NLF, the American advisers radioed instructions for a coordinated counterattack. But the Vietnamese staff officers chain-smoked the afternoon away engrossed in their maps and debate. At nightfall the Ranger unit retreated across the river, and the Vietcong faded into the dark, leaving five decapitated prisoners behind.

A few weeks later, an estimated five hundred guerrillas crossed the Cambodian border northwest of Saigon and overran five strategic hamlets. The Vietcong then dug in and fought a paratroop battalion supported by dive bombers and artillery. Ninety-four government soldiers were killed, the most in any engagement up to that point in the war.

Throughout April, NLF guerrillas roamed the Mekong Delta. At Kien Long, a district capital on the Ca Mau Peninsula, two battalions joined in a coordinated attack. After overpowering the Self Defense Corps, the Vietcong executed dozens of government supporters and disemboweled the district chief and his two children, and shot his wife in the head. ARVN reacted by moving in a paratroop battalion and two airlifted infantry battalions, which linked up with Rangers and South Vietnamese Special Forces already in the area. Despite the onslaught, the Vietcong broke out, picked up a third battalion—thus becoming the first regiment-sized NLF force of more than one thousand guerrillas ever mounted—and returned for a two-day fight that left more than a hundred dead on each side. An American adviser with one of the ARVN units commented: "Up to now, this war has been a patient cat-and-mouse game. Now it is becoming lions against tigers."

In April the government suffered 610 killed (2,500 casualties overall), versus an estimated 1,700 Vietcong killed. The American toll was 6 killed, 101 wounded.

While their allies and suppliers to the North stepped up their infiltration of the South, the Vietcong also launched a systematic campaign of terror against the American colony in Saigon. A terrorist threw an airline bag containing a bomb into the lobby of the Kin Do Movie Theater, killing an American major and a military policeman, and bringing portions of the ceiling down on the audience. One Saturday morning a mortar shell detonated beneath the bleachers of an American baseball field adjacent to Tan Son Nhut Air Base, where families were watching a softball game. Two Americans died. Underwater terrorists sank the U.S.S. *Card*, a transport ship, in Saigon Harbor, and another terrorist tossed a bomb into the crowd gathered to observe the salvage. A "Chinese businessman" left a suitcase bomb beneath the bed in his fifth floor Caravelle Hotel room. Miraculously, no one was hurt in the explosion that blew part of the fifth-floor wall into the street.

A regular noontime guest to the Cercle Sportif where he swam and lunched, Ambassador Lodge varied his schedule after police intelligence discovered a plot for a noon grenade attack on the club. In May, at the start of a scheduled visit by Secretary McNamara, police defused explosives beneath a bridge over which the secretary's car, also carrying Lodge, was to pass an hour and a half later. For the remainder of his trip, McNamara wore a bulletproof vest.

Dismayed at the declining security in Saigon and the continuing Vietcong control of the countryside, McNamara recommended increasing American personnel in Vietnam. Thus in July, eight months after NSAM 273 had scheduled a phased withdrawal of troops, the U.S. added 5,000 men to its 16,000-man advisory force. (In fact the withdrawal of 1,000 men did take place, but it was largely a normal rotation turnover. The troop level remained constant.) More planes, trucks, jeeps, and armored cars were also provided, raising the rate of U.S. investment in South Vietnam from $625 million to $700 million a year.

By midyear, however, the NLF's escalation had exacted its price: Vietcong Main Force battalions and regional militia units had endured heavy casualties. Few regroupees—southerners taken North for training and used to fill out below-strength units—remained in the North as a troop reservoir, and the promised build-up of North Vietnamese support only trickled down the Ho Chi Minh Trail. Moreover, the NLF's effort to win the loyalty of the population was faring far less well than its propagandists claimed.

To ease the problems of manpower and supply, the NLF altered its tactics in the villages. Time-consuming agitprop was inadequate to meet the pressing needs for guerrilla recruits, rice, and money, so the front began to rely more on force and terror. The

At Kien Long in the Mekong Delta, ARVN soldiers battled for two days against the first regiment-sized NLF unit. The body of an American adviser killed in the battle lies beside a mortally wounded South Vietnamese as their more fortunate companions continue to take fire.

NLF instituted a compulsory draft order which, said a captured propaganda cadre, "was often denounced for its dictatorial and harsh nature." The draft often took the form of kidnapping, followed by threats of assassination against the family of the recruit. The cadres increasingly appropriated rice, "without explanation," and hiked taxes. A farmer's contribution to the front ranged from one-sixth to one-half his income, and treatment for nonpayment turned less sympathetic: "Don't talk to me," Kim Loan, a feared Vietcong woman tax collector in Long An Province often warned, "talk to my pistol."

As a result, villagers who "believed everything the cadres said, and esteemed and respected them in 1962–63," according to one captured guerrilla, grew suspicious in 1964. Said one probably over-optimistic squad leader taken prisoner in Vinh Long Province, "If the Vietcong had continued their smooth propaganda lines of 1962–63, the population would be in their hands entirely."

Infiltration from the North

North Vietnam began in mid-1964 to fulfill its commitment proclaimed the previous December to increase support to the southern insurgency. Regular North Vietnamese Army units began preparing to in-filtrate. Some North Vietnamese soldiers had already appeared in the South, but in the summer of 1964, regiments of the 325th People's Army of Vietnam (PAVN) Division underwent training in the hills and forests of Quang Binh Province, just above the demilitarized zone.

Soldiers participated in practice attacks and political indoctrination sessions, in which they heard from cadres that the southern insurgents longed for the help of PAVN soldiers to unify the country. After completing training in September or October, the first regular North Vietnamese infantry regiment moved west toward Laos to begin the arduous journey down the network of paths, trails, and roads known collectively as the Ho Chi Minh Trail.

The march began in Ho Village, a clearing of grass-roofed barracks several days' walk from the Laotian border. There the soldiers exchanged army uniforms for the black pajamas of the NLF. After resolving "to attain the objective and protect my weapon," the soldiers departed, a company of a hundred men or a battalion of several hundred at a time,

Village life resumes the morning after a fierce battle in October 1964 near the town of Go Dau Ha near the Parrot's Beak on the Cambodian border. Bodies of some of the forty-six VC killed in the battle, covered crudely with straw mats, await removal.

Nung soldiers on patrol with U.S. Special Forces follow a section of the Ho Chi Minh Trail along a mountain stream.

at two- or three-day intervals. For security, the soldiers were not informed of their whereabouts.

Each journey took two months or longer. Men carrying sixty-pound packs and weapons hiked hundreds of miles through nearly impenetrable jungle and crossed mountains up to six thousand feet high. Usually no more than a footpath, the trail occasionally widened to two or three meters. When someone fell ill, another shouldered his load. The infiltrators walked from 6:00 A.M. to 7:00 P.M., fifty minutes out of every hour, four days out of five. If they had to move at night, the men smeared fireflies on each other's backs so each soldier could follow the man ahead through the darkness.

A liaison agent who knew only his sector of the trail guided the troops to the next rest camp, normally no more than a jungle clearing. A few larger camps contained sleeping quarters and storage facilities, but only one, Tchepone, existed on any map. This eastern Laotian town was the most important spur on the trail, serving as a way station and as a resupply depot. North Vietnam supplied the town via airdrops. (Early in 1965 American and Laotian bombers at-

tacked Tchepone, and the North Vietnamese broke down the assembly areas into small, fortified, camouflaged camps.)

From staging points montagnard guides led the infiltrators on month-long, back-breaking marches through the highlands of Laos to the Vietnam border of Kontum Province. There the regiments joined forces with NLF units operating in the province. By March 1965, three regiments, totaling fifty-eight hundred men, had joined the fighting in the South.

In a 1964 interview in *Le Monde*, Dr. Pham Ngoc Thach, North Vietnam's minister of health, described two trips he had made along the Ho Chi Minh Trail:

This is an extremely difficult and long road to negotiate with sixty pounds of equipment on one's back. Americans believe one can easily organize a two-way traffic between the North and . . . the front. That makes me laugh. . . . It shows they know nothing of war in the bush.

The United States pauses

On May 23, William P. Bundy, who had replaced Roger Hilsman as assistant secretary of state, produced, as requested in NSAM 288, a possible thirty-day scenario for the initiation of a bombing campaign. Aiming toward "D-Day," the script involved public statements from Saigon and Washington and diplomatic moves including consultation with allies and a third-party mission to Hanoi. It was to culminate in a bombing campaign against war-supporting targets, after an evacuation of U.S. dependents from South Vietnam. A joint resolution from Congress "approving past actions and authorizing whatever is necessary with respect to Vietnam" was a key requirement.

Bundy's scenario was not adopted as policy, but at a conference in Honolulu on June 1 and 2 the administration's top policy makers refined the plans. They judged the South Vietnamese government incapable at the time of mounting a bombing campaign by itself or of repelling any retaliatory attacks against Saigon. Without stronger military action, the planners realized that other means were required to display American resolve. It was felt that a Congressional resolution would both express American firmness and alert the public to the stakes at risk in Southeast Asia. Bundy believed that the June Honolulu confer-

Hop Tac — Anatomy of a Failure

"My God, our soldiers were so close!" wailed a South Vietnamese peasant. "Why couldn't they have done something for us?" Before dawn on April 9, 1964, an entire Vietcong battalion, about four hundred men, crept into the militia training camp of Go Den village, barely ten miles from Saigon. With bursts of machine-gun fire, they killed twenty-eight and wounded or captured all but one of the camp's ninety-eight defenders, then departed as swiftly as they had come. The event was shocking: The Vietcong were drawing their net ever tighter about South Vietnam's capital.

The Go Den massacre was scarcely an isolated incident. In that year, Vietcong units were attacking with impunity closer and closer to the capital. To counter this advancement, U.S. Ambassador Henry Cabot Lodge devised a plan of pacification to spread out from Saigon in concentric "rings of steel." As he conceived it, South Vietnamese forces within sixteen weeks would secure the territory in a fifty-mile radius from the environs of Saigon to the Cambodian border in the west and to the South China Sea in the east. General William Westmoreland, in charge of im-

plementing the plan, named it "Hop Tac," the Vietnamese word for cooperation.

Lack of cooperation turned out to be one of Hop Tac's major failings. Vietnamese officials did not consider Hop Tac to be a program of their own. Westmoreland and Ambassador Maxwell Taylor, Lodge's successor, presented it to Premier Khanh as a fait accompli. Khanh established the Hop Tac Council to accommodate the Americans, but he gave it little authority. He was far more interested in protecting his regime from a coup attempt than in inaugurating a wide-ranging pacification program with a "Made in USA" label. Khanh fired even the most effective province chiefs and military commanders whenever he could replace them with more loyal followers, while Hop Tac's success depended on well-trained soldiers and administrators. He also withheld supplies from the civic action programs and kept the best marine and airborne brigades for his personal protection.

On September 12, 1964, the 51st ARVN Regiment embarked on the first Hop Tac operation, a sweep through the VC stronghold closest to Saigon, a series of pineapple groves southwest of the city. On the second day, Vietcong guerrillas waited until part of the regiment advanced into a minefield and then sprang an ambush. Taking heavy casualties, the 51st regiment called off the rest of the operation and melted back to Saigon. The following day, incredibly enough, the unit joined in a short-lived coup d'état attempt instigated by General Lam Van Phat.

Poor planning and execution characterized Hop Tac from its inception. Pockets of Vietcong strength varied in each region slated for pacification, but no consideration was given to the fact that certain

areas remained more difficult to secure than others; the artificial schedule had to be met. The undertaking was plagued by rigid deadlines, unrealistic expectations, broken promises, and careless mistakes. American strategists, for example, did not take into account, as General Westmoreland later admitted, that "most of the South Vietnamese soldiers came from a specific region in the manner of American national guard units." When the 25th ARVN Division was moved into the Saigon area from its home province of Quang Ngai in I Corps, homesick and disgruntled soldiers deserted in droves.

Hop Tac's minor successes were continually flaunted as examples of significant progress, but security remained questionable at best. Parents of South Vietnamese Boy Scouts forbade their children to camp overnight at sites bordering Tan Son Nhut Airport, and government supporters still passed beyond the city limits of Saigon at their own risk.

In Long An Province—in which the first Hop Tac "ring of steel" was supposed to impose security—the 506th Vietcong Battalion continued to operate and even expand. By late 1964, recruitment was so high, in fact, that the battalion was split into two units. On January 8, 1965, the 506th overran an ARVN company command post and weapons platoon.

Despite this convincing demonstration of Vietcong strength, the bureaucratic overseers of Hop Tac deemed the area secure in January 1965—right on schedule—and laid plans for pacifying the second ring of steel in four months' time.

The fantasy of pacification under the Hop Tac program continued until 1966, when it was "merged" with other counterinsurgency programs.

ence marked a pause in the plans for escalation. It was, he said, "the beginning of a drawing back."

After the conference the staffs of the Departments of Defense and State and the White House drafted a Congressional resolution. It was ultimately shelved, however. With no immediate expansion planned in military activity, and thus no sense of military urgency, the administration recognized the difficulty of rallying Congress—and the public—to approve future actions. In addition, the Senate was debating the Kennedy/Johnson civil rights bill, after which it faced the sizable agenda of LBJ's "Great Society" programs. In July and August the Republicans and Democrats would hold their presidential nominating conventions, and there would not be enough time for adequate debate about Vietnam policy.

J. Blair Seaborn, the Canadian member of the International Control Commission, performed the intermediary role proposed by Bundy, traveling to Hanoi on June 18 to feel out the North Vietnamese on negotiations. Although he knew of the contingency bombing plans, his instructions precluded any explicit threats of bombing. Meeting with Prime Minister Pham Van Dong, Seaborn said, "American patience is not limitless" and that with escalation, North Vietnam would suffer "the greatest devastation."

The prime minister passed over the veiled threat, but he did reiterate Hanoi's requirements for an end to the war: American withdrawal, a neutralist coalition settlement in the South with NLF participation, and a reunification of the country. The prospects for the U.S., he said, showing his own country's stiff resolve, were "sans issue" ("a dead end"), and the only options for Vietnam were neutrality or "guerre à outrance" ("war to the end"), which, Dong maintained, the U.S. would not win.

With attacks against the North and the Congressional resolution in abeyance, the war-making machinery of the United States government slipped into neutral. A White House memorandum written by presidential adviser McGeorge Bundy charted a middle course, one designed to avoid a show of weakness or a widening of the war. Planning for direct military action against the North would continue, but approval would be granted only to covert programs already being carried out by South Vietnam and stronger actions against North Vietnamese infiltration through Laos. "Defense of U.S. interests is possible, within these limits, over the next six months," the memorandum concluded. That half year would carry the government to the national election, deliver a resounding mandate for a heretofore caretaker president, and lead into the year 1965.

The Taylor mission

Late in June, Ambassador Lodge resigned his post to return home for presidential politicking. In February

Two months before his promotion to commander of U.S. forces in Vietnam, General William C. Westmoreland escorts his eventual commander in chief, former Vice President Richard M. Nixon, through the village of Phu My near Saigon in April 1964.

he had won his party's New Hampshire primary. A moderate Republican, Lodge's own expectations for the nomination had collapsed with the primary victories of Barry Goldwater. Yet Lodge felt he must head off the Arizona senator and work for the nomination of a more progressive Republican.

To replace him, President Johnson appointed General Maxwell D. Taylor, one of several top advisers (including cabinet officers Rusk, McNamara, and Attorney General Robert F. Kennedy) who had reluctantly volunteered. Described by the New York Times as residing "somewhere between Virgil and Clausewitz," Taylor had followed an excellent performance as commander of the elite 101st Airborne Division in World War II with a distinguished postwar career that included every important rung on the military ladder—superintendent of West Point, army chief of staff, and, after a brief retirement and service as President Kennedy's military adviser, chairman of the Joint Chiefs of Staff. Fluent in German, French, and Japanese, he spoke in a clipped, self-confident voice and marshaled his strength by lying down for fifteen minutes every day after lunch. Though considered a loyal Kennedy man in matters of counterinsurgency, he was also committed to attacks against the North. Taylor arrived in Saigon July 7 with a broad grant of presidential authority—responsibility for the whole military effort in Vietnam with whatever degree of command and control he deemed appropriate.

General William C. Westmoreland, who had succeeded General Harkins as MACV commander only three weeks earlier, would therefore have to clear all policy cables to Washington through Taylor. With perfect discipline, Westmoreland accepted the commander in chief's order. "Taylor was the boss," he wrote. "I was, in effect, his deputy for military affairs." Westmoreland had developed a healthy respect for Taylor while serving as his secretary during Taylor's tenure as army chief of staff. In fact, Taylor had pinned on Westmoreland's second star when he became the army's youngest major general in 1956.

A lean and rigid six-footer, Westmoreland had advanced in his own impressive career track. The first captain of cadets in the West Point class of 1936, he returned there in 1960 as superintendent after World War II combat in Tunisia, Sicily, and Normandy, and postwar command of the 101st Airborne Division. A week after taking command of the 101st, he led a routine paratroop drop that ended tragically when treacherous winds dragged seven men to their deaths. From that day the general refused to permit a drop until he had jumped first to gauge the winds. A deeply moral man, committed to the military academy's code of ethics, Westmoreland was married to a fellow officer's daughter whom he met at his first post at Fort Sill, Oklahoma, when she was just nine years old. They married eleven years later.

As MACV commander, Westmoreland proposed to

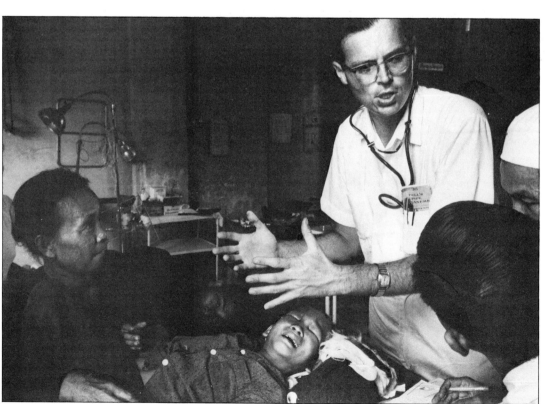

Dr. Robert Norton of the U.S. Operations Mission attends a wounded child at Can Tho Hospital. USOM, with USAID, was charged with parcelling out U.S. economic aid to South Vietnam.

USAID trucks arrive in a delta village with truckloads of piglets. By 1967, the U.S. was spending one quarter of its foreign aid budget in South Vietnam.

the new ambassador that MACV become the executive agent for the lagging pacification programs. But Ambassador Taylor rejected the proposal, preferring instead to establish a Mission Council that brought together all the major embassy officers weekly, including the military, as a miniature National Security Council. At Taylor's request, General Khanh organized a similar Vietnamese council to work more closely with the Americans. In addition to pacification plans and military activities, the U.S. Mission administered a host of civilian programs. During Taylor's tenure, one listing showed that of sixty programs actively underway in coordination with the Khanh government, only nineteen were directly related to military affairs.

In Khanh, the new ambassador faced an obstreperous ally. The Vietnamese premier was suspicious because of Taylor's earlier, highly publicized tennis matches with General "Big" Minh, Khanh's rival and nominal, though powerless, superior. Furthermore, Khanh's wavering irritated the decisive Taylor. General Khanh, he wrote, had "a propensity to abandon a course of action as soon as an obstacle was encountered and to start something new and less demanding."

In May Khanh had flip-flopped on the question of attacking the North, telling Secretary McNamara in midmonth that action must be delayed until the southern political base was solidified and informing Secretary Rusk two weeks later that the war must be carried north. On July 19, the day before the ten-year anniversary of Vietnam's partition, Khanh incited the crowds with an indiscreet speech calling for a march "to the North," which clashed with the American policy of patience and brought Khanh into sharp conflict with Taylor. The ambassador protested the "march to the North" campaign as an effort to force the U.S. hand.

In his first monthly report, filed on August 10, Taylor noted that the Khanh regime had lasted six months and "has a 50–50 chance of lasting out the year. The government is ineffective, beset by inexperienced ministers who are jealous and suspicious of each other." Popular support in the countryside continued to be poor, causing Khanh to "use the 'march North' theme to rally the home front and offset the war weariness."

Taylor summarized the U.S. objectives as improving pacification, working on social and economic projects, and bolstering the Khanh regime. The American public, he felt, should be kept informed of what the U.S. government was doing and educated about the reasoning behind such actions. A further aim, he wrote, was preparation "to implement contingency plans against North Vietnam with optimum readiness by January 1, 1965."

In short, the man in control of the U.S. effort in Vietnam felt that by the turn of the year, with the presidential elections over, the time would have come to carry the war to the North.

Covert Action, Hidden War

One summer day in 1959, 107 Special Forces soldiers departed Fort Bragg, North Carolina, for outposts in the distant mountains of Laos. The soldiers had been dropped from military rolls— "sheep-dipped," in military lingo. They wore civilian clothes and carried civilian identification and hunting rifles. Each man traveled with his own cover story; some, for example, claimed to be merchant marine sailors who had jumped ship and fled to landlocked Laos.

Under Lieutenant Colonel Arthur D. "Bull" Simons, a tough, brush-cut veteran of World War II Ranger operations, the disguised Special Forces were to join up with Laotian hill tribes singled out by the Central Intelligence Agency. If the tribesmen proved willing, the Special Forces would arm and train them as resistance fighters against the Communist-dominated Pathet Lao. This mission, designated Operation Hotfoot, was hazardous and secret. In addition to exploring

Rebel Pathet Lao troops sing marching songs and display their weapons during a rally at Sam Neua, Laos, in April 1958. The growing strength of the Communist-led Pathet Lao provoked President Eisenhower to send the Laotian government American economic and military aid.

uncharted territory, American soldiers had to contend with a diplomatic obstacle: They were prohibited by international treaty from setting foot in Laos.

Until 1965, most Americans were unaware that their countrymen were engaged in combat in Southeast Asia. Sporadic casualties (137 Americans killed by the end of 1964) were perceived as the inevitable result of the growing number of American advisers who accompanied Vietnamese units into the field, for Americans had orders to fire only if fired upon. Yet when American advisers poured into the area, they discovered that the CIA and Special Forces had already been conducting hidden actions.

Operation Hotfoot was but one of the activities that comprised the murkiest aspect of America's early involvement in Southeast Asia. Other programs from this period, like the Civilian Irregular Defense Groups, changed from covert to overt when the army took them over from the CIA in 1963 and their histories became known. A few, like the MACV Studies and Observation Group (SOG), remain shrouded in government secrecy. Many men who participated hesitate to reveal anything about their clandestine activities; others talk only guardedly. Because of the nature of covert activities, some operations were performed without the knowledge of officials who might have been expected to know. And one group may not have known of another's operations. Much of the history of America's clandestine activities remains classified "top secret," and the story may never be told in full. Enough information has been obtained, however, to allow some of the events to be pieced together.

One fact is clear: Even before President John Kennedy approved a Counterinsurgency Plan for Vietnam in 1961, some American troops were fighting in Indochina.

Operation White Star

Five years before U.S. Special Forces arrived in Laos, that country had won its independence under the Geneva Accords of 1954, which stipulated that only France could train the Royal Laotian Army. America was allowed to send limited amounts of hardware but not personnel. America also provided economic aid. The threat of a Communist takeover, however, persuaded President Eisenhower's secretary of state, John Foster Dulles, that Laos needed to build an army of twenty-five thousand to counter the Pathet Lao and their North Vietnamese allies. To that end the U.S. sent a military delegation, which it designated the Programs Evaluation Office (PEO). Dressed in civilian clothes, Americans trained the Royal Laotian Army in conventional military tactics. In 1959 the prowestern government asked Eisenhower to bolster the PEO, and the U.S. responded with Operation Hotfoot.

Bull Simons's Special Forces A teams spread out to form ten training centers for conventional warfare. Groups of soldiers then filtered out among the isolated tribes in the central and northern mountains. To gain their confidence, the team medic entered the village first and conducted a sick call. Once the tribes-

---

Preceding page. Camouflaged and in blackface, an American soldier trains for guerrilla warfare. The U.S. Army Special Forces, detached to the Central Intelligence Agency, arrived in Southeast Asia in 1959.

people were awed by the "magic" of medicine, the Americans talked to them about the war. By the end of six months, the intelligence assessment was clear: The tribes could be motivated to bear arms against Communist guerrilla forces. The Meo tribesmen, for example, were willing to fight because the war had disrupted their trade in opium, which they produced in order to buy iron, salt, and other necessities in the lowland cities and towns.

Training the Meo tribesmen began in earnest in 1960 amid political turbulence. Just after the inauguration of President Kennedy, General Phoumi Nosavan, heavily backed by the United States, lost a decisive battle to the Communist forces for the strategic Plain of Jars. This presented Eisenhower's successor with his first international crisis. The new president began an intense effort to negotiate a settlement (ultimately achieved at the Geneva Conference of 1962) with the Soviet Union that would neutralize Laos. Kennedy made several moves to demonstrate American power—alerting troops on Okinawa and stationing marines aboard troopships off Thailand. He also unveiled the American military presence by up-

grading the PEO to a Military Assistance and Advisory Group and ordering American soldiers to wear uniforms. To emphasize the change, Operation Hotfoot was renamed Operation White Star.

By mid-1961, White Star mobile training teams were openly training nine thousand Meo tribesmen to combat the Communists in the central and northern mountains. A typical "graduation exercise" was to mount a company-sized attack against Pathet Lao forces, with Americans leading the Meo. At the same time, Bull Simons started another program, sending the Special Forces into the Laotian panhandle to recruit Kha tribesmen, numbering about ten thousand, whose homelands stretched from the southern Bolovens Plateau to the Annamite Mountains. Through those mountains ran the lower end of the Ho Chi Minh Trail.

The Kha program proved so successful for a brief time that North Vietnam moved troops to the Bolovens Plateau to support the Pathet Lao. To elude Kha patrols, Communist attackers frequently retreated into Cambodia, and the Kha and their U.S. Special Forces advisers occasionally "bent the border" in

A Royal Laotian soldier practices cover and concealment with his face blackened and foliage attached to his uniform.

pursuit, running the Pathet Lao into preplanned ambushes. "Which bamboo tree was the border?" White Star Captain Leon Hope joked. "The attitude of Special Forces in Laos was so different from Vietnam where you couldn't push or be aggressive. We were a cocky damn bunch. There wasn't a damn thing we couldn't do."

To supply the remote villages, the CIA used Air America, on paper a subsidiary of a Nationalist Chinese commercial airline but in reality a CIA "proprietary." The highly skilled civilian pilots, flying small short-takeoff-and-landing planes, delivered supplies to small clearings in the mountains. Lacking the usual navigational aids, the pilots performed legendary feats of negotiating treacherous, cloud-covered terrain to find the remote landing strips.

North Vietnam was less interested in conquering Laos than in simply maintaining control over certain regions—two northern provinces and the section where the Ho Chi Minh Trail lay. Hanoi recognized that Vietnam was the main arena of conflict. If those eastern regions of Laos fell under prowestern control, infiltration of cadres and materiel to South Vietnam would be jeopardized.

North Vietnam won its objectives when the fourteen-nation Geneva conference settled the Laos crisis by establishing the neutralist coalition government advocated by U.S. Assistant Secretary of State W. Averell Harriman. The July 1962 accords resulted in a de facto partition of the country along the cease-fire line, with the Communists controlling the northern and eastern regions. To obtain a neutralist settlement, the U.S. had no choice but to accept the status quo at the time of the cease-fire.

The Geneva agreements required foreign nations to withdraw their military forces and cease assistance to the contending factions. The MAAG and White Star mobile training teams, totaling 666 men, withdrew in October, as did the Soviet planes that had been supplying the Pathet Lao and the North Vietnamese. But North Vietnam, which had always denied the presence of any of its troops, formally recalled only forty soldiers. The CIA estimated that seven thousand North Vietnamese remained in Laos.

At first, the United States complied with the accords. But the Communists continued to expand their holdings and to drive the Meo from their lands. They consolidated their control of the Plain of Jars by building more antiaircraft batteries equipped with Soviet-made 37 MM guns. To counter the Communist gains, the United States began to supply the Meo

once again, flying in food and materiel from bases in Thailand. (With the American withdrawal, the smaller Kha resistance had ceased altogether.) With help from the CIA, the Meo continued for a decade to battle the Communists.

The Ho Chi Minh Trail retained its strategic importance throughout the Vietnam War. A 1962 State Department intelligence estimate predicted that North Vietnam would use the trails circumspectly and would make no effort to turn the trails into roads. As the war ground on, however, the North made steadily increasing use of the trail. President Kennedy recognized the trail's importance. Early in 1962, while the Geneva conference on Laos was in session, the president told an aide: "No matter what goes wrong or whose fault it really is, the argument will be that the Communists have stepped up their infiltration and we can't win unless we hit the North. Those trails are a built-in excuse for failure, and a built-in argument for escalation."

Infiltration, sabotage

The Ho Chi Minh Trail was not the only pressing concern of South Vietnam and the United States. The two nations also feared a repeat of the Korean War experience—an invasion of the South by North Vietnam. Indeed, the Korean War shaped American strategic thinking throughout the 1950s. As a result, Vietnam trained its armies to fight set-piece battles against an invading army, ignoring the lesson learned at such great expense by the French.

In February 1956, the 1st Observation Group was formed by the South Vietnam military command to organize guerrilla bands just below the seventeenth parallel in the event of an invasion. The guerrillas' missions were to provide early warning of North Vietnamese military activity along the DMZ and to sabotage lines of communication behind an invading force. Trained at Nha Trang, the 305-man group functioned outside normal military channels; all its operations required the approval of Diem himself. Many of its members, all carefully screened, originally came from North Vietnam.

By 1961, the 1st Observation Group had already made "shallow penetrations" into Laos and limited forays into North Vietnam. The group's potential for intelligence gathering and disrupting North Vietnamese operations in and around the DMZ impressed military strategists both in Saigon and Washington. Based on the recommendations of his advisers in

Vietnam, President Kennedy, within his first days in office, adopted a Counterinsurgency Plan that mandated a twenty-thousand-man increase in the Vietnamese armed forces, including a five-hundred-man expansion of the 1st Observation Group. Soon after, Kennedy's "Presidential Program for Vietnam," enacted in May 1961, expanded 1st Observation Group missions by ordering more covert actions—sabotage and light harassment—in Laos and North Vietnam and proposing operations into VC-controlled territory in South Vietnam.

Of the four hundred U.S. Special Forces deployed to Vietnam in the spring of 1961, many arrived in Nha Trang to train the Vietnamese Special Forces (called *Luc Luong Dac Biet*, or LLDB), of which the 1st Observation Group was an elite unit. To provide at least a nominal cover for its clandestine missions, the group changed its name to the equally obscure "Office 45" of the Topographical Exploitation Service, a branch of the Presidential Survey Office.

The Combined Studies Group, an arm of the CIA, set up and monitored the covert operations. To insure the option of American "deniability," CIA Station Chief William Colby, a veteran of World War II OSS infiltrations behind enemy lines in France and Nor-

way, established a dummy Vietnamese private air transport corporation (VIAT). In Colby's opinion, Air America had become too well known as a CIA operation to provide a cover. The unmarked aircraft and pilots for VIAT's infiltrations were furnished by the Vietnamese Air Force Transport Squadron, commanded by a young colonel, Nguyen Cao Ky. Elegantly mustachioed and dressed in a flashy flight suit with trailing silk scarf, Ky was as aggressive as he was flamboyant. To persuade Colby of his skills as a pilot, he took the CIA chief on a knuckle-whitening, radar-eluding flight at wave-top level. Then, as squadron commander, he insisted on leading the first infiltration mission over the North, boasting on his return of having seen the lights of Hanoi off his wingtip.

The infiltration teams of four to six men operated "black"—carrying no identification, bearing "sterile" nonmilitary issue weapons, and wearing black or brown peasant clothing.

Despite all the planning, training, and secrecy, the missions fell far short of expectations. Of the fifteen to twenty teams infiltrated up to 1964, nearly all were captured after a short time. Those who landed in jungle areas often faltered and ventured to nearby villages for supplies or simply companionship. They

Operation White Star. Above. Members of an American Special Forces A Team share a hut with Kha tribesmen in southern Laos. Below. Kha tribesmen NCOs in Pak Se move through an obstacle course and target range built by a White Star training team.

were captured. In more populated areas, local militiamen proved unsurprisingly alert to the presence of strangers in the structured, closely knit communities.

Infiltrators who reported by radio were suspected of having been captured and turned into double agents by the North Vietnamese. "Some did manage to operate for a while before they were captured," said a Vietnamese Office 45 veteran. "But in those instances where we knew they were 'doubled,' we retained contact with them and fed false information to double them back." Radio Hanoi sometimes announced a team's capture, but many were never heard from.

Other problems bedeviled the program. A Vietnamese Air Force aircraft, patrolling near the demilitarized zone, once shot down a "black" plane returning from a resupply mission to the North. A second plane crashed into a mountain in Laos near the seventeenth parallel. Meo tribesmen, working with the CIA in Laos, trekked for two weeks through the jungles of the Annamite Mountains to reach the wreck and remove top-secret materials before the enemy stumbled upon them.

Unusual weather conditions in the region of the Annamite Mountains also caused problems for pilots. Vietnam endured a summer rainy season; in winter the rains shifted to Laos, west of the mountains. One country generally experienced clear skies and dry roads, while the other was drenched by rains. Aircraft taking off under ideal conditions in one country would meet stormy weather in the other.

Discouraged by the failure of the infiltrations, the CIA decided to scrap the program and concentrate on psychological warfare. "It just didn't pan out," Gilbert Layton, a Combined Studies Group agent, said later. "Most Vietnamese are not jungle people. They're village people and town people. They work in rice paddies. An American trained in our Special Forces is better able to survive in the jungles, with no one to contact and facing a problem of resupply. If you're not a fanatic or a professional, you're not going to make it under those circumstances."

A better strategy, thought William Colby, would be to resort to propaganda broadcasts, leaflet drops, and "deception actions" to spread the idea in North Vietnam that political collaboration, economic development, and coexistence were preferable to an armed insurgency in the South. But Defense Secretary McNamara insisted on continuing the infiltrations. The CIA's lack of success, McNamara believed, resulted from the limited resources of a civilian agency such as the CIA. Instead he assigned the military to take over the missions. With the military's greater resources, McNamara foresaw an enlarged, effective program. The secretary ordered the formation of a joint military-CIA team to implement the program, and MACV established the Studies and Observation Group.

Psychological operations

Before McNamara's order the CIA had begun work on psychological operations, or "psyops." In March 1963, Special Forces soldiers under the CIA reopened a rudimentary camp in Long Thanh, twenty kilometers east of Saigon, to continue training Vietnamese to infiltrate into North Vietnam.

Training concentrated on Special Forces skills, especially night airborne jumping for men embarking on northern infiltrations. Beginning in September 1963, they also trained two companies of Vietnamese troops destined for Operation 34-Alpha, a campaign of border control and maritime harassment, including shellings, commando landings, and sabotage of North Vietnamese coastal communities that would commence in 1964. But the CIA now added an element of psychological warfare to the training. Infiltrations into the North had failed dismally, and the CIA and its military advisers recognized that the South Vietnamese lacked patriotic motivation. No rigid loyalty, like that of the North Vietnamese for Ho Chi Minh, existed, and the repressive, anti-Communist regime of Ngo Dinh Diem provided little inspiration.

In an effort to develop team loyalty, the CIA reached back to an old Vietnamese legend* to create the Sacred Sword Patriots League. This patriotic "front" emulated the National Liberation Front's methods with daily courses of political indoctrination against communism and sessions of self-criticism. "We were trying to generate confidence for them to operate in a hostile environment. We oriented them on the beginning of a new era in North and South Vietnam," said one American. "We hoped we could develop an esprit, a devotion to a cause, a loyalty."

---

* In 1418 Le Loi, a wealthy landowner in Thanh Hoa Province (above the seventeenth parallel), organized a ten-year resistance against the Chinese Ming occupation. The tale is told that he pulled a sword from a lake while fishing and used it to lead his country to freedom. He then cast the sword back into the lake, where with a clap of thunder it leaped from its scabbard, changed into a dragon, and disappeared.

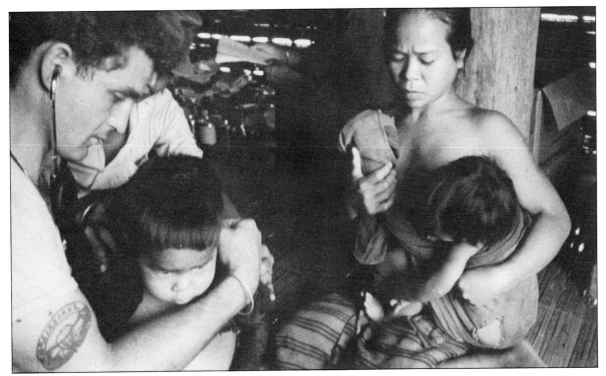

The Special Forces used medical care to help win the confidence of the montagnards. Here Sergeant Gerald "Doc" Grant of the A team at Buon Mi Ga treats a young Rhade girl.

Trainees at Long Thanh were inducted into the league with great ceremony. But disappointment again followed. For all the Sacred Sword flourishes, infiltrations into the North produced no dramatic successes. The Sacred Sword Patriots League nonetheless remained in the psyops arsenal. It would later be used in an attempt to rally a North Vietnamese-based resistance movement against the Hanoi government.

The most ambitious psychological operation took shape in the fall of 1963 when MACV and the CIA jointly established Radio Freedom and staffed it with Vietnamese civilians to broadcast to North Vietnam. The "Voice of Freedom" went on the air in February 1964, under the auspices of SOG. A ten-thousand-watt transmitter and three radio towers erected just south of Hue sent broadcasts to most of North Vietnam. A "white" station, that is, one that admitted its location in the South, Radio Freedom signed on the air in the early morning hours, closed down during the day, and returned at night with a repeat of its programming, for a total of eight hours daily. Because the peasants arose early to till their fields, evening hours were considered to be most productive.

The programs combined traditional Vietnamese music and theater, some western popular music, and a great deal of news and commentary. Blatant propaganda was avoided. Although favoring the South Vietnamese viewpoint, the news was written as honestly as possible. SOG also maintained some clandestine "black" radio stations, which purported to be located in North Vietnam. Operating on short-wave frequencies, these stations broadcast more propagandistic information, including reports on activities of the Sacred Sword Patriots League.

Combined studies group

Psychological operations, begun by the CIA and taken over by SOG, were but one aspect of the intelligence work conducted by the CIA station in Vietnam, which by 1964 totaled four hundred employees. In the early 1960s, the CIA and its operative paramilitary arm, the Combined Studies Group, was a free-wheeling agency that benefited from an ability unique in government: Its projects received rapid approval from its Langley, Virginia, headquarters after discussion by the 303 Committee. Named for the room number of the Executive Office Building across from the White House where it met weekly, the 303 Committee was formed after the April 1961 Bay of Pigs fiasco to clear all covert CIA activities. Its membership included Deputy Secretary of Defense Roswell Gilpatric, Deputy Undersecretary of State U. Alexis Johnson, Special Assistant to the President McGeorge Bundy, and CIA Deputy Director of Intelligence Richard Helms. The 303 Committee gave the CIA in Vietnam direct access to Washington decision makers. "Every time we got in a jam with some general, somebody would get 303 to approve what we were doing," said one Combined Studies agent.

In late 1961 the Special Forces, detached to Com-

The U.S. Air Force Joins The War

In 1961, when the Kennedy administration proposed using Vietnam as a laboratory for testing techniques of counterinsurgency, the U.S. Air Force had two projects to contribute—a squadron of air commandos for combat and training missions and an experimental program of defoliation. The air role would prove crucial in a guerrilla war, for the air force not only had to supply troops garrisoned in remote outposts, but also had to relieve soldiers caught in the withering fire of ambushes. Defoliation likewise assumed major importance in a country whose ecology featured dense tropical forests and mountain jungles. Herbicides cleared landing zones for helicopters and destroyed the concealing foliage surrounding air bases and army posts. A massive campaign of defoliation would eliminate much of the roadside cover for the insurgents' favored tactic—the ambush.

★　　★　　★

The coming of Agent Orange

Vietnam defoliation had its genesis in the laboratory of Professor E. J. Kraus, chairman of the University of Chicago's botany department, during World War II. Kraus contacted the War Department's chemical review committee to report the discovery of plant hormones that regulate growth. A heavy dose of 2, 4-dichlorophenoxyacetic acid (2, 4-D) killed broadleafed plants by inducing a wild and uncontrolled growth. The army center for biological warfare research tested the hormones, but the war ended before any field use was contemplated. Testing continued, however, and some versions of the herbicides appeared on the postwar market to control dandelions in suburban lawns or to clear railroad rights-of-way and power line routes.

By 1959 army scientists had developed a potent mixture of 2, 4-D and a close chemical relative, 2,4,5-trichlorophenoxyacetic acid (2,4,5-T), which made its way into the U.S. military arsenal. After experimental spraying in 1961 deemed them ready for possible use in antiguerrilla warfare, the herbicides were shipped to Vietnam. The various mixtures took their names from the color-coded strips girdling the packing crates—Agent Purple, Agent White, Agent Blue. The one containing the greatest proportion of 2,4,5-T was called Agent Orange.

Their use in Vietnam opened a new and controversial chapter in U.S. aerial warfare: the eradication of foliage and the destruction of crops. In January 1962, three air force C-123s, fitted with 1,000-gallon drums carrying herbicides, took to the air from Tan Son Nhut airfield to commence Operation Hades. (Although Hades was its official code name, the operation was more popularly known as Ranch Hand.) This first mission failed because the sprayed vegetation was dormant, and the herbicides worked only on growing plants. When the rainy season came in September, Ranch Hand operations went into full swing, with air force C-123s dusting nine thousand acres of mangrove forest bordering rivers and canals of the Ca Mau Peninsula, a Communist stronghold. The spraying defoliated an estimated 95 percent of the targeted area. Shortly thereafter American officials in Vietnam were given authority to approve Ranch Hand missions at their own discretion. Thus began a program that was to haunt Vietnamese and Americans in the years to come.

At the time, the serious, sometimes deadly, toxic effects of Agent Orange were not considered. No one bothered, before its use was widespread, to investigate the possible impact on civilians remaining within a sprayed area or soldiers patrolling in contested territory where defoliants had improved visibility. In fact, the herbicide's principal route into the human system was through drinking water, which in many areas came from rainwater cisterns and shallow wells. In Agent Orange, concentrations of the highly toxic 2,4,5-T averaged thirteen times the dosage recommended for domestic use in the United States.

Ranch Hand operations continued to expand. In 1964 alone, American and Vietnamese planes defoliated more than eighty-three thousand acres of vegetation, and, to deprive the enemy of food, destroyed crops covering another ten thousand acres. Within three years, the annual total laid waste would soar to 1.7 million acres, an area equivalent to half the state of Connecticut. By 1970 about one-seventh of Vietnam's land area had been sprayed with herbicides. In the ready room of Ranch Hand operations, airmen posted this sign: "Only You Can Prevent Forests."

The first inkling of the damaging effects of Agent Orange did not come until 1968, when the Bionetics Research Laboratories of Bethesda, Maryland, completed a study of domestic pesticides for the National Cancer Institute. The lab found no carcinogenic properties in 2,4,5-T, but the chemical was discovered to cause malformations in the fetuses of laboratory mice and rats. The abnormalities included lack of eyes, impaired vision, cystic kidneys, cleft palates, and enlarged livers.

Results of the Bionetics study did not, until 1969, come to the attention of the White House, which soon after reduced the use of Agent Orange. In April 1970, its use was suspended altogether. Yet the harm to Vietnamese and to American soldiers exposed to Agent Orange had already been done. The gruesome probability existed that the lives of uncounted thousands had been altered and the health of their offspring impaired.

★　　★　　★

Covert air combat

Responding to President Kennedy's emphasis on counterinsurgency, the air force in April 1961 formed the 4400th Combat Crew Training Squadron, nicknamed Jungle Jim, at Eglin Air Force Base, Florida. Selected for their combat skills, 352 air commandos, dressed in fatigues, combat boots, and Australian bush hats, were eager to fight; instead their primary mission was to train Vietnamese pilots, and many were not well suited to that.

Following the president's decision in October of that year to conduct covert operations in Vietnam, half of the 4400th Squadron acquired a new code name,

Farmgate. It was deployed to Bien Hoa, a dilapidated French air base with a single battered steel runway, fifteen miles northeast of Saigon. Bien Hoa was surrounded by swamps and jungles that easily concealed Vietcong raiding parties. Security had to be strengthened. Soon after Farmgate's arrival, seven hundred Vietnamese soldiers, using mortars, howitzers, and armored personnel carriers, patrolled the landing strip, tents, and lean-to huts.

In addition to training Vietnamese to fly propeller-driven AD-6s (later called A-1H Skyraiders), Farmgate also experimented with psychological warfare—dropping leaflets over enemy-controlled territory and making broadcasts above rural villages—and helped to supply Vietnamese Rangers and CIDG camps along the South Vietnamese border.

From the start, the Farmgate pilots felt shackled in the role of providing covert support to overt Vietnamese actions, and they began to assume more responsibility on operations. Just three months after their arrival, a low-flying SC-47 on a leaflet-dropping flight crashed near Da Lat, killing eight Americans and one Vietnamese. Embarrassed by the loss of so many Americans on a purported training flight, Defense Secretary McNamara ordered leaflet and speaker missions turned over entirely to the Vietnamese.

The eager air commandos bristled at restrictive rules of engagement (ROE) that required them to fly with Vietnamese copilots in aircraft bearing Vietnamese insignia. The pilots believed they had come to Vietnam to fight and disliked the subordinate role dictated by Washington. In addition, the highly motivated Americans found the Vietnamese too cautious and slow in reacting to calls for assistance from embattled ARVN units.

In their impatience, Farmgate pilots increasingly violated the rules of engagement by flying combat missions accompanied by raw Vietnamese recruits (whom they called "sandbags") in the second seat. This system was arranged by Air Vice Marshal Nguyen Cao Ky and MACV Air Force General Joseph H. Moore, who disagreed with Washington's restrictions and saw a need to improve reaction time on distress calls. By early 1964, eighty-nine U.S. Air Force pilots were flying combat missions in Vietnamese aircraft.

Because of a nearly total publicity blackout of air force activities, newsmen had been barred from Bien Hoa, and the public learned nothing about the expanding role of Farmgate. But the evasion came to light after a T-28 piloted by Captain Edwin G. Shank lost a wing and crashed near Soc Trang, killing Shank and his

U.S. Air Force Captain Edwin G. Shank, Jr., leans against the machine gun of a T-28 fighter-bomber. Shank's letters home exposed the fact that U.S. pilots sent as instructors to Vietnam under Operation Farmgate were also flying combat missions.

Vietnamese crewman. The pilot's bitter letters to his wife in Indiana broke in the U.S. press in May 1964, and the illicit combat operations were exposed. "What gets me most," Captain Shank had written a few months earlier,

is that they won't tell you people what we do over here. I'll bet you that anyone you talk to does not know that American pilots fight this war. We—me and my buddies—do everything. . . . [The "sandbags"] are stupid, ignorant, sacrificial lambs, and I have no use for them. . . . They're a menace to have on board.

These revelations angered Secretary McNamara. In discussions of Farmgate's function, he had repeatedly emphasized its training role. Now he reiterated that U.S. forces were not to take part in combat and made known in the Pentagon his intention to redeploy the Farmgate squadron to the United States within four months. In view of a greatly increased need for air support, however, McNamara relented. Instead of being phased out, Farmgate remained in Vietnam but was confined strictly to training missions.

bined Studies, built the Hoa Cam Training Center at Da Nang for several specialized programs. One group trained at Hoa Cam was mountain commandos, or mountain scouts, who performed long-range reconnaissance missions in remote jungle and mountain areas to gather intelligence on NLF activities. Trail watchers, or border surveillance units, performed essentially the same reconnaissance function along the Cambodian and Laotian borders, with the added mission of killing or capturing Vietcong whenever possible. Under a "Fighting Fathers" program, the Special Forces trained five companies of Catholic parishioners from Tay Ninh Province where insurgents had attacked Catholic priests and their followers. Virtually overnight the priests fielded an army of several hundred men.

The largest, and most successful, Combined Studies activity was the Civilian Irregular Defense Groups, which from experimental beginnings in January 1962 had grown within eighteen months to encompass eleven thousand strike force troops and forty thousand hamlet militia in thirty-seven self-defense camps. CIDG camps, and their widening areas of pacification, dotted the map of South Vietnam. The Special Forces A teams, detached to Combined Studies and thus under civilian control and often wearing civilian clothes, implemented the program as advisers to the commanding Vietnamese Special Forces in each camp.

With minimum manpower and at comparatively small expense, the CIDG program succeeded in bringing large areas under government control and enlisting numerous montagnards who would otherwise have been recruited by the enemy. In fact the program was designed not so much to combat the enemy as to deny him territory and recruits. "Most of the montagnards who were VC when we got there were VC only because the enemy was there first and recruited them," explained Gilbert Layton, one of the architects of CIDG. "We preferred to recruit them ourselves instead of killing them." The strong and wiry "mountain people" knew every inch of their tribal lands and had a history as fierce warriors. Hated and mistreated by the Vietnamese because of their primitive civilizations, the montagnards had proven easy prey for the politically wily Vietcong, who offered opportunities to rectify their mistreatment by combating the South Vietnamese. Yet they were as easily lured by the American Special Forces who persuaded them that to kill VC, who had controlled and taxed them, was at least as worthwhile as killing South Vietnamese. With their crossbows and other primitive weapons exchanged for rifles, the montagnards developed into effective irregular troops.

The South Vietnamese, however, were somewhat dissatisfied with the program. The arming of the montagnards bothered them because of the historical antipathy between the two groups. Montagnards from various tribes populated the CIDG camps in the central highlands of II Corps. But many Vietnamese soldiers joined the strike forces in camps in I, III, and IV Corps. When montagnards and Vietnamese were present in the same camp, the situation, according to one Green Beret, was akin to mixing Indian tribes and white settlers in the American West. And the Green Berets preferred the "Indians."

There was also friction between the Vietnamese Special Forces and their American counterparts. The

A Vietcong guerrilla is flushed out of a tunnel by a montagnard soldier.

U.S. Special Forces Deployment

- ■ Special Forces Detachments (A teams)
- ★ Special Forces Headquarters
- .... ARVN Corps boundaries

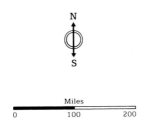

N
S

Miles
0   100   200

1962

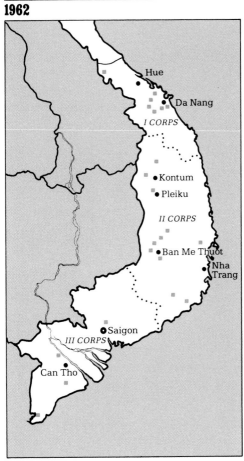

Hue
Da Nang
I CORPS
Kontum
Pleiku
II CORPS
Ban Me Thuot
Nha Trang
Saigon
III CORPS
Can Tho

1963

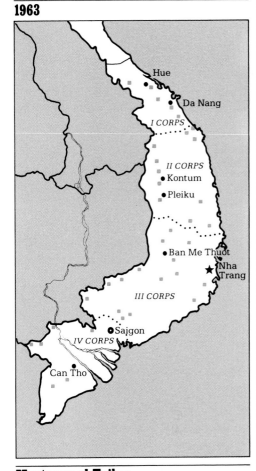

Hue
Da Nang
I CORPS
II CORPS
Kontum
Pleiku
Ban Me Thuot
★ Nha Trang
III CORPS
Saigon
IV CORPS
Can Tho

1964

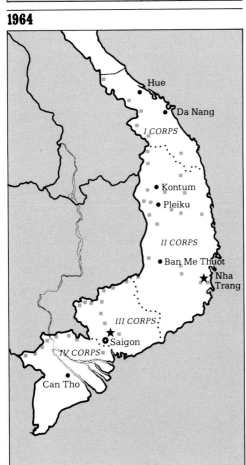

Hue
Da Nang
I CORPS
Kontum
Pleiku
II CORPS
Ban Me Thuot
★ Nha Trang
III CORPS
Saigon
IV CORPS
Can Tho

Montagnard Tribes

Hue
BRU
KATU
Da Nang
SEDANG
Kontum
BAHNAR
Pleiku
JARAI
Ban Me Thuot
RHADE
Nha Trang
STIENG
MNONG
CHAU MA
Saigon
Can Tho

Leading a routine patrol across a rice field, U.S. Special Forces Sergeant Robert Navarro and Vietnamese strike force troops from Tan Phu camp in the Mekong Delta are attacked with grenades and machine-gun fire.

Sergeant Navarro directs fire toward a machine gun pinning down the patrol.

LLDB, a proud unit considered to be the personal troops of Diem and Nhu, disliked acting the role of poor relation to the rich American adviser. For their part, the Americans viewed the Vietnamese as unaggressive and vehemently disagreed with their policy of refusing to patrol at night when the enemy was on the prowl. Americans often referred disparagingly to the LLDB as "Look long, duck back."

Unable to rely on the Vietnamese and jittery about the squabbling between the Vietnamese and montagnards, the U.S. Special Forces felt obliged to protect themselves against internal treachery. Sometimes they separated their teams into different bunkhouses or swapped bunks. An American usually walked guard duty, checking on his own strike forces. The Americans periodically checked the defenses during the night to insure that no camp spy had opened the gates for a Vietcong attack or turned machine guns and mortars inward on the camp. After some camps were attacked with inside help in 1964, the Special Forces in I and II Corps hired Nungs, a tribe of Chinese origin, as bodyguards. Better paid than the LLDB, the Nungs proved loyal to their pay. The Green Berets positioned them around the camps and took them along on operations.

This enhanced security, but it also caused bickering in the camps. One night in 1964 in an I Corps CIDG camp, members of the LLDB trained a machine gun on the Special Forces hut, turned on a spotlight, and called the Americans out. They demanded that the Nungs be expelled from the camp. "We came out to find a .30-caliber machine gun on a tripod, with an ammunition belt fed in, and the lever jacked back. One guy's laying there ready to shoot

up the whole team hut, and the officer's making demands," related one American who was there. "The Nungs lived in a grass hut that they built themselves off to one side. The team captain said, 'There will be no discussion, but I suggest you look to your right.' The LLDB soldiers looked over. The Nungs turned the headlights on in a truck and they're standing there with their rifles pointed on these guys." The Vietnamese gave up their demands.

Border surveillance

The Combined Studies Group turned over the CIDG program to the military in July 1963 under Operation Switchback, and MACV altered its mission dramatically. From the defensive strategic hamlets, which denied the enemy territory and manpower, the program turned to an offensive mission charged with halting infiltration via the Ho Chi Minh Trail.

Beginning in July, many of the camps in central Vietnam closed down and the Special Forces A detachments moved with their strike forces to even more remote outposts along the Laotian and Cambodian borders. In populated areas, new recruitment took place. But now strike forces alone were trained, and the defensive program for hamlet militia ended. Within a year twenty-five camps manned by Special Forces and eleven thousand strike force troops stretched along the Vietnam border.

Originally recruited to defend their own districts, the transferred strike forces grumbled at being moved away from their homes. Problems of discipline and desertion abounded. In one camp, several Vietnamese, who hesitated to desert because they feared negotiating the dense jungle, shot themselves in the feet and arms just before a medical helicopter ar-

The machine gun quieted, Navarro sprints through a paddy to troops hit in the first burst.

Navarro crouches beside a wounded Vietnamese soldier.

rived to evacuate a wounded soldier. They got out. Another camp in I Corps posted a 67 percent AWOL rate.

Although the Vietnamese LLDB still officially commanded the camps, the Americans ran most of the operations, particularly night ambushes they set for Vietcong moving through the area.

The teams used the local population to learn of enemy movements. Buffalo boys, who took their livestock out daily, often provided the best information. "They knew every foot of the area," said one Green Beret, "and for a couple of Tootsie Rolls, they'd tell you where the new trails were."

Despite army control of the CIDG program, uniforms and gear on operations were still optional. One Green Beret wore jungle boots and either black pajamas or Yarborough fatigues, a nylon tropical fatigue designed by Special Forces Commander Major General William P. Yarborough. In a simple Vietnamese rucksack, he carried two hundred 9 MM rounds for his Swedish K submachine gun, a poncho, hammock, and plastic baby formula bottles containing his coffee and salt. GI socks, filled with cooked rice and tied end to end, hung around his neck.

From their outposts along the border some Americans, using old French maps, crossed into Laos and Cambodia in late 1963 and 1964 to reconnoiter the Ho Chi Minh Trail. In operations lasting from five to as many as eighteen days, the teams searched for the trail's varying routes. Although such excursions were officially prohibited by the military command, the Americans, along with montagnards or Nungs, crossed the borders to scout the infiltrators. "They could sneak up on us at any time and mortar our camp," explained one Green Beret who regularly entered Cambodia, sometimes to a depth of fifteen kilo-

meters. "We went in because it was necessary to protect the lives of us all."

The Americans knew that if they engaged the enemy, they were on their own; they knew they would get no air support and no medical evacuation helicopters. In fact, if a man were wounded or killed, the team had to carry him back to Vietnam before calling a "dustoff" helicopter. But the teams tried to avoid combat: With only a couple of hundred rounds each and the certainty of no air support, they could not sustain a fire fight. Returning to Vietnam, the Americans carefully edited the intelligence they forwarded to their headquarters—giving no hint of their true location—and reported any engagement as having occurred in Vietnam.

The Ho Chi Minh "Trail" was amorphous in the war's early years. A vast network of trails and paths through Laos and Cambodia comprised the trail. It shifted as the infiltrators broke new trails or used existing ones where they found the least resistance, generally at a distance from the CIDG border surveillance camps. The trail could run for a stretch in Laos, shift over the border into Vietnam, and lead back into Laos or Cambodia. Many of the paths were used but once. In later years the Ho Chi Minh Trail became a jungle highway, and the United States mounted an extensive bombing campaign and cross-border ground operations run by SOG. But in 1964, the trail was more primitive. One Green Beret, who observed the trail while hiding in the Laotian jungle in late 1964, described it as "a highway. Next a foot trail. Next a bicycle path. I never saw a truck, but I heard them in the jungle and saw the tracks. They'd drive their trucks as far as they could. Carriers would offload the trucks, throw the goods in homemade rucksacks, go 'x' more clicks [kilometers] on down the trail, and they'd have to climb, but the steps were already built into the mountain. They'd pass their stuff on to bicycles, rigged with saddlebags and something like a yoke across the front so they could steer the bike as they pushed it."

"You will all be killed"

Every Special Forces soldier recognized the vulnerability of the CIDG camp, especially after nightfall: Because of their isolation, and the Vietcong skill at ambush, the camps could not count on reinforcements during the night, should the enemy attack.

When CIDG camps were first established, the Vietcong had given them wide berth, preferring to change their routes of travel and avoid contact. But the CIDG program had grown into a far-reaching program of pacification and, moving closer to the border, it threatened the life line of infiltration. Faced with this menace to NLF territory, the insurgents mounted an increasing number of assaults against the camps in late 1963 and 1964.

On July 5, 1964, outside Nam Dong camp in I Corps, fifteen miles from Laos, two reinforced Vietcong battalions massed for an attack. Situated in a bowl with two-thousand-foot mountains rising on every side, Nam Dong had proved to be a poor

Aftermath. The Nam Dong Special Forces camp is reduced to ruins after the all-night attack of July 5, 1964, by an estimated nine hundred guerrillas. Bodies of fifty-seven defenders and sixty-two Vietcong were found in and around the camp.

source of recruits; the largest of three strike force companies could muster only eighty-nine men. The camp was scheduled to be turned over to the local Civil Guard for protection. Camp defenses had deteriorated, and grass had grown up beyond the outer perimeter, obscuring fields of fire.

Captain Roger H. C. Donlon had brought his twelve-man A-726 detachment to Nam Dong a month earlier to preside over the transfer. Then his team was slated to establish a new border surveillance camp closer to Laos. At Nam Dong, on July 5, shooting broke out in the evening between Vietnamese and Nungs over some petty grievance. Five hundred rounds were fired before Captain Donlon and the Vietnamese LLDB commander were able to restore order. Fearing VC agitators had fomented the disturbance preparatory to an attack, Donlon moved the Nungs out of their barracks and tripled the night guard around the jittery camp. "All hell is going to break loose here," Staff Sergeant Merwin Woods wrote to his wife before turning in for the night.

At 2:30 A.M. Donlon was walking through the compound to check on the guards when the mess hall blew up with a blinding flash. His first thought was that his strike force troops were firing again, but his hope fled: Only white phosphorous mortar shells could cause such a brilliant explosion. In an instant, mortar rounds and grenades poured into the camp. Automatic weapons fired from all sides. Men raced from their huts as mortar blasts set the rattan and thatch buildings ablaze. Radio operator Sergeant Keith Daniels tapped out a fragmentary alarm to

The bodies of Vietcong sappers who carried satchel charges lie at Nam Dong's main gate where they were killed by Special Forces Team Captain Roger Donlon.

headquarters at Da Nang before a close mortar round sent him diving bare chested out the door. The next round obliterated the radio shack.

Men scurried for firearms, ammunition, grenades, and illumination shells. The Americans and Vietnamese rescued ammunition from a burning shack and returned machine-gun and mortar fire, alternating ordnance with illumination rounds. At the end of a fifteen-minute barrage, dead and wounded lay all about the camp. Then the Vietcong assault rolled over the outer perimeter.

With his men firing madly from every position, Captain Donlon dashed to reinforce the main gate. Spotting three demolition men inside the gate, he killed them with a burst from his AR15. Like nearly everyone else, Donlon was wounded, with a shrapnel hole in his stomach, cuts and burns on his arms and face. Three times explosions knocked him into the air. He ordered a 60 MM mortar withdrawn to a less exposed position and covered the retreat. He pulled the wounded team sergeant from the mortar pit, but an enemy shell exploded, killing the sergeant and driving shrapnel into Donlon's left shoulder. Crawling to an 81 MM mortar pit, Donlon directed fire while the deafening battle raged. The American, Vietnamese, and Nung defenders fired furiously at close range as the guerrillas surged forward. By dawn the defenders' ammunition would be gone.

At 4:04 A.M., after an hour and a half, the skies lit up. A flareship had arrived from Da Nang, thirty-two miles to the east.

In the din of the battle, a high-pitched voice suddenly crackled over a loud-speaker from beyond the perimeter. In Vietnamese and then in English the voice declared: "Lay down your weapons! We are going to annihilate your camp. You will all be killed!" The eerie voice shocked both sides into silence, until Sergeant Thurman Brown cranked off ten rapid mortar rounds in the direction of the loud-speaker.

The firing resumed, but with less fury. "I can't take any more of this crud," swore Sergeant Woods, dressed only in GI drawers and a pistol belt and blackened with soot and powder burns from the 81 MM mortar. The appearance of the flareship signified the imminent arrival of reinforcements, and the attack began to taper off. Soon medical supplies, radios, and ammunition were dropped by parachute. At 9:20 Vietnamese A-1H Skyraiders arrived and pursued the retreating Vietcong into the mountains.

The battle left fifty-five dead on the government side, including two Americans, and sixty-five wounded. Sixty-two Vietcong dead were found, and an inspection revealed that other VC bodies had been dragged from the field.

Nam Dong had held against an estimated nine hundred Main Force Vietcong guerrillas. The A-726 detachment collected two posthumous Distinguished Service Crosses, four Silver Stars, and five Bronze Stars. And Captain Roger Donlon became the first American in Vietnam to be awarded the Medal of Honor. Two months later a rebuilt Nam Dong, with

redesigned defenses, was formally transferred to the Vietnamese Civil Guard.

Project Delta

Trustworthy intelligence on the enemy's activities remained an essential ingredient of the American and Vietnamese military commands. Conflicting information continued to be a problem, but intelligence in the spring of 1964 indicated a build-up of enemy forces. Needing more first-hand intelligence, MACV, under the auspices of the U.S. and Vietnamese Special Forces, inaugurated yet another sensitive program in May 1964—Project Leaping Lena—to conduct long-range reconnaissance into Laos. Under Leaping Lena, five eight-man teams of Vietnamese commandos parachuted into the rugged mountains around Chavane—between Kontum Province in Vietnam and the Bolovens Plateau—to reconnoiter the Ho Chi Minh Trail. They were strictly reconnaissance teams and had orders to fight only in self-defense.

Once again, these "over the fence" (cross-border) missions failed to achieve their objectives, for a number of reasons. The teams were poorly trained and poorly led, and the North Vietnamese aptitude for detecting infiltrators produced an understandable lack of motivation on the part of the troops. "You had to damn near force them on the plane at the point of a gun," said one U.S. Special Forces colonel.

One team parachuted into an enemy-occupied village and was never heard from. A second team also failed to make radio contact. Three teams reported for a short time before they left the air, having failed

President Johnson awards the first Medal of Honor of the Vietnam War to Captain Roger H. C. Donlon in December 1964 for his leadership in the courageous defense of Nam Dong.

This North Vietnamese photo shows porters on the Ho Chi Minh Trail ascending wooden steps up a mountain. Despite Vietnamese and American efforts at interdiction, men and supplies flowed steadily into South Vietnam.

to meet their objectives. By early July, remnants of the Leaping Lena teams straggled back into Vietnam and reported on their missions, but they had little of useful consequence to report. The failure of Leaping Lena interrupted MACV's plans for phased operations in Laos and set back the mounting of cross-border operations for a year.

At about the time that Leaping Lena failed, the Special Forces initiated Project Delta to conduct long-range reconnaissance and combat patrols into enemy-controlled territory within South Vietnam. But military planners added an important element to Project Delta. From the Leaping Lena debacle, they had determined that American soldiers must accompany the patrols. Volunteers were thus recruited from both the Vietnamese and American Special Forces. To eliminate the friction that existed between the LLDB and Green Berets in CIDG camps, the Vietnamese and Americans formed reconnaissance teams (also called Hunter-Killer Teams) of eight Vietnamese and two Americans that performed every

function together during their extensive training. The joint exercises resulted in better coordination and built a "team spirit."

The teams infiltrated at night into the heart of enemy territory, often by means of a daring airborne "leapfrog" maneuver. Two helicopters, flying one behind the other, approached the target area at tree-top level. The first helicopter, dropping to the landing zone, deposited commandos as the second passed overhead. Then the chopper on the ground quickly rose to take position behind its partner. This "leapfrog" maneuver was repeated at the next LZ. With the noise of one helicopter covering the landing of the other, it was made to seem to the enemy that the helicopters had simply flown over the area, and teams could be infiltrated with less likelihood of detection.

Once on the ground, a team hid a short distance from the landing zone in case it had been detected. Wearing grease paint on their faces and camouflage fatigues, called tiger suits, the men moved out at first light to their assigned objectives. The primary mission

Vietnamese Special Forces soldiers bring back Vietcong prisoners captured by a Project Delta patrol into enemy-held territory. The early success of Project Delta prompted MACV to create other long-range reconnaissance groups.

during five-day patrols was intelligence, but each team had several options. Upon discovering an enemy village or guerrilla bivouac, it might call for extraction. (To be extracted, a soldier had to climb a rope ladder dangling from a hovering CH–34 helicopter.) Once safely out of the area, the team could help conventional forces to formulate a plan of attack. The men could also attack the Vietcong or call for air or artillery strikes. In addition, the teams could summon reinforcement by airborne Rangers and lead them to the enemy.

Working primarily in I Corps, Project Delta quickly gained the favor of MACV Commander General Westmoreland. He was impressed by the quality of intelligence its soldiers collected from areas previously denied to U.S. and South Vietnamese commands (and was persuaded eventually to create two other teams like Delta—called Omega and Sigma—to operate in enemy territory in II, III, and IV Corps). As the war widened with the arrival of American combat troops, more intelligence about enemy activities was constantly required. Demands for the services of Hunter-Killer Teams, however, often exceeded the capacity of Project Delta, whose force never grew to more than six hundred men.

Studies and Observation Group

The joint MACV-CIA team, the Studies and Observation Group, took over most of the activities of the Combined Studies Group in January 1964. Created by the order of Defense Secretary McNamara, SOG received its first missions on January 16 when President Johnson approved a Joint Chiefs of Staff plan for expanded covert actions against the coast of North Vietnam.

SOG was a "top-secret" organization; it reported directly to the Joint Chiefs of Staff. MACV had no authority for actions beyond the borders of South Vietnam, while SOG was formed to operate exclusively out of country, in North Vietnam as well as in Laos and Cambodia. Every SOG operation had to be ratified in advance by Rusk and McNamara and by Johnson himself. Outside those offices, information on SOG existed on a "need-to-know" basis. Even MACV officers, with the exception of General Westmoreland and one or two others who were briefed for courtesy, had no knowledge of SOG activities. Monthly MACV staff reports arrived in Washington with the SOG page blank except for the notation: "This annex forwarded separately."

SOG consisted of volunteers from the 5th Special Forces Group, with specialists from other services and liaison personnel from CIA, and coordinated planning with its South Vietnamese counterparts. To reflect the change from civilian to military control, the Topographical Exploitation Service changed its name to Strategic Technical Services. SOG eventually grew to include twenty-five hundred Americans and seven thousand Vietnamese.

Colonel Clyde Russell, SOG's first commander, divided the group into five units—maritime (Op 31), air support (Op 32), psychological operations (Op 33), northern infiltrations (Op 34), and other airborne "over the fence" missions (Op 35).

SOG ran only limited operations in 1964, as Colonel Russell spent several months immersed in planning. SOG missions into Laos under Op 35 did not begin until Colonel (later General) Donald Blackburn succeeded Russell in 1965. Blackburn's recommendation for American-led strikes against the Ho Chi Minh Trail encountered stiff opposition from American military planners who remembered the Leaping Lena fiasco. But Blackburn prevailed, and twelve-man reconnaissance patrols—made up of three Americans and nine indigenous soldiers (usually Nungs)—began penetrations into Laos in the spring of 1966. The same year Blackburn's successor, Colonel (later General) John K. Singlaub, was given permission to operate in Cambodia.

From these initial patrols, MACV-SOG was to grow into a formidable force. From three forward operating bases in Vietnam, SOG developed a capacity to launch airborne Slam (seek, locate, annihilate, monitor) missions behind enemy lines in Laos and Cambodia and rescue pilots downed over the North. Since they were waging a secret war, SOG unit achievements went unreported, and soldiers failed to win deserved medals because America would not admit the presence of troops in forbidden zones. SOG men had no specific uniforms, and their only insignia was a grim shoulder patch depicting a skull dripping blood from its teeth that the men designed themselves. Their feats make up one of the unrevealed stories of the Vietnam War.

An elite secret organization, MACV-SOG had no official unit insignia, but the men designed a graphic patch of their own.

Operation 34-Alpha

SOG's primary activity in 1964 remained the expansion of covert actions against the coast of North Vietnam. This mission was destined to deepen U.S. involvement in Vietnam. In January the U.S. Navy transferred two 180-foot-long escort vessels to South Vietnam. Vietnamese crews from the Coastal Security Service (an arm of the Strategic Technical Services) set off in these ships from Da Nang to harass coastal shipping near the DMZ and to search fishing junks for infiltrators en route to join the Vietcong.

The fourteen-knot speed of the escort ships, however, was far too slow for attack missions, and SOG's naval advisers adapted twelve American-made Swift torpedo boats for clandestine operations. Aluminum crafts with a top speed of fifty knots, the PT boats were armed with 40 MM cannons and light machine guns. SOG brought fifteen-man PT crews and the commandos from Long Thanh together to train for seaborne infiltration and coastal bombardment. The teams trained at a closely guarded base on a peninsula south of Saigon. The boats made practice runs sixty to seventy miles out from the South Vietnamese coast; they had to approach North Vietnam from the open sea because dense coastal traffic made it impossible to sneak northward without being detected.

At the end of July, the SOG advisers, working from aerial reconnaissance photographs, drafted orders for the first two missions. On July 31, the raiders would strike installations on two islands—a radar station on Hon Me and a radio transmitter on Hon Ngu—located near Vinh, 115 miles north of the DMZ. Three days later they would shell a mainland radar station at Cape Vinh Son, south of Vinh, and a security station near Ron.

To reach the targets, the raiders would put far out to sea before turning toward the mainland. Leaving from Da Nang, they would circle north and approach the coast of North Vietnam through a body of water the Vietnamese called Bac Bo. It is better known, in the history books and in the debate about Vietnam, as the Gulf of Tonkin.

With the Green Berets

John F. Kennedy visited Fort Bragg, North Carolina, in the fall of 1961 to observe U.S. Army Special Forces maneuvers. Impressed by the unconventional warfare tactics, the president became convinced that the Special Forces could play a crucial role in defending against Communist "wars of national liberation." He approved their trademark—the green beret—as a "mark of distinction and a badge of courage in the difficult days ahead."

With Kennedy's imprimatur, the Special Forces blossomed. Volunteers had to meet stringent criteria of intelligence, courage, and discipline. After undergoing a training regimen of combat and survival skills, the soldiers selected a specialty such as heavy or light weapons, demolitions, or medicine, and cross-trained in a second specialty to assure their units' effectiveness in the event of casualties. Two officers and ten enlisted men formed a so-called "A" detachment, each of which was to be capable of raising and training a small guerrilla army. In 1962 the Special Forces were deployed to Vietnam to implement the CIA's Civilian Irregular Defense Group (CIDG) program among montagnard tribesmen.

Left. Living off the land. A staff sergeant eats snake meat during Special Forces survival training in the swamps of Fort Bragg.

Torched by a Special Forces–led montagnard patrol in the central highlands, a Vietcong staging camp burns while Captain Vernon Gillespie makes radio contact with other patrols in the area.

The Green Berets found a primitive people in Vietnam's strategic central highlands. The montagnards, often in poor health, were armed with little more than crossbows and blowguns to defend themselves against Vietcong. "It was like a setting for a Tarzan movie," said Ronald Shackleton, team captain of the first Special Forces A team at Buon Enao. The medics helped win the montagnards' confidence by teaching them to make soap and by dispensing vitamin pills, pulling teeth, and performing surgery. Other team members helped to fortify the villages while arming the montagnards and training them in military tactics. To cement the alliance, many Americans participated in a ritual of ceremonial drinking and animal sacrifice in which each received a brass bracelet as a symbol of acceptance and loyalty.

From its cautious beginning in February 1962, the CIDG program grew rapidly; by the end of 1964, forty-four Special Forces camps had been established throughout Vietnam.

Captain Gillespie plays with montagnard children of the Rhade tribe at Buon Brieng.

Above. From an embattled assemblage of longhouses, the Rhade village of Buon Brieng was transformed into a fortified hamlet. Inside defensive barbed wire perimeters are trenches, mines, mortar and machine-gun positions, and floodlights. The landing strip served as the lifeline for the remote CIDG outpost.

A signal fire burns as Captain William Grace, commander of the Special Forces team at Plei Mrong, calls in helicopters to return his patrol to its camp.

The montagnard rebellion

Despite the successes of the CIDG program, the historical enmity between the montagnards and the Vietnamese (who called them "moi," or "savages") continued to fester. In May 1964, montagnard strike forces were assigned to the Vietnamese army, a rankling decision for tribes that had sought not closer ties with the national government, but autonomy. On September 20, 1964, montagnard anger flared in an uprising at five Special Forces camps.

In four of the camps the rebellious montagnards killed thirty-four Vietnamese and disarmed the Vietnamese and American advisers. But at Buon Brieng Captain Vernon Gillespie, the camp's A team leader, seized command and placed the Vietnamese under the protection of the American Special Forces. Then he invoked a loyalty ritual, binding together the montagnard, Vietnamese, and American leaders in the camp. Thereafter, in one camp after another Americans defused the revolt. The uprising ended amid strained negotiations between montagnards and the Vietnamese government.

Left. The Special Forces camp at Bu Dop on the Cambodian border under attack by Vietcong guerrillas in October 1965.

Above right. At the rebel command post six miles from Ban Me Thuot, leaders of the montagnard rebellion ponder the warning of unarmed Colonel John Freund: "If you don't leave here, the Vietnamese will bomb you."

In a crucial moment, Gillespie, in tribal dress, sips rice beer as he accepts a bracelet from the Rhade sorcerer. By participating in this two-hour ritual, Gillespie eased the tensions of the rebellion.

Predated Declaration of War

At noon on July 31, 1964, the destroyer U.S.S. *Maddox* steamed into the Gulf of Tonkin on an electronic spy mission. The patrol's code name was Desoto. As the ship cruised along the coast of North Vietnam, technicians in a special communications center plotted enemy radar installations by homing in on the electronic signals tracking the intruder. Other technicians charted navigational information such as landmarks and river mouths. Three other Desoto patrols had already been carried out, all without incident.

That morning, as the *Maddox* refueled from a tanker at the entrance to the gulf, members of the crew had spotted four American Swift PT boats on the horizon, streaking home to Da Nang after midnight raids on two North Vietnamese islands. At Hon Me and Hon Ngu, the South Vietnamese attackers had encountered heavy defensive fire and had been unable to land commando teams. But they had bombarded the islands—the first shelling of North Vietnam from the sea—and had

created a series of harmless explosions by throwing their demolition charges overboard near shore. Withdrawing to the open sea, the two raiding parties met in the gulf and turned for Da Nang. They had attacked and gotten away with it but had caused little, if any, damage.

The *Maddox* had been given a scanty briefing on these so-called 34-A raids and in the communications center, technicians intercepted coded and uncoded radio traffic indicating that the Hanoi military was in an uproar. The monitors heard an order positioning a defensive ring of PT boats around the islands to prevent a recurrence of the attacks. The *Maddox's* number, DD-731, figured with increasing frequency in the radio messages as the North Vietnamese charted her northward course, obviously wondering about the ship's possible connection with the raids. Patrolling no closer than eight nautical miles from the coast, the *Maddox* remained beyond the three-mile limit. (Later North Vietnam, like many other nations, would claim a twelve-mile limit.) Desoto Commander Captain John Herrick viewed the intercepted messages with alarm. Briefing officers had promised a "Sunday cruise," as uneventful as any of the electronic intelligence missions that occurred routinely around the world.

After midnight on August 2, the *Maddox* passed Hon Mat Island, several kilometers to sea from Hon Ngu, shelled two days earlier by the 34-A raiders. Hundreds of fishing junks massed ahead of the destroyer, and the *Maddox* played its searchlight over the fleet, trying to pick out a navigable path. Herrick had been warned that some of the junks could contain paramilitary soldiers, and any could have drifted alongside to lay mines or other explosives. Suddenly the lighthouse beacon on Hon Mat shut down.

Herrick sounded a general-quarters alarm, rousing crewmen sleeping on the deck in the sweltering heat. The *Maddox* turned seaward, skirting the fishing flotilla. At 3:50 A.M. Herrick sent a radio message through channels to the commander of the 7th Fleet, the commander of the Pacific Fleet, CINCPAC, and the Joint Chiefs of Staff, warning of "possible hostile action" against the *Maddox* by the North Vietnamese. Three hours later Herrick again cabled: "Consider continuance of patrol presents an unacceptable risk."

Preceding page. An A-1 Skyraider on the U.S.S. Constellation flight deck is readied for takeoff. After the second Gulf of Tonkin "incident," Skyraiders from the Constellation joined the retaliatory attacks against North Vietnam.

The attack of August 2

Herrick had an answer, from the 7th Fleet commander, almost immediately: "Resume itinerary. You are authorized to deviate from itinerary at any time you consider unacceptable risk to exist."

The *Maddox* continued north, picking up its route in daylight. After a few hours, the ship turned south, as dictated by its orders. Approaching Hon Me Island, scene of the second 34-A attack, crew members saw three Soviet-made PT boats disappear behind the island. The PT boats caused little concern until the monitoring crews intercepted a startling message: The PT boats received an order to attack the *Maddox* as soon as they refueled. Sixteen miles offshore, the *Maddox* altered course to the southeast and picked up speed.

Commander Herbert L. Ogier, captain of the *Maddox* itself but subordinate to Herrick's Desoto command, sounded battle stations and addressed the crew. "This is not a drill," he said. In the combat information center, the vessel's nerve system, radar operators picked up the PT boats as they left Hon Me. Traveling at a speed of fifty knots, they would close within an hour. Herrick notified the Pacific command: "Being approached by high-speed craft with apparent intent to conduct torpedo attack. Intend to open fire in self-defense if necessary." He also requested air support from the carrier U.S.S. *Ticonderoga*, stationed off South Vietnam. Herrick and Ogier decided that if the PT boats closed to within ten thousand yards (5.8 miles), they would fire warning shots across their bows.

At 3:08 P.M. two of the ship's six five-inch guns roared. Plumes of water rose in front of the speeding PT boats, but they didn't hesitate or change course. Three minutes later, with the boats spread five hundred yards apart and approaching torpedo range, the *Maddox* fired with all six guns.

For twenty minutes the *Maddox* fired furiously. Crew members spotted the first torpedo when the boats were twenty-seven hundred yards away. The *Maddox* swung to port, and the torpedo passed one hundred to two hundred yards to starboard. At the distance of one mile, the boats opened fire with machine guns, but the bullets, with the exception of one that struck a gun mount, went awry. The *Maddox* evaded another torpedo and the gunners continued firing. The lead boat was finally hit by one of the five-inch shells. The boat stopped dead in the water, and a great cheer arose on the *Maddox*. Astern of the

ship a second PT boat, apparently hit, lost speed, and the third boat sped over as if to assist the crew.

At that moment four F-8 Crusader jets from the *Ticonderoga* appeared overhead, emptying their 20 MM guns and firing Zuni rockets in successive passes. Two of the rockets hit. The aircraft broke off the engagement after eight minutes, and the *Maddox* closed for the kill. But one pilot reported damage to his jet and feared he might have to eject. Herrick turned and followed the plane south for fifteen or twenty minutes until the pilot radioed that he would make it. Just as Herrick gave the order to return to the scene, he received a cable from his superiors: "Do not pursue and proceed to the southeast and await further instructions."

"Resume Tonkin patrol"

Official Washington awakened that Sunday morning in an air of mild crisis (time in the Tonkin Gulf is twelve hours ahead of that in Washington). President Johnson gathered his advisers at noon. Intelligence officers suggested the North Vietnamese might somehow have confused the *Maddox* with the 34-A operations, and gradually that explanation took precedence over any others. Retaliatory raids were suggested, and immediately rejected by Johnson, who had overriding political concerns. The president and his aides were not of a mind to allow any expan-

A photograph taken from the U.S.S. Maddox *shows a Soviet-made North Vietnamese PT boat skirting the American destroyer during the August 2 Gulf of Tonkin attack.*

sion of the war before the election in which he faced hawkish Senator Barry Goldwater, nominated by the Republicans two weeks earlier. Johnson's campaign image of resolution with restraint precluded reprisals after this relatively minor incident. But the president chose to display his resolution.

Summoning the White House press corps to the Oval Office Monday morning, Johnson announced that he had ordered the patrols in the Gulf of Tonkin continued, another destroyer added, and constant air support provided. The commanders had instructions to attack any force that attacked them "with the objective not only of driving off the force but of destroying it." Through the ICC, the United States sent a severe note of protest to Hanoi, vowing "grave consequences" for further unprovoked military action. With the aid of Secretary of State Dean Rusk, Johnson also drafted a personal message for Soviet Premier Khrushchev stating that the U.S. did not wish to widen the war in Vietnam but intended to continue naval patrols in international waters. Transmitted over the Washington-Moscow teleprinter link set up after the Cuban missile crisis, the message was the first use of the so-called "hot line." Johnson would turn to it three more times in the next two days.

Aboard the *Maddox*, refueling at Yankee Station off Da Nang, Captain Herrick received the order from the Pacific Fleet commander: "Resume Gulf of Tonkin patrol earliest." A follow-up cable from *Ticonderoga* Task Force Admiral R. B. Moore carried a warning: "It is apparent that DRV has thrown down the gauntlet and now considers itself at war with the United States. . . . [DRV boats] will be treated as belligerents from first detection. . . ." With the destroyer *C. Turner Joy* trailing one thousand yards astern of the *Maddox*, the Desoto patrol steamed back into the Gulf of Tonkin on August 3.

The mood aboard the ships was tense. North Vietnamese radar kept the ships under constant surveillance. After making feints toward the shore to stimulate and record more electronic impulses, the *Maddox* and *Turner Joy* withdrew to sea for the night.

Herrick worried about the appearance of provocation because of the 34-A operations scheduled for the same night. But Admiral Thomas M. Moorer, the Pacific Fleet commander, ordered the ships to patrol fifty to sixty miles farther north, which would "eliminate Desoto patrol interference with 34-A ops, and possibly draw NVN [North Vietnam patrol boats] away from the area of 34-A ops."

At 4:00 P.M. the South Vietnamese 34-A raiders departed on schedule, with two PT boats heading to Cape Vinh Son to bombard a mainland radar station and the other pair destined to attack a security station near Ron. Steering far out to sea, the PT boats paralleled the route taken that day by the two destroyers. Striking around midnight, the boats shelled the installations for half an hour. As they withdrew toward Da Nang, a North Vietnamese patrol boat pursued a team of raiders for an hour, giving up the chase as the faster PT boats pulled away.

Although MACV in Saigon and the senior naval commanders in the Pacific knew of these attacks, word passing through channels apparently did not reach top government officials in Washington until August 6. Therefore, all the decisions made in Washington over the next two days, it seems, were made without the knowledge that a series of 34-A attacks had been repeated.

The incident of August 4

The *Maddox* and *Turner Joy* cruised back toward the mainland at sunrise on August 4 to find the North Vietnamese coastal radio network in a frenzy over the 34-A attacks. By midmorning intercepted messages persuaded Herrick of his precarious position, and he advised his Pacific commanders that North Vietnam considered the destroyers part of the 34-A operations, hence as enemy craft. At 5:00 P.M. the *Maddox* intercepted a transmission to some Swatows—Chinese-built patrol boats armed with machine guns but no torpedoes—alerting the patrollers to the destroyers' presence. The *Maddox* later intercepted another message to two Swatow patrol boats and one PT boat directing them to prepare for military operations. For the remainder of the night, significantly, Herrick maintains that the *Maddox* reported no further radio intercepts.

By nightfall, when the ships retired to the open sea, the weather had turned nasty. A high wind had picked up, and rainsqualls blew violently. "There was some lightning, no moon, completely dark, an inky black night," said Herrick. A *Maddox* crewman recalled, "You could see the *Turner Joy*'s running lights, and the phosphorescence of our wake, but only when you looked right down on it." It was likewise a poor night for radar because the beams were "ducting"—bouncing off low clouds, recording false images, and picking up objects beyond the horizon.

As the ships moved east to the center of the gulf, the *Maddox* radar detected unidentified objects thirty-six miles ahead, in the area where the destroyers had spent the previous night. Herrick suspected the enemy might be lying in wait. The blips showed up clearly on the screen and then disappeared, possibly because of the weather. The radar also picked up three "unidentified aircraft," but they too disappeared from the screen. Jet aircraft from the *Ticonderoga*, stationed at the mouth of the gulf, scrambled to investigate a contact thirteen miles distant from the destroyers and closing at thirty knots. Finding nothing, the planes returned to the carrier.

Nerves in the combat information center tightened with each radar contact and scarcely relaxed when the contacts proved false. The *Maddox* sonarman, a relatively inexperienced twenty-three-year-old, continued to listen intently to the myriad sounds beneath the sea, including the *Maddox*'s own propellers and the treacherous swells slapping the hull of the ship. As yet, he had reported nothing.

At 9:30 P.M. the blips on the *Maddox* radar screen began closing at high speed. The *Turner Joy*, which had previously had no contact, now also plotted the advancing objects. Both destroyers fired illumination shells into the air, but the rounds burst above the clouds and failed to lighten the gloom. With the blips four thousand yards away, the *Turner Joy* commenced firing into the darkness.

Almost simultaneously, the *Maddox* sonarman cried, "Torpedo in the water!" Four crew members on the *Turner Joy* reported seeing a torpedo wake passing the port side, at a distance estimated between one hundred and four hundred feet. The *Turner Joy*'s sonar, however, did not register any torpedo noise.

The *Turner Joy* continued firing in the direction of the radar contacts. Watching on the *Maddox* radar screen, Herrick saw one projectile from the sister ship merge with a radar blip, and the blip immediately disappeared. In the light of the five-inch gun flashes, the *Turner Joy* captain claimed to see a column of black smoke rising almost two miles away, and the *Turner Joy* claimed one boat sunk. The *Maddox*, meanwhile, continued firing the nearly useless illumi-nation shells. The pilots of eight Skyhawk jets, launched from the *Ticonderoga* and flying at an altitude of one thousand feet, never saw any attackers.

Even as the *Turner Joy* sonarman listened futilely for torpedoes, his *Maddox* counterpart continued to report torpedo-like noises, and both ships twisted in evasive maneuvers. The *Maddox* sonar heard sounds suggesting twenty-two torpedoes. (Herrick finally determined that the rapid, weaving turns of the *Maddox* resulted in the screw beats of the propeller reflecting off the rudder, with the vibrations projecting forward to the sonar monitor on the hull of the ship. The sound was similar to that of a torpedo. When he ordered the *Maddox* to cease its evasive maneuvers, reports of torpedoes also stopped.)

The *Turner Joy* captain reported seeing a search-light flicker skyward, which he interpreted as a recall signal to the attackers. Radar contacts ended, and

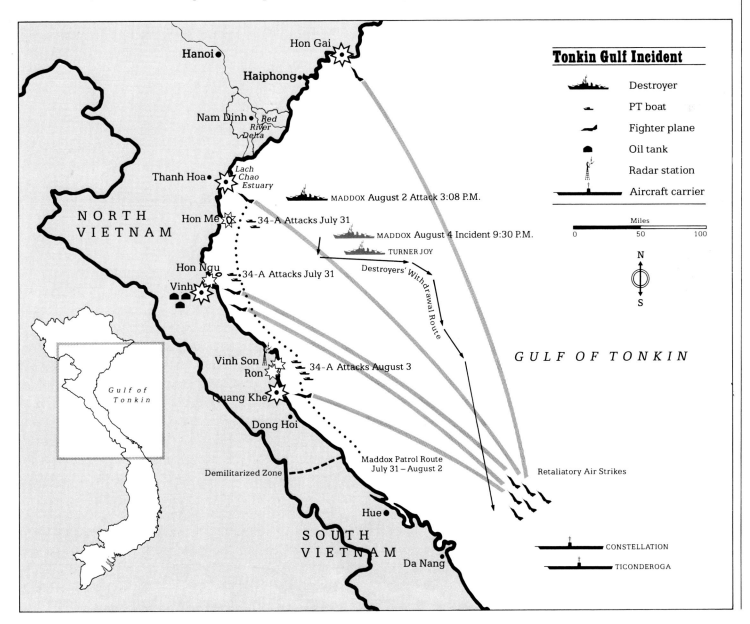

Tonkin Gulf Incident

	Destroyer
	PT boat
	Fighter plane
	Oil tank
	Radar station
	Aircraft carrier

Miles
0   50   100

Hon Gai

Hanoi

Haiphong

Nam Dinh · Red River Delta

Thanh Hoa · Lach Chao Estuary

MADDOX August 2 Attack 3:08 P.M.

NORTH VIETNAM

Hon Me · 34-A Attacks July 31

MADDOX August 4 Incident 9:30 P.M.

TURNER JOY

Destroyers' Withdrawal Route

Hon Ngu · 34-A Attacks July 31

Vinh

GULF OF TONKIN

N

S

Gulf of Tonkin

Vinh Son · Ron · 34-A Attacks August 3

Quang Khe

Dong Hoi

Demilitarized Zone

Maddox Patrol Route July 31 – August 2

Retaliatory Air Strikes

Hue

SOUTH VIETNAM

Da Nang

CONSTELLATION

TICONDEROGA

the destroyers broke off the "engagement." As the ships steamed southward at full speed, Herrick plunged into an immediate review of the incident, interviewing the crew and ordering more experienced technicians to listen to sonar tape recordings.

"Bona fide" ambush

Washington was in turmoil. At 9:20 A.M. August 4, the day after Hanoi had been warned sternly not to interfere with American patrols, the National Military Command Center—known as the War Room—in the Pentagon basement received the flash cable from the Far East reporting the North Vietnamese order to prepare for military operations. There Dean Rusk and Robert McNamara listened to sketchy dispatches from the Gulf of Tonkin announcing torpedo "sightings" and the destroyers' answering fire. Interspersed with battle descriptions from the *Maddox* came two other radio intercepts: one reporting that in the attack an American aircraft was falling, another stating that the North Vietnamese had shot down two aircraft and had themselves lost two boats. The discrepancy between the North Vietnamese intercepts and the *Maddox* reports caused no alarm; in the confusion of battle, situation and damage reports are often exaggerated. For those monitoring the incident in the Pentagon, the fact of the August 2 attack made the August 4 reports easy to believe.

August 5, 1964. One hot summer day's front-page news, most of it gloomy, is topped by President Johnson's announcement of American retaliatory raids against North Vietnam.

"All the News That's Fit to Print"

The New York Times.

LATE CITY EDITION
U.S. Weather Bureau Report (Page 66) forecasts:
Variable cloudiness today; clear tonight. Fair and cool tomorrow.
Temp. Range: 86—65; yesterday: 81—57.
Temp.-Hum. Index: low 70's; yesterday: 73.

VOL. CXIII—No. 38,910. © 1964 by The New York Times Company Times Square, New York, N.Y. 10036. NEW YORK, WEDNESDAY, AUGUST 5, 1964. TEN CENTS

U.S. PLANES ATTACK NORTH VIETNAM BASES; PRESIDENT ORDERS 'LIMITED' RETALIATION AFTER COMMUNISTS' PT BOATS RENEW RAIDS

F.B.I. Finds 3 Bodies Believed to Be Rights Workers'

GRAVES AT A DAM

Discovery Is Made in New Earth Mound in Mississippi

By CLAUDE SITTON
Special to The New York Times

JACKSON, Miss., Aug. 4—Scattered violence broke out again here tonight as roving groups bodies believed to belong to three civil rights workers missing since June 21 were found early tonight near Philadelphia, Miss.

Federal Bureau of Investigation agents recovered the bodies from a newly erected earthen dam in a thickly wooded area about six miles southwest of Philadelphia, in east-central Mississippi.

The dam is several hundred yards off State Highway 21, near the Neshoba County fairgrounds.

Fulton Jackson, the county coroner, made a preliminary examination at the scene. The bodies were then sealed in plastic bags and moved by ambulance to the University of Mississippi Medical Center in Jackson, 70 miles to the southwest.

Pledge by Governor

Roy K. Moore, special agent in charge of the Jackson F.B.I. office, said physicians and fingerprint experts would seek to make positive identification and establish the cause of death.

[In Washington, authoritative sources said that President Johnson had telephoned Gov. Paul B. Johnson Jr. of Mississippi after having learned of the discovery of the bodies. However, this could not be confirmed immediately.]

Johnson said in

Scattered Violence Keeps Jersey City Tense 3d Night

400 Policemen Confine Most of Rioters to 2 Sections—Crowds Watch in Streets Despite Danger

By FRED POWLEDGE
Special to The New York Times

JERSEY CITY, Aug. 4—Scattered violence broke out again here tonight as roving groups of Negroes hurled crude Molotov cocktails in the streets. There was some gunfire but no injuries were reported.

About 400 city policemen contained most of the young rioters to two predominantly Negro neighborhoods. There were at least 22 arrests.

Although it was dangerous to be on the streets on this third night of violence, many people watched from sidewalks and front porches as police cars, their red lights flashing, sped from one pocket of violence to another.

On Ocean Avenue the police trained spotlights on the roof of a three-story block of apartments. A man had been seen on the roof, and it was feared that he was armed with a rifle, fire bombs, or both. Yet on the sidewalk below, a woman walked her dog, apparently without concern, through throngs of helmeted policemen. From a front porch across the street, a baby cried.

Since the rioting started Sunday night, more than 30 persons have been injured, two of them with gunshot wounds. None of the wounds was critical. More than three dozen persons have been arrested.

Five hundred more Jersey City policemen stood ready to

Text of Whelan's statement will be found on Page 36.

Continued on Page 36, Column 1

JOHNSON SEEKING EXTREMISM PLANK

Favors a Stand Against Far Left and Right Without Naming Any Groups

Special to The New York Times

Rockefeller to Join Goldwater's Parley On Campaign Unity

Special to The New York Times

ALBANY, Aug. 4—Governor Rockefeller has accepted the invitation of Senator Goldwater to attend a meeting of Republican Governors at Hershey, Pa.,

REDS DRIVEN OFF

Two Torpedo Vessels Believed Sunk in Gulf of Tonkin

By ARNOLD H. LUBASCH
Special to The New York Times

WASHINGTON, Aug. 4—The Defense Department announced tonight that North Vietnamese PT boats made a "deliberate attack" today on two United States destroyers patrolling international waters in the Gulf of Tonkin off North Vietnam.

The attack came two days after North Vietnamese torpedo boats attacked the *Maddox*, one of the destroyers in today's incident.

The destroyers and covering carrier-based aircraft fired on the vessels in today's attack, drove them off and apparently sank at least two of them, according to the announcement. The Pentagon said there were no United States casualties or damage.

The attack was made by an "undetermined number of North Vietnamese PT boats" during darkness about 65 miles from the nearest land, the Pentagon reported. It said the attack came at 10:30 P.M., North Vietnamese time, or 10:30 A.M., Washington time.

'Fabrication,' Reds Say

[The North Vietnamese regime said Wednesday that the report of another attack on United States ships was a "fabrication."]

The second attack was described in Washington as much fiercer than the first one, which was said to have lasted half an hour. The second

2 CARRIERS USED

McNamara Reports on Aerial Strikes and Reinforcements

By JACK RAYMOND
Special to The New York Times

WASHINGTON, Wednesday, Aug. 5 — Secretary of Defense Robert S. McNamara said at a postmidnight news conference that the United States planes that attacked North Vietnam came from the carriers Constellation and Ticonderoga in the Gulf of Tonkin.

He said that the attacks had been directed against the bases used by the North Vietnamese PT boats that attacked two United States destroyers in international waters yesterday.

The Secretary added that the naval planes, believed to have included propeller-driven as well as jet-powered craft, had also conducted strikes against "certain other targets directly supporting the operation of the PT boats."

The United States planes used conventional weapons.

Separate Targets

Mr. McNamara, who held his news conference shortly after President Johnson had addressed the nation on television, emphasized in his report that the PT boat bases and the supporting facilities in North Vietnam had been separate targets.

He said it was a guess, based on incomplete reports, that in the exchange of fire between the attacking PT boats and the United States destroyers and aircraft in international waters, possibly four

Associated Press Wirephoto
DECISION: President Johnson, in a nationwide broadcast, tells of action he ordered taken against North Vietnam.

The President's Address

Following is the text of the President's address on Vietnam last night, as recorded by The New York Times:

My fellow Americans:

President and Commander in Chief, it

FORCES ENLARGED

Stevenson to Appeal for Action by U.N. on 'Open Aggression'

By TOM WICKER
Special to The New York Times

WASHINGTON, Aug. 4—President Johnson has ordered retaliatory action against gunboats and "certain supporting facilities in North Vietnam" after renewed attacks against American destroyers in the Gulf of Tonkin.

In a television address tonight, Mr. Johnson said air attacks on the North Vietnamese ships and facilities were taking place as he spoke, shortly after 11:30 P.M.

State Department sources said the attacks were being carried out with conventional weapons on a number of shore bases in North Vietnam, with the objective of destroying them and the 30 to 40 gunboats they served.

The aim, they explained, was to destroy North Vietnam's gunboat capability. They said more air strikes might come later, if needed. Carrier-based aircraft were used in tonight's strike.

2 Boats Believed Sunk

Administration officials also announced that substantial additional units, primarily air and sea forces, were being sent to Southeast Asia.

This "positive reply," as the President called it, followed a naval battle in which a number of North Vietnamese PT boats attacked two United States with torpedoes

Rusk and McNamara hurried to the White House to meet with Johnson and McGeorge Bundy. In a luncheon meeting, consensus arrived swiftly. The U.S. would retaliate by bombing torpedo boat bases, an action for which the Joint Chiefs had already drawn contingency plans. The attack (code-named Pierce Arrow) would come at daylight the next morning.

The president and his advisers made two other decisions: They would brief Congressional leaders that evening and they would at last seek a Congressional resolution approving their actions. Drafts of a resolution had been written in May and June when administration officials realized they had better seek some approval from Congress to continue their policies in Vietnam. Both drafts had been abandoned, however, because the heavy agenda on Capitol Hill precluded a full-fledged debate before the presidential nominating conventions. Now, with instructions from Rusk, State Department officials composed a draft in two parts—endorsing the retaliation and allowing the president latitude in the event of wider hostilities in Southeast Asia. The finished document, reviewed by Undersecretary George Ball and legal adviser Abram Chayes, would have only two sentences in common with the May draft and but one phrase similar to that written in June.

An hour and a half had passed since the incident, and official Washington buzzed with activity. Aboard the *Maddox*, meanwhile, Captain Herrick had completed his preliminary review of the incident, and he reluctantly sent a flash cable that he later admitted "I had to squeeze out." It read:

Review of action makes many reported contacts and torpedoes fired appear doubtful. Freak weather effects and overeager sonarman may have accounted for many reports. No actual visual sightings by *Maddox*. Suggest complete evaluation before any further action.

An hour later Herrick followed up with a second cable:

Turner Joy also reports no actual visual sightings or wake. . . . Entire action leaves many doubts except for apparent attempt to ambush at beginning. Suggest thorough reconnaissance by aircraft at daylight.

With those messages, Herrick brought the weight of the Pentagon onto his shoulders. Cables flew across the Pacific, as officers in the chain of command bombarded the sleepless Herrick with questions to verify the attack. After persistent badgering,

Herrick allowed ambiguously that "details of action present a confusing picture although [I am] certain that original ambush was bona fide." Under pressure from his superiors, he had upgraded the intent to ambush from "apparent" to "certain."

Herrick had emphasized the "confusing picture," but Admiral Ulysses S. Grant Sharp, Jr., the CINCPAC, reassured Secretary McNamara that the "ambush was bona fide." Demanding queries continued to arrive on the bridge of the *Maddox* long after Washington's need for confirmation had passed. In any event, eyewitness verification of the attacks was not necessary to McNamara, because the intercepted Vietnamese messages reporting the attack and damage to American aircraft sufficed, in his mind, as independent proof.

Following McNamara's last conversation with Ad-

The destroyer U.S.S. Maddox *operates off the coast of Oahu, Hawaii, in the spring of 1964. Five months later, the* Maddox *steamed into the Gulf of Tonkin on an electronic spy mission called the Desoto Patrol.*

Zuni rockets are loaded on a Crusader jet aboard the U.S.S. Ticonderoga, *which provided air cover for the Desoto Patrol. Two Zunis hit PT boats in the August 2 attack.*

On the U.S.S. Ticonderoga, Navy pilot Lieutenant Ralph James returns from a Pierce Arrow retaliatory strike over North Vietnam. He carries a .38-caliber pistol and bandolier, knife, sea biscuits, and first aid kit—standard survival gear for pilots in case they are shot down.

miral Sharp at 6:00 P.M. Washington time, the alert orders to the planes waiting off South Vietnam were confirmed. President Johnson and his top advisers briefed an approving Congressional leadership just before 7:00 P.M. on the events of the day and the retaliation to come. Then he worked on the speech he would deliver to the American people. At 10:43 P.M. the jets catapulted from the deck of the *Ticonderoga*. The *Constellation*, steaming toward Yankee Station, launched its aircraft slightly later.

At 11:37 P.M. Lyndon Johnson appeared on television to report on the first major international crisis of his presidency. Addressing his "fellow Americans," the president announced the attack and added that the United States's "reply is being given as I speak to you tonight. . . ."

Pierce Arrow was aloft. Flying through a heavy overcast that forced a low altitude approach, six F-8 Crusader jets from the *Ticonderoga* descended on the southernmost target at Quang Khe at 1:15 P.M. Vietnam time (1:15 A.M. Washington time), bombing the patrol boat base. Ten minutes later a second *Ticonderoga* attack group struck the patrol boat base

at Phuc Loi, farther up the coast. It also bombed the oil storage depot at nearby Vinh, blowing up eight oil tanks that sent smoke billowing fourteen thousand feet into the air, a sight visible to Captain Herrick on the *Maddox*, far to the south. Fourteen aircraft returned to Vinh more than three hours later to strike the depot again and set two more tanks ablaze.

Aircraft from the *Constellation* joined the air offensive at 3:45 P.M. as ten A-4 Skyhawks, two F-4 Phantoms, and four A-1 Skyraiders bombed patrol boats at their docks at Hon Gai, north of Haiphong. The planes streaked down on their targets through heavy flak from 37 MM and 57 MM batteries situated on a hilltop to protect the harbor. Farther south, in the midpoint of the coast, *Constellation* aircraft unleashed their bombs over PT boats in the Lach Chao estuary.

Pierce Arrow pilots reported sinking twenty-five PT boats, more than half of North Vietnam's fleet. In addition, Washington estimated that 10 percent of North Vietnam's total petroleum storage capacity had been destroyed. But the U.S. also suffered losses: Antiaircraft gunners damaged two planes and downed two others. Hit over Lach Chao, Lieutenant Richard Sather of Pomona, California, ditched his Skyraider into the gulf and died. Lieutenant Everett Alvarez of San Jose, California, ejected from his Skyhawk after it was hit over Hon Gai. His jet crashed, and Alvarez became the first American pilot taken prisoner by the North Vietnamese.

Southeast Asia Resolution

The Southeast Asia Resolution was submitted to a receptive Congress. Senate Foreign Relations Committee Chairman J. William Fulbright had agreed to serve as the bill's floor manager. Now he listened as Secretary Rusk, in his opening statement to the joint Foreign Relations and Armed Services committees, promised that in spite of the resolution's open-ended phrasing, "there will continue to be regular consultations" between the president and Congress on American conduct in Southeast Asia.

Only Oregon Senator Wayne Morse, a tenacious lone-wolf politician who had been both Democrat and Republican but was a captive of neither party, probed and prodded for more detail. Having heard from a Pentagon tipster about the 34-A raids, Morse queried the Secretaries of State and Defense about the connection to the Gulf of Tonkin incidents. McNamara replied unambiguously. "Our navy played absolutely no part in, was not associated with, was not

The first pilot taken prisoner by the North Vietnamese, Lieutenant Everett Alvarez, listens skeptically to an amused guard in this Soviet news agency picture released in 1967. Alvarez ejected from his damaged A-4 Skyhawk at Hon Gai on August 5, 1964.

aware of any South Vietnamese actions, if there were any. . . . This is the fact," he said.

After an hour and forty minutes of discussion, the Foreign Relations Committee took a roll call and delivered a nearly unanimous vote, with only Senator Morse booming out a solitary "no." The resolution passed to the full Senate and debate continued through the following morning. Morse continued to press, and be rebuffed, on the matter of the 34-A attacks. Maryland Senator Daniel Brewster, veteran of World War II Asian campaigns, asked Fulbright whether the resolution would approve "the landing of large American armies in Vietnam and in China."

"There is nothing in the resolution, as I read it, that contemplates it," answered Fulbright. "However, the language of the resolution would not prevent it."

As the debate came to a close, Alaska Senator Ernest Gruening denounced the resolution as "a predated declaration of war." The irascible Senator Morse had the final word: "I believe that history will record that we have made a great mistake in subverting and circumventing the Constitution of the United States. . . . We are in effect giving the president . . . war-making powers in the absence of a declaration of war. I believe that to be a historic mistake."

With only Morse and Gruening dissenting, the Senate on August 7 voted 88-2 to allow "the president, as commander in chief, to take all necessary measures to repel any armed attack against the forces of the United States and to prevent further aggression." Senate deliberations on the resolution had totaled only eight hours and forty minutes. The House of Representatives agreed with the Senate, supporting the president with a unanimous vote of 416-0.

The American people apparently consented as well. Eighty-five percent of the public approved the reprisal raids, pollster Louis Harris reported on August 10. The same day LBJ signed the resolution.

Two weeks later, the president rode that crest of popularity into Atlantic City, where the Democratic party nominated him to run for his own full term. Senator Fulbright, who would later turn into a vehement opponent of the war and denounce the administration for providing doctored testimony to Congress, seconded his friend's nomination. Praising Johnson's "sense of responsibility," Fulbright cited the events in the Gulf of Tonkin and the American reprisal as evidence of the president's reliance upon "restraint which lessens rather than enhances the possibility of a major war in that area."

Continuing controversy

The Johnson administration came to view the Southeast Asia Resolution as a call to arms, one that granted advance approval to whatever escalation the president and his advisers deemed necessary "to prevent further aggression." Indeed, Undersecretary of State Nicholas deB. Katzenbach told a querulous Senate Foreign Relations Committee in 1967 that the resolution was the "functional equivalent" of a declaration of war. "What," he asked rhetorically, "could a declaration of war have done that would have given the president more authority and a clearer voice of the Congress than that did?"

The resolution passed because of the August 4 incident, yet doubts that began to arise on the bridge of the *Maddox* immediately afterward have never been convincingly dispelled. Even President Johnson came to doubt the occurrence of a second attack. Two or three days after the events of August 4, he remarked to George Ball, "Hell, those dumb, stupid sailors were just shooting at flying fish!"

In September 1964, before any controversy arose in the United States, North Vietnam published a lengthy statement on the Gulf of Tonkin incidents. In somewhat overblown prose, the North Vietnamese described the 34-A raids and boasted of their own August 2 attack on the *Maddox*. After their patrol boats were fired upon, the boats took "defensive action" and "drove the intruder out of Vietnamese waters." As for the August 4 incident, however, North Vietnam flatly denied any participation. At about the time when PT boats allegedly attacked the *Maddox* and *Turner Joy*, the report states, "gun shelling was heard, flares and planes were seen off the shores . . . on international waters." The senior North Vietnamese naval commander, who had written the after-action reports from the August 2 attack, was taken prisoner in 1966. He declared "definitively and emphatically," according to interrogation notes, that no attack had occurred on August 4.

Despite this evidence, defenders of the administration maintain that the radio intercepts in themselves proved that an attack was taking place. Yet critics of the administration raise two important points about those intercepts: Captain Herrick stated that the *Maddox* did not intercept the radio messages during the actual August 4 "engagement." Second, the intercepted messages shown in private to selected members of the Senate Foreign Relations Committee in late 1967 appear to describe the attack of August 2. Could the messages have been mishandled or filed incorrectly by the Pentagon, critics and historians have since asked.

As late as 1982, those disputed messages were still classified by the Department of Defense. Their release could possibly answer the question of whether an attack occurred on August 4. Yet one knowledgeable source who has seen the classified cables describes them as confusing. Thus, these major pieces of evidence may in the end neither corroborate nor repudiate the August 4 attack, and the Gulf of Tonkin incident may remain one of history's imponderables. Unless conclusive documentation is presented, however, it appears likely that no attack took place in the Gulf of Tonkin on August 4, 1964.

The Vung Tau Charter

The air attacks on North Vietnam had buoyed America's South Vietnamese allies. General Khanh, Ambassador Taylor cabled to Washington, "is now in a fairly euphoric state as a result of our Gulf of Tonkin action." Khanh had issued his "March to the North" call in July, and now, a few weeks later, he felt like a vindicated prophet. In a radio address, he called on the Vietnamese people "to keep calm so as to clearly see your responsibilities in the face of events, brush aside private differences, and willingly submit yourself to the national discipline." He urged regular tit-for-tat bombings and on August 7 declared a state of emergency, reimposing press censorship and causing the government to control food distribution.

Then Khanh committed a most serious blunder. Having ignored the various drafts that had been proposed for a new constitution, he unveiled a hastily written constitution that created an all-powerful presidency, an office that Khanh intended to occupy. He would finally oust the sulking figurehead General Minh. Khanh's Military Revolutionary Council approved the Vung Tau Charter on August 16, thereby installing the general as president. Khanh vowed to establish a broadly based civilian government to work under him.

Students and Buddhist factions grated at Khanh's grab for power and took to the streets in a series of violent demonstrations. As marchers and rioters surged through Saigon, Khanh capitulated. On August 27, after two stormy sessions with the Military Revolutionary Council, he withdrew the charter, an act that humiliated many of the generals.

Suffering from nervous exhaustion, Khanh fled to Da Lat. Rumors of coups swirled in the vacuum he had left in Saigon, but on September 3 Khanh returned. He announced a triumvirate government consisting of himself, General Minh, and General Tran

Thien Khiem that would evolve into a civilian constitutional government. A national council of elder professionals would design the government. The immediate crisis ended.

Another arose less than two weeks later in the form of a coup attempt by the relatively obscure Brigadier General Lam Van Phat. The U.S. quickly announced its support for Khanh, Minh, and Khiem, thus defusing the coup. A countercoup by a group of younger officers called the "Young Turks," including Nguyen Cao Ky, Nguyen Van Thieu, and Nguyen Chanh Thi, restored Khanh to power.

For the next several weeks, the government of South Vietnam seemed to be in suspension as the political crises settled and a new constitution was prepared. At the end of October, the High National Council selected a respected elder statesman, Phan Khac Suu, as chief of state, and former Saigon mayor, Tran Van Huong, as prime minister. General Khanh stepped down to become commander in chief of the armed forces and promised to keep the army out of domestic politics.

The president decides

On the night of October 31, sampans carrying a detachment of Vietcong drifted along one of the many streams near Bien Hoa airfield. Putting ashore at a previously determined site, the guerrillas set up 81 MM mortars. The distance of several thousand yards from the stream bank to the airfield had already been paced off by Vietcong posing as local farmers. An attack opened, and for several minutes mortar shells rained down on the air base killing four Americans, destroying five B–57 light bombers, and damaging eight others. As suddenly as it had begun, the bombardment ended, and the guerrillas reloaded their equipment aboard the sampans and sailed away.

While traveling by helicopter to inspect the damage, Ambassador Taylor concluded that the deliberate attack on a U.S. installation marked a turning point in Vietcong tactics. Whereas attacks on American personnel serving with South Vietnamese units had not been uncommon, this attack on a U.S. air base represented a first. Arguing that such a change in tactics had undoubtedly been instigated by Hanoi, Taylor on his return to Saigon fired off a recommendation to Washington for immediate reprisals against North Vietnam.

With only two days to go until the elections, President Johnson and his advisers declined to retaliate. Throughout the campaign Johnson had contrasted his own restraint with the policies of escalation advo-

An air force crew clears the wreckage of the B–57 bombers demolished in the October 31, 1964, Vietcong mortar attack on Bien Hoa airfield. The NLF issued a stamp (inset) to celebrate the first VC attack on an American facility.

cated by Goldwater. Instead the president ordered a review of U.S. policies to develop future options for escalation.

Under the leadership of Assistant Secretary of State William P. Bundy, the Working Group on South Vietnam convened at 9:30 A.M. on November 3—election day. Before the end of the day, American voters delivered the largest plurality to Lyndon Johnson that any president had ever won. Sixty-one percent of the voters embraced the candidate whose keynote campaign theme was a refusal to allow "American boys to do the fighting for Asian boys."

Exploring every conceivable aspect of the war, the Working Group labored throughout November and produced a report at the end of the month. It outlined three options, none of which called for more restraint:

• Option A would continue current policies of support to South Vietnam, with bombing reprisals against North Vietnam for incidents such as the Gulf of Tonkin attacks or the shelling of Bien Hoa.

• Option B would increase military pressure systematically and rapidly until "at some point" the military actions would lead to negotiations.

• Option C would expand Option A by initiating a program of graduated bombing against infiltration targets, first in Laos, then in North Vietnam, and progressing to other military and industrial targets in North Vietnam. Military pressure would be accompanied by communications with Hanoi and Peking showing willingness to negotiate.

On December 1, with Ambassador Taylor in Washington, President Johnson made his decision. He would stay with Option A. The president was uncertain that actions against North Vietnam should be taken. But in the event they became necessary, the planning had already been done. The bombing campaign (Option C) would be held in reserve.

"Among all the top command," wrote George Ball, who had prepared a logical and lengthy memorandum opposing the bombing, "I found President Johnson the most reluctant to expand America's involvement. He was wary, among other things, of repeating MacArthur's error of attacking too close to the Chinese border; he did not want American boys to have to fight the Chinese hordes once again. Yet the failure of our efforts in the South tended more and more to strengthen the hand of those who—in default of other tactical alternatives—were agitating for bombing attacks on the North."

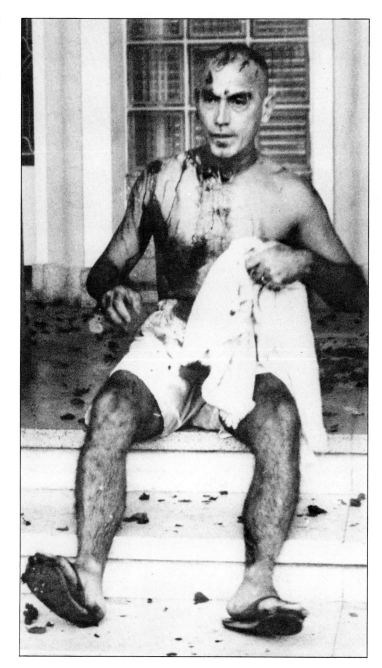

A bloodied U.S. Army officer awaits care outside his quarters in Saigon's Brink Hotel after an explosion ripped out the underside of the building on Christmas Eve, 1964.

Khanh's power play

Ambassador Taylor returned to Saigon with two important messages from Washington for the Vietnamese: Joint planning for reprisal air action against North Vietnam could begin and political stability would be absolutely essential. To reaffirm the latter point, Taylor invited a score of senior South Vietnamese officers, including Thieu, Ky, and the four corps commanders, to a dinner at the home of General Westmoreland. Speaking French, the ambassador exhorted the officers to rally around the Huong government. He also exacted an informal pledge from the generals to work with the government.

Political machinations continued, however. One major concession sought by the Young Turks from the High National Council was a provision that all military men with twenty-five years of service be forced to retire, thus allowing the younger officers to rise to positions of power and command. The council curtly rejected the proposal, and Khanh reacted petulantly by abolishing the council and jailing many of its members.

Infuriated, Taylor called Khanh for an explanation. Khanh sent four emissaries, Generals Thieu and Thi, Marshal Ky, and Admiral Chung Tan Cang, to the embassy. Greeting them coldly, Taylor shed his diplomatic manners. "Do you understand English?" he began bluntly. The irresponsible behavior of the generals was suicidal nonsense that the U.S. found unacceptable, he said. Furthermore they had broken their pledge to him and had harmed plans to form a civilian government.

After the generals reported to Khanh, they complained publicly about the tirade of the American ambassador. "He must have thought we were cadets," Marshal Ky fumed to a friend. "I've never been talked to in my life like that. I wouldn't let my father talk to me like that."

The political battle in Saigon raged for a month, until the Armed Forces Council voted to oust Prime Minister Huong and charged Khanh with establishing a new government. Khanh once again planned to set himself up as chief of state, but Taylor hurriedly notified the other key generals that the U.S. could no longer work with Khanh. His influence eroding, Khanh settled for a new civilian government. He retained Phan Khac Suu as chief of state and named Nguyen Xuan Oanh, a Harvard-trained economist, acting prime minister while he cast about for a candidate he could control. Khanh still manipulated events, but his days were clearly numbered.

Clear the decks

Amid the political bickering, the Vietcong struck again at Americans, this time in the heart of Saigon. On the afternoon of Christmas Eve, when the Americans eagerly awaited the arrival of entertainer Bob Hope, a panel truck was driven into the basement garage of the Brink Hotel, which served as an American bachelor officers' billet. The driver parked the truck and walked away. Shortly thereafter explosives packed in the truck detonated, killing a naval officer and a civilian and ripping out the underside of the building. More than a hundred people, including fifty-eight Americans, were wounded by the blast and resulting fire.

At his Christmas-day performance at Tan Son Nhut Airport, Hope drew his biggest laugh from the hardened troops with his opening remark: "I've gone from many airports to my hotel, but this is the first time I've found the hotel on its way out to meet me."

Ambassador Taylor was not amused. An act of terror directed at Americans demanded quick retaliation, he believed, and he immediately cabled his recommendations to Washington. But President Johnson refused to retaliate, lest the United States give the appearance that "we are trying to shoot our way out of an internal political crisis."

New Year's Day 1965 marked the date that Ambassador Taylor had earlier advocated as the beginning of the bombing campaign against the North. Now, in January, Taylor argued once again for bombing. Irrespective of the resolution of the Saigon political crisis, Taylor and his advisers saw the graduated air strikes as the appropriate course of action. Without them, he cabled, "we see slight chance of moving toward a successful solution."

Taylor's argument paralleled other reassessments going on within the Departments of State and Defense. "The situation in Vietnam is now likely to come apart much more rapidly than we had anticipated in November," wrote Assistant Secretary of State William Bundy. He stopped short of recommending the bombing campaign but suggested looking for "an early occasion for reprisal action" and withdrawing U.S. dependents. Assistant Secretary of Defense John T. McNaughton agreed. In a memorandum to Secretary McNamara, McNaughton urged the evacuation of dependents and retaliatory bombings. "Strikes against DRV should be done anyway," he wrote, "first as reprisals."

On January 25 Taylor received a cable asking whether U.S. dependents should be evacuated to "clear the decks." While still needing an "occasion for reprisal action," the administration was clearly poised to move against the North. But that occasion would not likely arise for a week or longer, for the Vietcong had declared a unilateral seven-day cease-fire to celebrate Tet. The lunar holiday would close out the Year of the Dragon and herald the Year of the Snake.

Enter the U.S. Marines

The week-long Tet cease-fire had ended at midnight, February 6. Now, two hours into the Year of the Snake, 300 guerrillas stole through the high grass outside Camp Holloway, near the provincial capital of Pleiku. Slipping one by one beneath the barbed wire perimeter, they evaded a slack cordon of South Vietnamese sentries.

Relaxed by the lull in hostilities, the four hundred Americans of the 52nd Combat Aviation Battalion settled down for a good night's sleep before the war resumed. Four miles away another 180 U.S. advisers to the 22nd ARVN Division at Pleiku's II Corps headquarters also retired. Intelligence analyses had predicted a massive post-Tet offensive to link the central Pleiku Province to the enemy-held coastal plains of neighboring Binh Dinh Province. The Americans believed the Communists aimed to sever Vietnam across its waist.

While the Vietcong had not fought for a week, neither had they rested. During the cease-fire, the

Communists had cached explosives around Camp Holloway and trained captured American 81 MM mortars on the Americans' barracks.

At 2:00 A.M. the bombardment opened. Mortar shells rained on the barracks and guerrillas sprinted to the airstrip, blowing up parked helicopters and reconnaissance planes with satchel charges. The mortars were right on target: Some barracks blew up, others caught fire. Several men died in their bunks from the first salvo. Tracers streaked wildly through the night as aircraft ammunition erupted.

Holloway came alive in an instant. Men raced to defensive positions. Able-bodied soldiers pulled the wounded from collapsing barracks. Firemen darted amid detonating rockets and ammunition, dousing fires on the airstrip. Four helicopters missed by the saboteurs—three gunships and a flareship—roared to life and lifted into the darkness. Flares illuminated attackers scurrying through the chaos. One of the helicopters crashed, killing the pilot.

After fifteen minutes the Vietcong pulled back. They left behind seven dead Americans, more than a hundred wounded, and a painfully clear picture of their objective: to kill Americans. Not one of thirteen hundred South Vietnamese at Holloway was injured.

Four miles away, before the first explosion at Holloway, another guerrilla squad slipped past South Vietnamese guards and snipped two barbed wire aprons surrounding the U.S. advisory compound. The two attacks were coordinated. But Specialist 5 Jesse Pyle of Marina, California, on back-up guard duty, spotted the crawling guerrillas and fired, killing one. The fire roused the sleeping Americans. The guerrillas killed Pyle, hurled the rest of their homemade beer-can grenades at the building, and quickly melted away. Pyle had kept them from entering the building, but the exterior explosions wounded twenty-five advisers.

Word of the attack flashed to Saigon, and General Westmoreland hurried from his villa to an emergency predawn meeting with Ambassador Taylor, Deputy Ambassador U. Alexis Johnson, and presidential assistant McGeorge Bundy, in Vietnam on a fact-finding trip. Together they weighed an appropriate American response.

Superseding the two four-star generals in the room, Bundy, who had been an army captain and

staff officer in World War II, led the discussions. Politically astute, Ambassador Taylor considered it good fortune to have the presidential assistant on the scene. But to Westmoreland, Bundy appeared abrupt, even arrogant, in outlining an American reaction. "Like numbers of civilians in positions of some governmental authority," Westmoreland acidly wrote in his memoirs, "once he smelled a little gunpowder he developed a field marshal psychosis." The United States had retaliated after the August Gulf of Tonkin incidents, and the mechanism for tit-for-tat strikes, decided the previous March, was in place. The Saigon group thought it should be used. Bundy phoned the White House with the consensus: strike back.

But the presence in Hanoi of Soviet Premier Aleksei Kosygin posed thorny diplomatic problems. American planners assumed that the North Vietnamese were at least aware of the Vietcong attack, if they had not in fact ordered it themselves. Thus, with Kosygin visiting Hanoi, the Pleiku attack seemed to be a deliberate provocation to which the U.S. could respond by retaliation, risking a grievous affront to the Soviets, or by doing nothing and incurring "paper tiger" insults from Hanoi. American diplomats, therefore, took pains to reassure Moscow that retaliation was not meant to embarrass the Soviet Union.

Flaming Dart I

News of the Pleiku disaster reached Washington in midafternoon, and the decision making was almost automatic. The president used frontier images to express his anger. "We have kept our guns over the mantel and our shells in the cupboard for a long time, and what is the result? They are killing our men while they sleep in the night. I can't ask our American soldiers to continue to fight with one hand tied behind their back. ... I want three things. I want a joint attack [by Vietnamese and U.S. planes]. I want it to be prompt. I want it to be appropriate."

Alerted by Admiral Sharp, the CINCPAC, the crew of the navy aircraft carrier U.S.S. *Ranger*, within range of North Vietnam, readied aircraft for takeoff. Two other carriers, the U.S.S. *Hancock* and *Coral Sea*, steamed toward North Vietnam.

Westmoreland and Bundy flew to Pleiku aboard the general's personal C-123, the *White Whale*, for a rendezvous with General Khanh. Bundy's Pleiku visit introduced the former Harvard dean to the bloody reality of guerrilla war. He wandered through the shambles of the American advisory compound, ap-

A memorial service is conducted for the eight Americans killed in Vietcong attacks at Pleiku on February 7, 1965. An aircraft waits to return the flag-draped coffins to the United States.

palled not only by the devastation but also by the rudimentary defenses. Continuing on to the 8th Field Hospital at Nha Trang to which the Pleiku wounded had been evacuated, a tense and pale Bundy followed Westmoreland on rounds through the wards. Viewing the wounded soldiers prompted Bundy to place another call to President Johnson in the Oval Office, underscoring the need for retaliation. The president remarked to George Ball, "Old Mac's really got himself stirred up. Those poor wounded boys in the hospital sure as hell got to him."

Twelve hours after the first mortar fell on Pleiku, forty-nine navy A-4 Skyhawks and F-8 Crusaders catapulted from their carriers' flight decks and streamed north of the seventeenth parallel in an operation called Flaming Dart. Dropping through heavy clouds above Dong Hoi, the aircraft unleashed their bombs and rockets on guerrilla training and staging areas.

Because of the poor weather over the mainland, South Vietnamese planes had not launched. But the following day a fleet of twenty-four VNAF Skyraiders and American F-100 Supersaber jet fighters streaked north from Da Nang to raid guerrilla staging and communication centers at Vinh Linh and Chap Le,

just above the DMZ. Air Vice Marshal Nguyen Cao Ky led the attack and was grazed by shrapnel. Back in Da Nang, Ky, resplendent in a black jumpsuit, violet scarf, and white crash helmet streaked with orange, climbed down from his cockpit to beam, "This is the most beautiful day of my life."

In fact, bomb damage reports indicated that of nearly five hundred buildings targeted for the air strike, only forty-seven had been destroyed and twenty-two damaged. It was a performance that Secretary McNamara criticized.

For the U.S., the two days of raids marked a costly turning point in its Vietnam involvement. Premier Kosygin announced in Hanoi that the Soviet Union would increase its aid if the North were invaded. Formerly, North Vietnam had depended almost exclusively on aid from China.

Returning from Vietnam aboard Air Force One, McGeorge Bundy drafted a memorandum for the president. "These [Pleiku] attacks and our reaction to them have created an ideal opportunity for the prompt

169

development and execution of sustained reprisals," he wrote. Such reprisals, he suggested, could begin in reaction to highly visible incidents such as the attacks on Pleiku. But "once a program of reprisals is clearly underway, it should not be necessary to connect each specific act against North Vietnam to a particular outrage in the South." Rather, "weekly lists of outrages" should suffice as justification for the bombing. Recognizing the limitations of bombing, Bundy wrote, "The object would not be to 'win' an air war against Hanoi, but rather to influence the course of the struggle in the South."

Attack on Qui Nhon

In announcing the Flaming Dart reprisals, Johnson said, "We have no choice now but to clear the decks and make absolutely clear our continued determination to back South Vietnam." He deployed a Hawk (homing-all-the-way-killer) missile battalion and five hundred and fifty marines from Okinawa to Da Nang. Mobile surface-to-air guided missiles, the Hawks would guard the air base against the slim possibility of North Vietnamese air attacks. "Other reinforcements, in units and individuals, may follow," added the president.

He also ordered the evacuation of over eighteen hundred U.S. dependents from South Vietnam, an action long recommended by the country team. In Hue and Saigon, mothers with hastily wrapped packages and tearful children boarded commercial airliners barely thirty-six hours after the president's directive. At Tan Son Nhut, an acquaintance taunted sixteen-year-old Katherine Westmoreland about the evacuation being her father's fault, and she snapped, "It is not! It's the fault of Lynda Bird's father, not mine."

Radio Hanoi exhorted the Vietcong to "strike hard, very hard, at the enemy on all battlefields." The guerrillas complied. In a night raid, the Vietcong battered two South Vietnamese companies bivouacked in the mountains near Phu My, a coastal city north of Qui Nhon. Answering plaintive calls for help, an ARVN battalion, reinforced by an armored troop, set off along Highway One. At a narrow pass, three companies cautiously scouted the jungle hills. They made no contact. After the scouts had passed, a disciplined battalion of guerrillas swarmed out of camouflaged foxholes and poured down machine-gun and recoilless rifle fire on the trapped troops. When the three scouting companies doubled back to the battle, a second guerrilla battalion attacked them from the rear. The armored troop and four U.S. advisers escaped, but the infantrymen were butchered. It was the South Vietnamese army's worst defeat of the war up to that point. The toll: three hundred soldiers killed, an equal number wounded.

On its clandestine Liberation Radio, the NLF had vowed that U.S. servicemen would soon "pay more blood debts." Thereupon the guerrillas struck a U.S. enlisted men's hotel in Qui Nhon on February 10. The

U.S. soldiers dig through the remains of the Qui Nhon enlisted men's hotel destroyed by a Vietcong bomb.

newly constructed, four-story Viet Cuong ("Strength of Vietnam") Hotel housed sixty-two members of the 140th Maintenance Detachment, an aircraft repair unit. Forty-three men were in their rooms or in the ground-floor bar when the Vietcong attacked just after 8:00 P.M. Shooting erupted as roof-top sentries spotted black-clad guerrillas in the street. Specialist 5 Robert Marshall, reading in his third-floor room, grabbed his loaded 7.62 MM rifle and rushed to the balcony. He killed two guerrillas firing up at him. Other guerrillas rushed the hotel and, in the confusion of the shooting, placed friction charges at the front and back wall of the hotel. A hundred-pound plastic charge, concealed inside the hotel, exploded simultaneously with the other charges, destroying the central staircase supporting the building. The hotel collapsed in a twenty-foot high pile of rubble.

Back in his room to collect more ammunition, Spec 5 Marshall acted instinctively. "My first impulse was to grab my steel folding bed and pull it over me," he said. "This must have saved my life. The hotel simply disintegrated beneath me." Inching toward gaps where he saw light, Marshall managed to gouge his way to safety after three hours.

A coordinated guerrilla attack on the local power station blacked out Qui Nhon and delayed rescue operations till dawn, but the rescuers themselves proved to be tempting targets for the Vietcong. Soon after the hotel collapsed, fifty junks, commandeered from local fishermen, carried guerrillas into Qui Nhon's darkened harbor. As they neared the docks, Vietnamese gunboats opened fire and U.S. helicopter gunships swooped down, making one run before they were called off by U.S. officials. "We orbited in frustration under specific orders not to attack until we were provided ARVN observers," related fire team leader Frederick F. Mentzer. The junks fled.

The rescuers picked through the hotel rubble with increasing bitterness. They would ultimately pull twenty-one bodies and twenty-two wounded soldiers from the wreck of the hotel. "They were all noncombat troops," said Colonel Theodore Mataxis, senior U.S. adviser to II Corps. "These are people who fix airplanes. Now the murderous Vietcong are attacking them directly." A sergeant, digging with a shovel, added, "I hope we blast the hell out of them."

Flaming Dart II

As the rescuers cursed the Qui Nhon terrorists, the planes of Flaming Dart II streaked northward. Dis-

agreements in Washington and Saigon over targets had stalled the launch for a day, but on the morning of February 12, more than one hundred navy warplanes from the *Ranger, Hancock,* and *Coral Sea* thundered toward Chanh Hoa, a supply and staging area near Dong Hoi. A short time later twenty USAF F-100 jet fighters and twenty-eight VNAF A-1H Skyraiders left Da Nang for Chap Le to destroy targets missed during the first Flaming Dart strike.

The navy aircraft advanced on Chanh Hoa at eight hundred feet. Flying in wingtip-to-wingtip formation through heavy antiaircraft fire, the planes dove to strafe and bomb the base. Two hours later the air force jets from Da Nang zoomed down in fifteen-degree dives over the Chap Le compound, firing rockets and dropping bombs at antiaircraft guns. Six fighters were hit. Trailing the American planes, the Vietnamese Skyraiders dropped eighty tons of bombs over the buildings and motor pool area of Chap Le.

"They woke us up in the middle of the night, and we woke them up in the middle of the night," said a hardened President Johnson. "They did it again and we did it again." But this time the strikes were not characterized as a reprisal. Significantly, the joint U.S./Vietnamese statement described the raids as "air operations" provoked by "continued aggression." The White House published a long list of Vietcong incidents that had occurred since the attack on Pleiku, most of them not Vietcong "spectaculars" but normal guerrilla incidents. The terrorist attack at Qui Nhon was not mentioned. The McGeorge Bundy memorandum had clearly swayed the president.

The following day, February 13, President Johnson

Beneath the destruction lies the hand of one of the Vietcong saboteurs who set off the Qui Nhon barracks explosion.

took Bundy's counsel and that of other advisers, including Ambassador Taylor, the Joint Chiefs, and the secretary of defense and decided "to execute a program of measured and limited air action jointly with GVN against selected military targets in DRV . . . south of the nineteenth parallel [about eighty miles into North Vietnam]." The air attacks would be scheduled once or twice weekly, hitting two or three targets on each operation. The bombing campaign would be called Rolling Thunder.

In a brief public statement, the president announced the escalation and sounded his keynote themes. The American objective in Vietnam, he said, is "to join in the defense and protection of freedom. . . . We have no ambition there for ourselves. We seek no dominion. We seek no conquest. We seek no wider war."

Semicoup

In Saigon the continually shifting make-up of the Vietnamese government was undergoing yet another change. Dr. Phan Huy Quat, a medical doctor and General Khanh's foreign minister, had become prime minister, succeeding Acting Prime Minister Nguyen Xuan Oanh. Scarcely had the intellectual Quat named his cabinet, which included four other doctors—it was jokingly referred to as the "medicine cabinet"—when a new military coup attempt, aimed primarily at Khanh, shook Saigon.

On February 19 at 1:23 P.M.—during siesta hour—the post office clock stopped. Rebel troops had seized the post office and parts of the city without firing a shot. M24 tanks rolled over the barbed wire around the Vietnamese naval headquarters where General Khanh lived. But Khanh had fled.

Whose troops were they? From the lead tank emerged Colonel Pham Ngoc Thao. Thao had commanded the tanks that advanced on the presidential palace during the coup against Diem, but he never gained favor with the successive military regimes. Now he had joined forces with Brigadier General Lam Van Phat, instigator of the failed September coup against Khanh. In the yard of the naval headquarters, Thao declared the coup merely "an internal army purge" that would not affect the civilian government of Dr. Quat.

Troops under General Phat had meanwhile seized Tan Son Nhut Airport and the Vietnamese air force's operations center. In Bien Hoa, Air Vice Marshal Ky threatened to bomb the operations center and led his planes on a swooping flight over Tan Son Nhut. For several hours the stalemate continued, and by midnight General Phat's rebel troops had dispersed. Finding himself without protection, Phat peeled off his uniform to reveal civilian clothes beneath. He shook the hand of an American officer working in the center, said, "I go now," and disappeared into a waiting automobile.

Early in the morning, troops loyal to Khanh entered the city, and the remaining rebels retreated without protest. Colonel Thao slipped into Saigon's radio station and broadcast an appeal for Khanh to retire. Then, like Phat, he disappeared.

In midmorning the Armed Forces Council, led by "Young Turks" Thieu and Ky, convened and adopted a vote of no confidence in Khanh. Avoiding the meeting, Khanh boarded his airplane and flew to the delta, frantically courting support from other generals. His efforts a failure, he returned to Da Lat and, accepting the inevitable, resigned. A few days later he departed for exile as an ambassador-at-large to the U.S. and Europe. To allow Khanh to save face, the generals accorded him a ceremonial sendoff.

Ambassador Taylor, politely attending the ceremony, greeted Khanh's departure with bittersweetness. Pleased at the downfall of the wavering general, Taylor nonetheless was disappointed that Khanh had never realized his potential. "With some character and integrity added to his undeniable ability," a severe Taylor would write, "he might have been the George Washington of his country."

General Westmoreland, who had waited out events in the MACV operations room, eventually became convinced that the attempted coup d'état had been a farce staged by Thieu and Ky to demonstrate that Khanh could no longer control the military. In Westmoreland's astute scenario, Thieu and Ky had enlisted the services of Phat and Thao with a promise of amnesty and either safe passage out of the country or protection within it. Thieu and Ky, according to the MACV commander, recognized the importance of political stability to the war effort, and they had assumed the obligation of assuring that stability through the country's only viable institution, the armed forces. Very shortly, the Young Turks would be in power.

The roll of thunder

The political turbulence resulting from Thao's semicoup forced postponement, at Ambassador Taylor's

Nguyen Cao Ky led Vietnamese pilots on Flaming Dart reprisal raids on February 7, 1965, and his aircraft took four hits. He was an accomplished pilot whose daring inspired those under his command.

urgent suggestion, of the first Rolling Thunder strike scheduled for February 20. The Vietnamese air force remained on "coup alert," and thus could not fly north. After several more delays, pending resolution of the political turmoil, Rolling Thunder IV was finally set for February 26, the day following General Khanh's departure from Vietnam. But bad weather grounded the planes for another four days before Rolling Thunder V flew northward on the afternoon of March 2.

A fleet of 104 U.S. Air Force jets—B-57s, F-100s, and F-105s—unleashed 120 tons of bombs on the North Vietnamese supply and munitions dump at Xom Bang, ten miles north of the border. At the same time 19 Vietnamese Skyraiders swung farther north to the Quang Khe naval base. With U.S. jets diving to suppress antiaircraft fire, the Skyraiders dropped 70 tons of bombs through a cloudless sky, destroying repair shops, ammo dumps, and supply warehouses and sinking three PT boats at their berths. U.S. briefing officers claimed the ground fire was weak and inaccurate, but a Vietnamese pilot disagreed. "The flak was heavy and volleys of tracer bullets buzzed like wasps on their way to a new nest," reported a poetic Major Nguyen Huu Chan.

Indeed, antiaircraft fire downed six aircraft. U.S. helicopters of the 5th Air Rescue Detachment from Da Nang went after the pilots. Air force First Lieutenant James A. Cullen of Winchester, Massachusetts, ejected from his F-100 Super Sabre into the Gulf of Tonkin, practically into the midst of a fleet of patrolling junks and torpedo boats. The boats closed in as Cullen bobbed in the choppy sea, trying to hide behind his life raft. "I thought I was finished," he said.

Navy Skyraiders from a 7th Fleet aircraft carrier, swooping down to wave-top level, screeched over the boats, turning them aside. An amphibious HU-16 "Albatross" zeroed in on the homing beacon built into Cullen's life belt and sighted the brilliant orange dye the pilot had spilled into the water. Defying the five-foot swells, the Albatross set down, taxied to the downed pilot, and pulled him aboard thirty minutes after he had hit the water.

Over the mainland, an H43-F "Huskie" rescued a U.S. captain whose Thunderchief jet had crashed in the jungles near Quang Khe. Sighting the officer's signal fire, the Huskie descended to one hundred feet and hauled the captain up from the jungle floor with a steel cable and winch. "I love you, I love you," cried the pilot as he was bundled aboard. In all, five of the six downed pilots were rescued.

White-faced soldiers

With Rolling Thunder a continuing operation, the Joint Chiefs suggested improving "security and cover and deception measures" at U.S./Vietnamese air bases. General Westmoreland feared especially for Da Nang. As the launch site for most of the northern raids, it was vital to Rolling Thunder. Vietnamese troops under I Corps Commander General Nguyen Chanh Thi guarded the sprawling complex, but Westmoreland predictably doubted the Vietnamese capabilities. Moreover, ARVN troops tied to defensive positions were not combating the enemy. After a February 22 inspection visit to Da Nang, MACV Deputy Commander Lieutenant General John L. Throckmorton returned to Saigon with a grim assessment. The same day, Westmoreland cabled CINCPAC to recommend the landing at Da Nang of two marine infantry battalions to secure the air base. A third reserve battalion, said the commander, should remain aboard ship off the coast. Admiral Sharp forwarded the request to the Joint Chiefs with the urgent message that the marines be sent now, "before the tragedy."

Ambassador Taylor, by presidential fiat Westmoreland's military superior, had long opposed the commitment of American ground forces to Vietnam. But while he reluctantly agreed on the need to protect the Da Nang airfield, he spelled out his reservations in a separate cable to Washington. After an initial landing of troops, he wrote, "It will be very difficult to hold the line." The Vietnamese government, Taylor knew, was certain to react to the presence of American troops by relinquishing other "ground force tasks" to the Americans. Those "tasks," sure to escalate, represented the ambassador's greatest concern: "The white-faced soldier, armed, equipped, and trained as he is, is not a suitable guerrilla fighter for Asian forests and jungles. The French tried to adapt their forces to this mission and failed. I doubt that U.S. forces could do much better."

Four days after dispatching this cable, Taylor received word from Washington: The marines would land. Taylor secured approval from the Vietnamese government, but Generals Thieu and Tran Van "Little" Minh, concerned about the possibility of riots

in Da Nang, asked that the marines be "brought ashore in the most inconspicuous way possible."

"Close Da Nang"

Marine Brigadier General Frederick J. Karch, a stern veteran of the World War II Saipan and Iwo Jima beachheads, took charge. On previous visits to Vietnam, Karch had grown disgusted with the military situation. At one preoperation briefing he attended at Da Nang, the major of a Vietnamese Ranger battalion described a helicopter lift, scheduled for the next morning, to sweep a village four miles away. Karch was incredulous. "Why is it," he asked, "that you are going out there in helicopters at 8:00 in the morning and alert the whole countryside that you are coming, instead of walking out there tonight and surrounding the buildings?" The major answered, "I couldn't walk my troops out there tonight. They'd get shot at on the way." From his cursory survey in 1964, the general concluded: "Vietnam was just one big cancer." Karch had written in his report that if U.S. Marines were to land in Vietnam, "Make it North Vietnam, not South. If we go into Da Nang, we'll disappear into the countryside and never be heard from again."

In late February, he received orders to prepare a landing at Da Nang. Karch traveled there to inspect "Nam 0" Beach, and on March 7 he waited ten miles off Da Nang aboard the U.S.S. *Mount McKinley*, flagship of Naval Amphibious Task Force 76. The four ships of the task force carried the 2nd and 3rd battalions, 9th regiment, of the 9th Marine Expeditionary Brigade. The 3rd battalion would go ashore while the 2nd would fill a reserve role, remaining aboard ship.

In Washington the Pentagon announced the deployment of the marines, and aboard the *Mount McKinley*, Karch received a dispatch at noon: "Close Da Nang. Land the landing force."

Karch exclaimed, "Do you suppose in Washington they know what time it is in Da Nang? This means a night landing if we close Da Nang at this point." Perhaps worse, the ships rocked in what Karch considered the worst weather he had encountered in the South China Sea. Visibility extended no more than two hundred yards. The general got the order delayed until the following morning.

At dawn on March 8, the task force anchored four thousand feet from Nam 0 Beach, renamed Red Beach by the marines. Visibility had cleared, but the seas remained high; by 8:00 A.M. ten-foot swells slapped the sides of the ships, snapping landing craft

Three F-100 "Super Sabres," armed with napalm and 750-pound bombs, approach their Rolling Thunder target.

mooring lines. The landing hour was put back again, to 9:00, and three minutes later, at 9:03, Corporal Garry Powers leaped from an amphibian tractor into ankle-deep water and ran up the wet sand.

Wave after wave of marines streamed ashore in full battle regalia, their M14 rifles at high port. They had been taught to assume that no shore was friendly, but on this beach Vietnamese girls greeted them, hanging leis of yellow dahlias and red gladioli around their necks. General Thi and the mayor of Da Nang welcomed them too. General Karch, who had flown to shore in a helicopter, supervised the landing. Unsmiling, and appearing forlorn, the general wore a necklace of flowers over his starched fatigues. Overhead U.S. helicopter gunships combed the area for Vietcong.

While one company stayed on the beach to unload 105 MM howitzers, M48 medium tanks, and 106 MM recoilless rifles, the marines clambered into trucks for the ride to the air base. Over the road, banners welcomed the troops to this "free world outpost," and children lining the route smiled and waved. A morning of drizzling rain gave way to a hot, damp, and cloudy afternoon. At 1:00 P.M. the first air force C-130 transports, diving sharply to avoid small-arms fire, touched down with the U.S. Marines 1st Battalion, 3rd Regiment from Okinawa. Carrying sixty-five pound packs and rifles, the men filed out onto the airfield and milled about awkwardly. They watched as marines at the field's perimeter erected tents, dug foxholes, and filled sandbags. The new arrivals had

grumbled on hearing their assignment of security. "Defensive perimeter, shee-it," a rifleman had said. "This is a grunt battalion, not a buncha gate guards."

The marines could scarcely believe that this was a war-torn nation. Rice fields and bamboo groves lay verdant in the distance, as peasants in conical hats jogged to and fro carrying water. ARVN soldiers lounged nearby, sometimes getting up to beg cigarettes from the marines. "I scanned the countryside with my binoculars," wrote Lieutenant Philip Caputo, "but the only signs of war were our own Phantoms, roaring northward with their bomb racks full." The marines soon learned that in Vietnam the war happened after nightfall. Caputo described the sights and sounds of darkened Vietnam: "Grenades and mortars thumped. Small arms crackled like burning timber, and a couple of tracers streaked in silent, scarlet lines above the trees. Artillery boomed in another, more distant battle." With these distractions, and the fog of insects, the thirty-five hundred marines passed a restless first night "in-country."

In a swirling mist the following morning, a weary I Company assembled at the base of Hill 327—immediately renamed the "hungry i" for the company and the popular San Francisco nightclub. Their mission was to secure the 1,060-foot hill, located two miles west of the airfield, and install Hawk missiles at the peak. "All right, spread out around the forward

The U.S. Marines Land

Left. Marines of the 9th Expeditionary Brigade take cover on Da Nang's Red Beach Two soon after landing there on March 8.

Above and right. Instead of finding a hostile beachhead, the marines find Vietnamese college girls ready to welcome them with flowers.

General Nguyen Chanh Thi greets U.S. Marine General Frederick Karch, somber despite the colorful flowers given to him by Vietnamese girls. "When you have a son in Vietnam and he gets killed," Karch said later, "you don't want a smiling general with flowers around his neck."

edge," barked I Company Staff Sergeant Johnny Thompson. "Get down and keep your weapons ready." The marines would extend the defensive perimeter several miles from Da Nang and soon would begin patrolling to intercept any guerrillas intending to harass the base.

We're here for keeps

General Harold K. Johnson, U.S. Army chief of staff, returned to Washington from Vietnam shortly after the Da Nang landing. The general's opposition within the councils of the Joint Chiefs to a strategy dominated by air power had reached the ears of the president. Lyndon Johnson, in what was possibly a calculated move, sent him to Vietnam for a review of the military situation. Detailed briefings by General Westmoreland and Ambassador Taylor had sketched

a grim military picture, and now General Johnson, as expected, recommended further U.S. involvement because "what the situation requires may exceed what the Vietnamese can be expected to do." Only the United States was capable of applying sufficient pressure on North Vietnam to force it to desist in its support of the Vietcong. Johnson urged an increase in money, ships, aircraft, advisers, and hardware. To release Vietnamese forces from guard duty, he also advocated deployment of an army division either to secure Bien Hoa and Tan Son Nhut or to "defend" the highland provinces of Kontum, Pleiku, and Darlac.

Secretary McNamara emphasized that he would prefer to see South Koreans, rather than Americans, deployed, but in the margin of General Johnson's report he scribbled: "Policy is: Anything that will strengthen the position of the GVN will be sent."

While deliberations continued on ground troops,

Vietnamese children welcome U.S. Marine convoys rolling into Da Nang.

A marine aboard an M48 medium gun tank waits his turn to land on Red Beach Two.

"Launch!" signals the catapult officer aboard the U.S.S. Coral Sea and this A-4 Skyhawk is started on its Rolling Thunder flight.

Readying an A-1 Skyraider for a Rolling Thunder bomb run, crewmen aboard the carrier Ranger position a 2,000-pound bomb beneath the aircraft.

Rolling Thunder, expanding by design, continued to hammer the North. On March 14, in Rolling Thunder VI, more than a hundred air force jets and navy bombers struck an ammunition depot at Phu Qui—only one hundred miles south of Hanoi. For the first time, only American aircraft participated. Jets swooped low to burn out antiaircraft positions with napalm, then bombers dropped explosives over a square-mile area. Two hours later air force fighter-bombers returned to pound the depot a second time, trapping soldiers who were combing the wreckage.

Rolling Thunder VII roared north four days later and lasted for a week. Air force and navy aircraft hit supply depots at Vinh Son and Thuan, dropping 750-pound bombs and strafing with rockets and 20 MM cannons. Again, the bombers dropped napalm and, aided by good weather, the pilots reported "100

percent" damage to their targets. A few days later eight U.S. Thunderchiefs departed on the first "armed reconnaissance" mission. Searching for a "military target of opportunity," the jets descended on the early warning radar system at Vinh Son.

Vietnamese Skyraiders and American jets carried out a raid two days later on the Phu Xa radar and military radio station protecting Dong Hoi, and two days after that navy aircraft made their deepest penetration yet into the North, striking Bach Long Island, sixty miles out to sea and one hundred and twenty miles southeast of Hanoi. The next day, another armed recon mission bombed radar facilities at Ba Binh.

By the end of March a U.S. Embassy officer concluded that the air raids over North Vietnam had produced "the obvious results, in damage to installations and in showing Hanoi that we're here for keeps. But as for infiltration, we haven't seen any results one

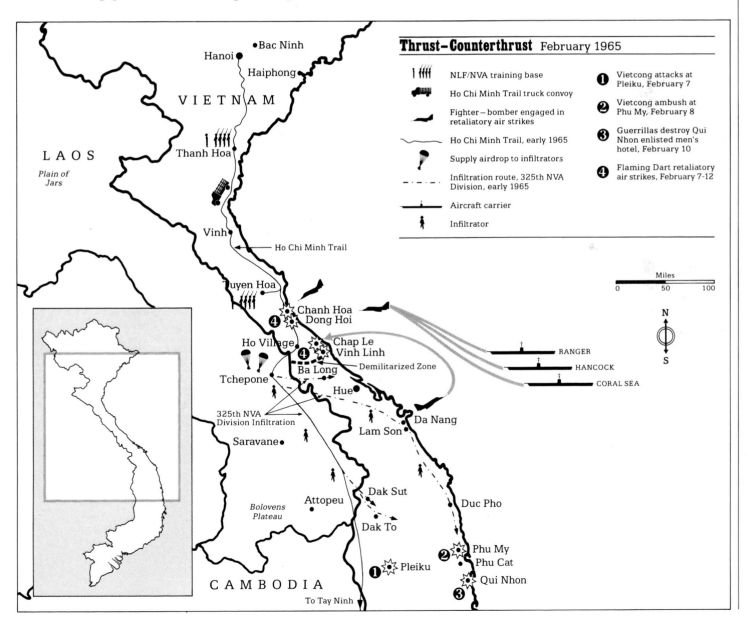

Thrust-Counterthrust February 1965

NLF/NVA training base	
Ho Chi Minh Trail truck convoy	
Fighter–bomber engaged in retaliatory air strikes	
Ho Chi Minh Trail, early 1965	
Supply airdrop to infiltrators	
Infiltration route, 325th NVA Division, early 1965	
Aircraft carrier	
Infiltrator	

❶ Vietcong attacks at Pleiku, February 7

❷ Vietcong ambush at Phu My, February 8

❸ Guerrillas destroy Qui Nhon enlisted men's hotel, February 10

❹ Flaming Dart retaliatory air strikes, February 7-12

Caught in the explosion at the U.S. Embassy on March 29, the body of a Vietnamese woman lies in front of burning wreckage of the building.

way or the other. So far, the message doesn't seem to have gotten across."

On March 28 Ambassador Taylor returned to Washington. On his arrival at Andrews Air Force Base, Taylor told reporters that while he had no assessment of the U.S. air raids on North Vietnam, they had produced a "very clear lift in morale" in the South. Discussing the overall progress of the war, he said it was "too early to talk about negotiations or ending the war." He added, however, that in general, "things are turning for the better in Vietnam."

The embassy bombing

The American Embassy, a dreary six-story concrete building, sat at the intersection of two of Saigon's busiest streets. After the Brink Hotel bombing on Christmas Eve, security had increased, and wooden police barricades placed around the embassy pre-

vented cars from parking on the sidewalks. Concern about an attack on the prime symbol of American presence in Vietnam had intensified in mid-March when police discovered thirty-five pounds of explosives cached by terrorists in a Saigon house.

On March 29 an inconspicuous gray Renault sedan stalled on Vo Di Nguy, a street next to the embassy, just before 11:00 A.M. The Vietnamese driver got out and raised the hood. An embassy policeman, armed with an M1 carbine, walked out to the curb, and the pair fell to arguing.

In his second-floor office, CIA Station Chief Peer de Silva, his foot on the windowsill, stood talking on the telephone and looking out on the street scene. Watching the common sight of a motorist and policeman arguing, his eyes fastened on wisps of gray smoke emerging from behind the driver's seat. Suddenly he saw a "time pencil," a cylindrical brass detonator filled with ignition powder.

LBJ Rallies His Party

Less than two months after the inauguration that capped his landslide electoral victory, President Lyndon Johnson was showing unmistakable signs of strain. "I don't know what will be written about my administration," he sighed in March to a group of educators visiting the White House. "Nothing seems to go right from early in the morning to late at night. ... When I was a boy growing up, we never had these issues of our relations with other nations so much. We didn't wake up with Vietnam and have Cyprus for lunch and the Congo for dinner. ..."

In early 1965 the clear voice that Congress expressed in the August Southeast Asia Resolution had been quiet for several months. As the planes of Flaming Dart and Rolling Thunder unleashed destruction over North Vietnam, the bombing touched off war jitters at home and abroad unequaled since the Cuban missile crisis.

Soon Johnson began to hear rumbles of dissent within his own party. Liberal Democrats such as Wayne Morse, South Dakota's George McGovern, and Frank Church of Idaho rose in the Senate to urge a negotiated solution to the war in Southeast Asia. "The question," Senator Church said, "is not whether we should negotiate, but when." Yet neither Hanoi, Peking, nor Moscow had evinced the slightest interest in peace talks. "Who the hell do they think I'm going to negotiate with?" the frustrated president thundered to an aide after another dovish speech on the Senate floor.

If he had possessed any leverage, Johnson would have locked Ho Chi Minh and the president of South Vietnam in the White House Cabinet Room, as he had done with railroad presidents and union leaders a year earlier on the eve of a threatened strike. He would have knocked their heads together until they reached a compromise that he could call his own. But in the confrontation with North Vietnam, which he once called that "raggedy-ass little fourth-rate country," the masterful "Johnson treatment" was useless. In 1965 Johnson believed his only leverage to be bombing.

In his own councils, the president placed himself between the hawks and doves and let the two sides argue. Beyond the executive branch, however, the president demanded a consensus. The survivor of Texas politics and Senate power struggles always hesitated to move without his colleagues' support, without solid approval ratings in public opinion polls. He now undertook a private campaign to silence his critics, vowing to talk to each one personally. One possibly apocryphal story spread around Washington of an encounter with Frank Church. Johnson approached him at a reception and complained, "Frank, you've been making some speeches that haven't been very helpful."

"Well, Mr. President," the senator replied, "if you read the speeches all the way through, it isn't the same as the headlines."

"The headlines are all I read, and all anybody reads," Johnson said. "When you were in trouble in your state, Frank, I used to come out and give you a hand, didn't I?"

"Mr. President," Church said defensively, "what I've been saying isn't much different from what Walter Lippman has been writing."

"Walter Lippman is a fine man," Johnson said. "I admire him. Next time you're in trouble out in Idaho, Frank, you ask Walter to come help."

In March the president initiated a series of receptions for Congressional leaders at the White House. Cozily assembled in the Blue Room while their wives chatted upstairs with Lady Bird, the men heard briefings by Secretaries Rusk and McNamara on the administration's policy in Vietnam. The president opened the floor to questions, including any dealing with classified material. "You can ask me anything you want," he assured them, "and I'll answer it."

The legislators enthusiastically endorsed the sessions. William Proxmire, the liberal senator from Wisconsin, voiced his appreciation by declaring there was "simply no precedent for this kind of candid dialogue between congressmen and the president in the history of the republic."

In late February, the Johnson administration had also gone public with what it believed to be a blockbuster State Department white paper entitled "Aggression from the North: The Record of North Vietnam's Campaign to Conquer South Vietnam." The sixty-four-page document, containing charts, reports, and photographs of interrogated prisoners, was intended to expose "Hanoi's elaborate program" of infiltration and supply and to justify America's intervention in Vietnam.

The white paper was not universally convincing, however. Of all the interrogated prisoners, only six were natives of North Vietnam. The remainder were "regroupees," natives of South Vietnam who had returned from the North to join the insurgency. That distinction was crucial in any attempt to prove an invasion. Likewise the evidence on Communist supply was flawed, since the figures showed that 97.5 percent of weapons captured from the Vietcong had originally been stolen or captured from the American-supported South Vietnamese army. Even Assistant Secretary of State William P. Bundy has suggested that "evidence on supply was numerically weak to the point of ridicule."

For those in the administration, the white paper served to validate Hanoi's role—however difficult to pin down—in the southern insurgency. But to those who reacted against the bombing, the white paper was hardly a persuasive document. Noted Alaska Senator Ernest Gruening, an administration critic, "That is nothing new. ... We have been aiding the South Vietnamese on a scale far surpassing the aid given [the VC] by the North Vietnamese."

Yet the combination of the white paper and Johnson's cajolery succeeded in luring many wayward Democrats back to the fold. Criticism in his own party waned for the time being, and the president had regained consensus. As he contemplated a further expansion of the United States commitment in Vietnam, Lyndon Johnson claimed to have the American people behind him. As it turned out, this support was short lived.

The motorist opened fire on the policeman, who unslung his rifle and was killed by gunfire from another terrorist on a halted motor scooter. The firing alerted embassy staff members. "It might be a bomb!" cried a first-floor worker who spotted the car. Workers ducked for cover. A floor above, de Silva, the phone still in his hand, spun away from the window. His world turned to "glue and slow motion" as three hundred pounds of plastic explosives packed in the trunk of the Renault erupted in a fireball.

The blast tore through the building's first three floors and sprayed shards of window glass. CIA secretary Barbara Robbins died at her desk, still clutching a ballpoint pen. A Filipino serving in the U.S. Navy also died. Broken glass blinded two other CIA officers. De Silva found himself on the floor with a gaping wound in his neck and his sight impaired. The vacant office of Ambassador Taylor was destroyed. "We all had glass in our eyes, hair, and pockets," said political officer Robert Burke. Deputy Ambassador U. Alexis Johnson, ensconced in his fifth-floor office, had his face cut by flying glass. Fifty-two Americans were wounded.

Dazed and bleeding embassy staff members stumbled out of the building to a devastating scene in the street. The explosion had killed twenty and injured one hundred and thirty Vietnamese who were passing by or dining in restaurants across from the embassy. Police had killed the fleeing motorist and wounded and captured the second.

President Johnson was presiding over a White House dinner for the visiting president of Upper Volta when a note about the bombing was brought to him. He read it and gave the note to Secretary Rusk, who hurried to the State Department. Ambassador Taylor, also at the dinner, felt "more than a little ashamed" at being away from his Saigon post. Had he been there, he might have died in the explosion.

The president reserved comment until the next morning when he declared, "Outrages like this will only reinforce the determination of the American people and government to continue, and to strengthen their assistance and support for the people and government of Vietnam."

Run in or run out?

During the following two days President Johnson met with Taylor and the members of the National Security Council for a wide-ranging review of U.S. policy in Vietnam. After the first meeting the president responded to press inquiries concerning dramatic new developments by saying, "I know of no far-reaching strategy that is being suggested or promulgated."

With that statement the president made inevitable the "credibility gap" that was to open between his administration and the public and press. For at that very moment on the table in the Cabinet Room rested a discussion paper written by McGeorge Bundy that summarized his views and those of other advisers and called for a dramatic expansion of the United States's involvement in Vietnam.

On April 2 the president made his decision. He approved the Bundy memorandum but added a proviso aimed at secrecy: "The president desires that with respect to [these] actions . . . premature publicity be avoided by all possible precautions. The actions themselves should be taken as rapidly as practicable, but in ways that should minimize any appearance of sudden changes in policy. . . ."

These new orders would send eighteen to twenty thousand additional soldiers—engineering and logistical units—to Vietnam. The tempo of Rolling Thunder would continue to ascend with attacks on lines of communication and possibly, within a few weeks, against rail lines that connected North Vietnam with China. The governments of South Korea, Australia, and New Zealand would be urgently entreated to send soldiers to Vietnam.

Further, two more U.S. Marine combat battalions, and one marine air squadron, would be deployed. For the marines, significantly, President Johnson authorized a "change of mission . . . to permit their more active use under conditions to be established and approved by the secretary of defense." The conditions approved by McNamara would release the Americans to patrol within a fifty-mile radius of their bases and to initiate offensive operations against the VC.

"I thought we either had to run in or run out," President Johnson said years later of his decision. "It had reached the desperate point . . . we had tried everything available to us to get to the peace table . . . from November 1963 to 1965. And we had not succeeded. And we either had to run in or run out."

On April 6, 1965, the day that NSAM 328 was promulgated, there were twenty-seven thousand American fighting men on the ground, in the air, and off the shores of Vietnam. Soon combat soldiers would be pouring into the country by the tens of thousands, and by midsummer, America would be at war.

Taking heavy sniper fire from the tree line, the 1st Battalion, 7th Marines storm ashore at White Beach on the Batangan Peninsula, near Quang Ngai, as part of Operation Piranha in September 1965.

Bibliography

I. Books and Articles

Andrews, William R. *The Village War. Vietnamese Communist Revolutionary Activities in Dinh Tuong Province, 1960–1964.* University of Missouri Press, 1973.
"The Atlantic Report: South Vietnam." *The Atlantic,* December 1962.
Austin, Anthony. *The President's War.* J.B. Lippincott Co., 1971.

Ball, George W. *The Past Has Another Pattern.* W.W. Norton & Co., 1982.
BDM Corporation. *A Study of Strategic Lessons Learned in Vietnam.* Vols. I, V, and VI. National Technical Information Service, 1980.
Berger, Carl, ed. *The United States Air Force in Southeast Asia, 1961–1973.* Office of Air Force History, 1977.
Blaufarb, Douglas S. *The Counterinsurgency Era.* The Free Press, 1977.
Braestrup, Peter. *Big Story.* Anchor Books, 1978.
Browne, Malcolm W. *The New Face of War.* Bobbs-Merrill Co., 1968.
Bundy, William P. *Memoirs.* Unpublished, no date.
Burchett, Wilfred G. *Vietnam: Inside Story of the Guerrilla War.* International Publishers, 1965.
Buttinger, Joseph. *Vietnam: A Dragon Embattled.* Vol. II. Praeger, 1967.

Caputo, Philip. *Rumor of War.* Holt, Rinehart and Winston, 1977.
Carver, George A., Jr. "The Faceless Viet Cong." *Foreign Affairs,* April 1966, pp. 347–72.
Chaffard, Georges. "Inside Vietcong Territory." *Viet-Report,* July 1965, pp. 3–11.
Charlton, Michael, and Anthony Moncrief. *Many Reasons Why: The American Involvement in Vietnam.* Hill & Wang, 1978.
Colby, William, and Peter Forbath. *Honorable Men.* Simon & Schuster, 1978.
Cooper, Chester. *The Lost Crusade: America in Vietnam.* Fawcett, 1972.
Corson, William R. *The Betrayal.* W.W. Norton & Co., 1968.

de Silva, Peer. *Sub Rosa, The CIA and the Uses of Intelligence.* The New York Times Book Co., 1978.
Devillers, Philippe. "The Struggle for Unification of Vietnam." *The China Quarterly,* 9(1962).
Donlon, Roger H.C., and Warren Rogers. *Outpost of Freedom.* McGraw-Hill, 1965.
Donnell, John C. *Viet Cong Recruitment.* Rand Corporation RM–5486–1, 1967.
DuBerrier, Hilaire. *Background to Betrayal: The Tragedy of Vietnam.* Western Islands, 1965.
Duiker, William J. *The Communist Road to Power in Vietnam.* Westview Press, 1981.

"Engagement in Saigon." *The New Republic,* March 12, 1962.
Eqbal, Ahmad. "The Theory and Fallacies of Counterinsurgency." *The Nation,* August 2, 1971.
Evans, Rowland, and Robert Novak. *Lyndon B. Johnson: The Exercise of Power.* New American Library, 1966.

Fairbanks, Henry G. "The Enigma of Ngo Dinh Diem." *Commonweal,* September 21, 1962.
Fall, Bernard. "Master of the Red Jab: Ho Chi Minh." *The Saturday Evening Post,* November 24, 1962.
Street Without Joy. The Stackpole Co., 1964.
The Two Viet-Nams: A Political and Military Analysis. Praeger, 1963.
FitzGerald, Frances. *Fire in the Lake: The Vietnamese and the Americans in Vietnam.* Atlantic–Little Brown, 1972.
Futrell, Robert Frank. *The United States Air Force in Southeast Asia, The Advisory Years to 1965.* U.S. Government Printing Office, 1981.

Galloway, John. *The Gulf of Tonkin Resolution.* Associated University Presses, 1970.
————, ed. *The Kennedys and Vietnam.* Facts on File, Inc., 1971.
Goulden, Joseph C. *Truth Is the First Casualty.* Rand McNally & Co., 1968.
Goure, Leon, and C.A.H. Thomson. *Some Impressions of Viet Cong Vulnerabilities: An Interim Report.* Rand Corporation RM–4699–1–ISA/ARPA, 1965.
Gravel, Sen. Mike, ed. *The Pentagon Papers.* Beacon Press, 1971.
Grose, Peter. "Vietcong's Shadow Government." *The New York Times Magazine,* January 24, 1965.

Halberstam, David. *The Best and the Brightest.* Random House, 1972.
"Getting the Story in Vietnam." *Commentary,* 39(1965), pp. 30–4.
The Making of a Quagmire. Random House, 1964.
Hammond, Dr. William Michael. "U.S. Intervention and the Fall of Diem." In *The Vietnam War,* edited by Ray Bonds, Crown Publishers, Inc., 1979.
Hickey, G.C., and W.P. Davison. *The American Military Advisor and His Foreign Counterpart: The Case of Vietnam.* Rand Corporation RM–4482–ARPA, 1965.
Hilsman, Roger. *To Move a Nation.* Dell, 1967.
Honey, P.J. "North Viet Nam's Workers' Party and South Viet Nam's People's Revolutionary Party." *Pacific Affairs* (1962–1963).

Johnson, Lyndon B. *The Vantage Point.* Holt, Rinehart and Winston, 1971.
Joiner, Charles A. "South Vietnam's Buddhist Crisis." *Asian Survey,* 7(1964), pp. 915–28.

Kahin, George McTurnan, and John W. Lewis. *The U.S. in Vietnam.* Dell, 1967.
Karnow, Stanley. "The Newsmen's War in Vietnam." *Nieman Reports,* 16, No. 4(1963), pp. 3–8.
Kattenburg, Paul M. *The Vietnam Trauma in American Foreign Policy, 1945–1975.* Transaction Books, 1980.
Kelly, Col. Francis J. *Vietnam Studies: U.S. Army Special Forces, 1961–1971.* Department of the Army, 1973.
Knoebl, Kuno. *Victor Charlie: The Face of War in Viet-Nam.* Trans. Abe Farbstein. Praeger, 1967.
Kraft, J. "Hot Weapon in the Cold War." *The Saturday Evening Post,* April 28, 1962.

Lacouture, Jean. "Inside North Vietnam." *The New Republic,* May 21, 1962.
"The Vietcong." *Cross Currents,* 1965.
The Vietcong: Who Are They, What Do They Want? *The New Republic,* March 6, 1965.
Vietnam: Between Two Truces. Random House, 1966.
Lamont, Nicholas S. "On Communist Organization and Strategy in South Vietnam." *Public & International Affairs* (1965).
Lewallen, John. *Ecology of Devastation: Indochina.* Penguin Books, 1971.
Lewy, Guenter. *America in Vietnam.* Oxford University Press, 1978.
Lindsay, F.A. "Unconventional Warfare." *Foreign Affairs,* January 1962, pp. 269–74.
Lodge, Henry Cabot. *The Storm Has Many Eyes: A Personal Narrative.* W.W. Norton & Co., 1973.
Lucas, Jim G. *Dateline: Vietnam.* Award House, 1966.

Maclear, Michael. *The Ten Thousand Day War: Vietnam: 1945–1975.* St. Martin's Press, 1981.
Martin, Robert P. "Americans in a War in Asia." *U.S. News & World Report,* March 5, 1962.
Mauldin, Bill. "Vivid Picture of the Attack on Pleiku—And Who Ordered It." *Life,* February 19, 1965.
Mecklin, John. *Mission in Torment.* Doubleday, 1965.
Millet, Stanley. "Terror in Vietnam: An American's Ordeal at the Hands of Our 'Friends.'" *Harper's,* September 1962.
Moore, Robin. *The Green Berets.* Crown Publishers, 1965.
Morgenthau, Hans J. "Vietnam—Another Korea." *Commentary,* May 1962, pp. 369–74.
Munk, Michael. "Why the Vietnamese Support the NLF." *New Politics* (1965), pp. 18–25.
Mus, Paul. "The Role of the Village in Vietnamese Politics." *Pacific Affairs* (1949), pp. 265–72.

Nighswonger, William A. *Rural Pacification in Vietnam.* Praeger, 1966.
"No Win in Vietnam." *The New Republic,* April 9, 1962.

O'Ballance, Edgar. *The Wars in Vietnam: 1954–1973.* Hippocrene Books, 1975.
Orshefsky, Milton. "Joan of Arc or Dragon Lady?" *Life,* October 26, 1962.
Ortner, E.H. "U.S. Special Forces: The Faceless Army." *Popular Science Magazine,* August 1961.
Osborne, Milton E. *Strategic Hamlets in South Vietnam: A Survey and a Comparison.* Cornell University Data Paper 55, 1965.

Pike, Douglas. "How Strong Is the NLF?" *The Reporter,* February 24, 1966.
Viet Cong: The Organization and Techniques of the National Liberation Front of South Vietnam. MIT Press, 1966.
War, Peace, and the Viet Cong. MIT Press, 1969.
Popkin, Samuel L. "Pacification: Politics and the Village." *Asian Survey,* August 1970, pp. 662–71.
Porter, Gareth, ed. *Vietnam: The Definitive Documentation of Human Decisions.* Vol. 2. Earl M. Coleman Enterprises, 1979.

Race, Jeffrey. "How They Won." *Asian Survey,* August 1970, pp. 628–50.
War Comes to Long An: Revolutionary Conflict in a Vietnamese Province. University of California Press, 1972.

Raskin, Marcus G., and Bernard Fall, eds. *The Viet-Nam Reader: Articles and Documents on American Foreign Policy and the Viet-Nam Crisis.* Random House, 1965.

Roberts, Charles. *LBJ's Inner Circle.* Delacorte Press, 1965.

Rose, Jerry A. "Elusive Vietcong." *The New Republic,* May 4, 1963.

    "I'm Hit, I'm Hit." *The Saturday Evening Post,* March 1963.

Rostow, W.W. "Guerrilla Warfare in Underdeveloped Areas." *Marine Corps Gazette,* January 1962, pp. 47–50.

Rovere, Richard H. "Letter from Washington." *The New Yorker,* March 20, 1965.

Schlesinger, Arthur M., Jr. *A Thousand Days: John F. Kennedy in the White House.* Houghton Mifflin Co., 1965.

    Robert Kennedy and His Times. Houghton Mifflin Co., 1978.

Scigliano, Robert. *South Viet-Nam: Nation Under Stress.* Houghton Mifflin Co., 1964.

    "Viet-Nam: A Country at War," *Asian Survey,* January 1963, pp. 48–54.

Shaplen, Robert. Articles in *The New Yorker,* 1962–1965.

    The Lost Revolution: The U.S. in Vietnam, 1946–1966. Rev. ed. Harper & Row, 1966.

Shulimson, Jack, and Charles M. Johnson, *U.S. Marines in Vietnam, The Landing and the Buildup 1965.* U.S. Government Printing Office, 1978.

Sochurek, Howard. "American Special Forces in Action in Vietnam." *National Geographic,* January 1965, pp. 38–65.

    "Report from Vietnam." Unpublished, March 1, 1962.

Sorenson, Theodore C. *Kennedy.* Harper & Row, 1965.

Sparks, W. "Guerrillas in Vietnam." *Commonweal,* June 29, 1962.

Stavins, Ralph, Richard J. Barnet, and Marcus G. Raskin. *Washington Plans an Aggressive War.* Random House, 1971.

Taylor, Maxwell D. *Swords and Plowshares.* W.W. Norton & Co., 1972.

Thayer, Carlyle A. "Southern Vietnamese Revolutionary Organization and the Vietnam Worker's Party: Continuity and Change, 1954–1974." In *Communism in Indochina: New Perspectives,* edited by Joseph Zasloff and MacAlister Brown, D.C. Heath Co., 1975.

Thich Thien An. *Buddhism and Zen in Vietnam.* Charles E. Tuttle, 1975.

Tregaskis, Richard. *Vietnam Diary.* Holt, Rinehart and Winston, 1963.

    "Vietnam Visit." *Travel,* March 1959.

Trumbull, Robert. "Mandarin Who Rules Vietnam." *The New York Times Magazine,* January 7, 1962.

Warner, Denis. "Agony in Saigon." *The Reporter,* October 10, 1963.

    The Last Confucian. Macmillan, 1963.

Washburn, A. Michael, and Willard H. Mitchell. Policy Memo #33, "Walt Rostow, Vietnam, and the Future Task of American Foreign Policy." Princeton University, 1967.

Westmoreland, William. *A Soldier Reports.* Dell, 1976.

"We Wade Deeper Into the Jungle." *Life,* January 25, 1963.

Whiteside, Thomas. *The Withering Rain.* Dutton, 1971.

Whitlow, Capt. Robert H. *U.S. Marines in Vietnam: The Advisory and Combat Assistance Era, 1954–1964.* History and Museums Division Headquarters, U.S. Marines, 1977.

Wulff, Erich. "The Buddhist Revolt." *The New Republic,* August 31, 1963.

"Z." "The War in Vietnam: We Have Not Been Told the Whole Truth." *The New Republic,* March 2, 1962.

Zasloff, Joseph J. "The Problem of South Vietnam." *Commentary,* February 1962, pp. 126–35.

II. Government and Military Reports

Andert, Lt. Joseph D. *Report of U.S. Advisory Detachment to 21st ARVN Infantry Division, 1964.* Unpublished, 1964.

Campbell, Capt. Joseph R., III. *History of the 121st Aviation Company, Formerly the 93rd Transportation Company, 1 January 1963–December 1963.* Unpublished, no date.

Center for Military History Open File. *Tay Ninh Monthly Province Report Summary.* February 1965.

Comptroller General of the United States. *Maintenance and Supply Support of United States Army Helicopters in South Vietnam.* U.S. General Accounting Office, 1963.

Conley, Michael Charles. *The Communist Insurgent Infrastructure in South Vietnam: A Study of Organization and Strategy.* Center for Research in Social Systems, American University, 1967.

Department of State. *Aggression from the North: The Record of North Vietnam's Campaign to Conquer South Vietnam.* U.S. Government Printing Office, 1965.

Duncan, Sgt. Donald W. *A Case Study in a Special Operations Advisory Effort (Project Delta), 5th Special Forces Group.* Unpublished, February 1965.

Ghaus, A.S., et al. "The Violation of Human Rights in South Vietnam." *United Nations General Assembly Official Records,* Agenda Item 77, Document A/5630, September 1963.

Murphy, Lt. Col. Paul J.G., Jr. *History of the Army Concept Team in Vietnam, 1 October–30 June 1963.* Unpublished, no date.

Serong, Col. F.P. "Current Operations in South Vietnam." Unpublished, October 1962.

Shay, Capt. Ruben W. "Debriefing of Colonel George C. Morton, Commanding Officer, U.S. Army Special Forces Vietnam, 1 September 1962 through 6 November 1963." Unpublished, 1963.

"Staff Office Report, Headquarters United States Army Special Forces Vietnam, October–December 1962." Unpublished, January 1963.

United States Mission. *Captured Documents and Interrogation, North Viet-Nam's Role in the South from Viet-Nam Documents and Research Notes.* June 1968.

Urick, Capt. Richard E., and Capt. M.L. McDonald, Jr. *History of the Twenty-third Special Warfare Aviation Detachment, 1 January–31 December 1963.* Unpublished, no date.

U.S. Senate Select Committee to Study Governmental Operations, 94th Congress, 1st Session, Interim Report No. 94-465. "Alleged Assassination Plots Involving Foreign Leaders." U.S. Government Printing Office, November 1975.

Vietnam Documents and Research Notes No. 96. Saigon Embassy, 1971.

III. Newspapers and Periodicals

The authors consulted the following newspapers and periodicals: *Newsweek, The New York Times, Time, Times of Vietnam,* and *U.S. News & World Report.*

IV. Archival Sources

LBJ Library, Austin, Texas. *Leadership Breakfast Meeting Notes File,* August 4, 1964.

    Oral History Interview: Lyndon B. Johnson, August 12, 1969, by William J. Jorden.

John F. Kennedy Library, Boston, Massachusetts. *Presidential Office Files:* Counterinsurgency; Vietnam, 1961–1963; Vietnam Security, 1961–1963.

    National Security Files: Vietnam 1/61–11/63; Attorney General Robert F. Kennedy Round the World Trip, 2/62; NSC meetings on Vietnam 9/63–11/63.

    Oral History Interviews: Robert F. Kennedy.

Marine Corps Historical Center, Washington, D.C. *Oral History Collection:* Brig. Gen. Frederick J. Karch, USMC (Ret.), January 15, 1972.

V. Interviews

Brig. Gen. Donald D. Blackburn, U.S. Army (Ret.), on August 25, 1981.

Lt. Col. Gary Brosch, U.S. Army, on August 29, 1981.

Lucien Conein, former CIA officer, on September 3, 1981.

Col. Roger H.C. Donlon, U.S. Army, December 1981.

Capt. Sully Fontaine, U.S. Army (Ret.), September 22, 1981.

Vu Thuy Hong, former GVN press analyst, on September 1, 1981.

Lt. Col. Leon Hope, U.S. Army (Ret.), on August 26, 1981.

Gilbert Layton, retired CIA officer, on October 20, 1981.

Maj. Morris Lewis, U.S. Army, on August 25, 1981.

Henry Cabot Lodge, former U.S. ambassador to South Vietnam, on February 10, 1982.

Graham Martin, former ambassador to South Vietnam, on August 27, 1981.

Rev. Walden Pell, former pastor, Episcopal Church of Saigon, on August 28, 1981.

Frank Scotton, U.S. International Communications Agency, on August 30, 1981.

Col. Charles M. Simpson, U.S. Army (Ret.), on September 1, 1981.

Maxwell Taylor, former presidential adviser, ambassador to South Vietnam, on September 1, 1981.

Barry Zorthian, former head of USIS Vietnam, on September 2, 1981.

Photography Credits

Cover Photo:
UPI

Chapter I
p. 7, Larry Burrows—LIFE Magazine, © 1963, Time Inc. p. 8, Wide World. p. 9, U.S. Army. p. 10, Howard Sochurek—LIFE Magazine, © 1962, Time Inc. p. 13, John Dominis—LIFE Magazine, © 1962, Time Inc. pp. 16-7, François Sully—Black Star. p. 21, Wide World. p. 24, Howard Sochurek—LIFE Magazine, © 1962, Time Inc. p. 25, Larry Burrows—LIFE Magazine, © 1963, Time Inc.

Choppers
p. 26, Rene Burri—Magnum. p. 27, Larry Burrows—LIFE Magazine, © 1964, Time Inc. p. 28, © James H. Karales, 1964. p. 29, top, Rene Burri—Magnum; bottom, Wide World. p. 30, top, UPI; bottom, U.S. Marine Corps. p. 31, Ned Broderick.

Chapter II
p. 33, Paris Match, courtesy of Life Picture Service. p. 35, top, UPI; bottom, Wide World. p. 39, top, UPI; bottom, Eastfoto. p. 40, Eastfoto. p. 41, Agence France-Presse. p. 43, Eastfoto. p. 47, Collection of James H. Pickerell.

Chapter III
pp. 49-50, Wide World. p. 51, Collection of John Spragens, Jr. p. 53, Wide World. p. 55, John Topham Picture Library. p. 57, Larry Burrows—LIFE Magazine, © 1963, Time Inc. p. 60, UPI. p. 61, Wide World. p. 64, Black Star.

The Soldiers of South Vietnam
p. 67, Larry Burrows—LIFE Magazine, © 1963, Time Inc. p. 68, © James H. Karales, 1964. p. 69, top, © James H. Karales, 1964; bottom, Burt Glinn—Magnum. p. 70, top, The Bettmann Archive, Inc.; bottom, Keystone. p. 71, Wide World.

Chapter IV
p. 73, Wide World. pp. 74-5, Henri Dauman—LIFE Magazine, © 1964, Time Inc. p. 76, Wide World. p. 77, Burt Glinn—Magnum. p. 78, James H. Pickerell. pp. 79-80, Burt Glinn—Magnum. p. 83, Larry Burrows—LIFE Magazine, © 1963, Time Inc. p. 89, Pictorial Parade. p. 90, James H. Pickerell-Black Star.

Chapter V
p. 93, Wide World. p. 95, Larry Burrows—LIFE Magazine, © 1964, Time Inc. p. 96, Harry Redl. p. 97, Wilfred Burchett—Roger Pic, courtesy of Life Picture Service. p. 98, François Sully—Black Star. p. 99, Harry Redl. p. 101, Larry Burrows—LIFE Magazine, © 1964, Time Inc. p. 104, Wide World. p. 105, U.S. Army.

The Brutal War
p. 107, © James H. Karales, 1964. p. 108, James H. Pickerell. p. 109, Akihiko Okamura, courtesy of PAN-ASIA. pp. 110-1, UPI.

Chapter VI
p. 113, Agence France-Presse. pp. 115-6, Collection of Frank Scotton. p. 117, Frank Scotton. p. 119, Akihiko Okamura, courtesy of PAN-ASIA. pp. 120-1, Wide World. p. 123, UPI. p. 124, © James H. Karales, 1964. p. 125, U.S. Army.

Chapter VII
p. 127, Ralph Morse—LIFE Magazine, © 1961, Time Inc. p. 128, UPI. p. 129, U.S. Army. p. 131, top, Leon Hope; bottom, Carl Winkler. p. 133, Jerry Rose—Camera Press Ltd. p. 135, Mrs. Connie Shank Fickes, courtesy of Life Picture Service. p. 136, Robin Moore. pp. 138-9, © James H. Karales, 1964. pp. 140-1, Roger Donlon. p. 142, Wide World. p. 143, Library of Congress. p. 144, Jim Morris. p. 145, Soldier of Fortune Magazine.

With the Green Berets
p. 146, Jay:Leviton-Atlanta. pp. 147-8, Larry Burrows—LIFE Magazine, © 1964, Time Inc. p. 149, top, Howard Sochurek; bottom, Jerry Rose—Camera Press Ltd. p. 150, Pictorial Parade. p. 151, Howard Sochurek.

Chapter VIII
p. 153, Robert Moeser. p. 155, Wide World. p. 158, © 1964 by The New York Times Company. Reprinted by permission. p. 159, top, U.S. Navy; bottom, U.S. Navy, courtesy of Lou Drendel. p. 160, Bill Ray—LIFE Magazine, © 1964, Time Inc. p. 161, Sovfoto. p. 163, inset, Collection of John Spragens, Jr. p. 163, UPI. p. 164, Wide World.

Chapter IX
p. 167, UPI. pp. 169-71, Burk Uzzle—Magnum. p. 173, Daniel Camus—Paris Match. p. 175, U.S. Air Force. p. 176, p. 177, top, Larry Burrows—LIFE Magazine, © 1965, Time Inc.; bottom, U.S. Navy. p. 178, Larry Burrows—LIFE Magazine, © 1965, Time Inc. p. 179, top, UPI; bottom, U.S. Navy. p. 180, top, U.S. Navy; bottom, Robert Moeser. p. 182, UPI. p. 185, Paul Schutzer—LIFE Magazine, © 1965, Time Inc.

Map Credits

p. 19—Map by Diane McCaffery. From *The Two Viet-Nams: A Political and Military Analysis*, Second Revised Edition by Bernard B. Fall. Copyright © 1963, 1964, 1967 by Frederick A. Praeger, Inc. Reprinted by permission of Holt, Rinehart and Winston, CBS College Publishing.

p. 22—Map by Dick Sanderson.

p. 52—Map by Diane McCaffery.

p. 65—Map by Dick Sanderson.

p. 137—Map by Diane McCaffery. Source: Department of the Army.

p. 157—Map by Diane McCaffery.

p. 181—Map by Diane McCaffery.

Acknowledgments

Boston Publishing Company wishes to acknowledge the kind assistance of the following people: William P. Bundy, editor, *Foreign Affairs*; James E. Butler and the Special Operations Association; Charles W. Dunn, professor and chairman, Department of Celtic Languages and Literatures, Harvard University; Neil Sheehan; Major General John K. Singlaub, U.S. Army (Ret.); the staffs of the Center for Military History and the U.S. Marine Corps History and Museums Division; numerous army and navy veterans of the Vietnam War and Central Intelligence Agency officers who wish to remain anonymous.

Index

A

Agent Orange, 134
Agitprop (agitation-propaganda), 37-8, 40-1, 46, 114, 118
Alvarez, Lieutenant Everett, 160, *161*
America, 94-5, 102, 128, 145, 162, 184; involvement in Southeast Asia, 128, 164, 183 (see also United States)
American, 51, 87, 89, 98, 114, 118, 132, 141-2, *143*; advisers, 10-2, 14, 20, 22-5, 51-2, *51*, 54-8, 60-2, 70, *70*, 91, 108, 118, *118*, 128, 131, 138, 151, 168; agents, 81, 85; aid, 61, 91, *128*; aircraft, 158-9, 181; backed coup against Diem, 82, 88; combat support, 10, 14, 36; commitment, 12, 60, 91, 102; conduct in Southeast Asia, 160; equipment, 18-20, 51-2, *51*, 54-6, *104*; influence over Diem regime, *77*, 83; interests in Vietnam, 60, 91; involvement in South Vietnam, 59, 62, 82-6, 89, 91, 95, 115, 172; military, 46, 59, 91, 99, 142; military personnel in Vietnam, 8, 11-2, 31, 57, 94, 118, 129, 163, 174, 182, 184; officers, 51, 68, 172; officials, 18, 58, 60, 78, 88, 100, 134; people, 24, 91, 102, 125, 160-1, 183-4; pilots, 52, 135, 160; planners, 100, 145, 168; policy, 78, 82, 85, 91, 125; reporters, 58-60, *61*, 62, 77, 88; soldiers, 11, 14, *50*, 128-9, *128*, 134, 143, 168; stance toward Saigon, 37, 79, 85; tactics, 79; technology, 31, 62; troops, 44-5, 91, 128, 174; -type war, 53; -Vietnamese cooperation, 63, 87 (see also United States)
Americans, 22, *25*, 32, 38, 46-7, 51, 53, 56-8, 62-3, 70, *70*, 81, 84-6, 88-9, 103, 114, *114*, 121-2, 125, 128-9, 134-5, 138-9, 141-3, 145, 148, 151, 160, 163, 165-6, 168, *169*, 174, 178, 184
An Xuyen Province, 54
Ap Bac, battle of, 48-52, *50, 51*, 54, 56, 59-60, 98
Army of the Republic of Vietnam (ARVN), 11-2, 14, 19, 23, *25*, 32, 50-2, 54, 56, 59, 61-2, 70, 98, *104*, 106, *108*, 115, 118, 122; atrocities, 56, 106-9, *108*; commanders, 11, 19, 54, 56-8, 62, 81; desertions, 102; I Corps, *10*, 11, 23, 81, 94, 99, 106, 122, 136, 138-40, 144, 174; IV Corps, 51, 88, 94, 104, 114, 136, 144; II Corps, 23, 81, 94, 136, 138, 144, 166, 171; 2nd Division, 11; 7th Division, 19, 22, 25, 48, 54-5, 59, 98; soldiers, *8*, 12, *53, 67*, 68, *69*, 70, *70, 71*, 108, *118*, 175; III Corps, 82, 88, 94, 136, 144; troops, 26, *26, 30*, 51, 174
Arnett, Peter, 59-60

B

Ball, George, 18, 82, 94, 159, 162, 164, 169
Ben Tuong, 15, 18
Bien Hoa, 135, 164, 172, 178; airfield, 163, *163*
Bigart, Homer, 58-9, 62
Binh Dinh Province, 18, 114, 166
Binh Duong Province, 15, *69*
Binh Xuyen, 34, 81
Bolovens Plateau, 129, 142
Boondodge, Operation, 20, 52
Browne, Malcolm, 59, *61*
Buddhist, 72-81; bonzes, 34; crisis of 1963, 64-5, 76, 84, 91, 95, 100, 112
Buddhists, 72-81, *74, 76*, 85, 88-9, 96; repression against, 82, 84, 88
Bundy, McGeorge, 89, 94, 123, 133, 159, 168-72, 184
Bundy, William P., 84, 121-3, 164-5, 183

Buon Brieng, *148, 149*, 151
Buon Enao, 12-3, 148
Burchett, Wilfred, 24

C

Ca Mau Peninsula, 13, 18, 20, 22, *41*, 54, 61, 118, 134
Cambodia, 20, 24, *26*, 97, 102, 118, *120*, 122, 129, 136, 138, 139, 144, 145, *151*
Camp Holloway, 166, 168
Can, Ngo Dinh, 63-5, 85
Cao, General Huynh Van, 25, 51
Cao Dai sect, 34, 96
Cape Vinh Son, 145, 156
Catholic; church, 87, 89; parishioners, 136; priests, 34, 38, 136; refugees from the North, 13
Catholicism, 75-6
Catholics, 75-6, 96
Central Committee of North Vietnamese Communist party, 34-6, 46, 97
Central highlands, 12-3, 22-4, *26*, 32, 47, 54, 59, 97, *146*, 148
Central Intelligence Agency (CIA), 12, *50*, 81-2, 85-6, 88, 94, 114-7, 126, 128, *128*, 130-3, 144-6, 182, 184
Central Office of South Vietnam (COSVN), 36, 41-2; successor to Nambo Regional Committee, 36
Chap Le, 169, 171
Chieu Hoi (Open Arms) program, 61
China, People's Republic of, 58, 100, 103, 164, 169, 183, 184; American armies in, 161; Cultural Revolution in, 103
Chinese; approval of de Gaulle's neutralist vision, 100; Communists, 14, 35; intervention in North Vietnam, 101
Chuong, Tran Van, 81
CINCPAC, 154, 156 (see also Sharp, Admiral)
Civil Guard, 10, 15, 19, 42, 50-1, 54, 59, 87, 106, 140, 142
Civil Guardsmen, 51 (see also Regional Forces)
Civil Operations and Revolutionary Development Support (CORDS), 116
Civilian Irregular Defense Group (CIDG), 12, 116, 128, 135-6, 138-40, 143, 146, 148, *149*, 151
Co, General Nguyen Huu, 104, 106
Colby, William, 94, 131-2
Collectivization, 43-6
Combined Studies Group, 131-3, 136, 138, 144
Communism; denying South Vietnam to, 91; foreigners help Vietnamese fight, 20
Communist; anti-, 59, 75, 90, 114, 116; domination of National Liberation Front, 35; domination of Southeast Asian peninsula, 91; escalation, risk of, 102; expansion, 81; forces, 117, 129; insurgency, 78, 100; insurgency in Malaya, 14; relationship with People's Revolutionary party, 36; strength in China, 58; takeover, 83-4, 128; "wars of national liberation," 146 (see also Lao Dong party, National Liberation Front, Vietcong)
Communists, *117*, 129-30, 166, 168
Conein, Lucien, 81, 85-6, 88-9
Cong, Vo Chi, 34
Congress (U.S.), 58, 94-5, 122-3, 159-62, 183
Counterinsurgency Plan (CIP), 128, 131
Counter-Terror Teams, 116-7
Crusader jets (F-8), 155, *159*, 160, 169
Cuban missile crisis, 57, 155, 183

D

Da Lat, 86, 100, 135, 162, 172
Dam, Colonel Bui Dinh, 48-51
Da Nang, 13, 21, 23, 84, 136, 141, 145, 152, 154, 156, *168*, 169-71, *173*-5, 178, *179*; American air base at, 11
Dang Tien (Let's Go), Operation, 18
Darlac Province, 97, 178

Defense Department (U.S.), 18, 23, 57, 82, 123, 162, 165; pro-Diem faction at, 84, 89
De Gaulle, Charles, 57, 100
Delta, Project, 143-4, *144*
Demilitarized zone (DMZ), 23, 130, 145, 169
Democratic Republic of Vietnam (DRV), 103, 156, 165, 172
De Silva, Peer, 115, 182, 184
Desoto patrol, 152, 154, 156, *159*
Dickerson, Lieutenant Colonel William, *10*, 11
Diem, Ngo Dinh, 18, 24, *41*, 42, 51, 53-4, 57-61, 63-5, 75-89, *77*, 91, 94-100, 106, 114, 130, 138, 172; and Buddhist crisis, 75-81, 85, 95; assassination of, 87-9, *89*, 94; authoritarian rule of, 76; censorship by, 54, 58, *60*; government of, 8, 14, 36, 38, 43, 54, 57-61, *61, 74*, 75, *76*, 77-82, *77, 78*, 84-5, 87, 90-1, *90*, 106, 132; land distribution program of, 42; refuses to let elections take place, 34; world opinion turns against, 81
Dien Bien Phu, 103
Dinh Tuong Province, 48, 55
Don, General Tran Van, 11, 81, 86-9, 96, 100
Dong, Pham Van, 123
Dong Hoi, 169, 171, 181
Donlon, Captain Roger H.C., 140-2, *141, 142*
Duc, Colonel Duong Van, 100
Duc, Thich Quang, 74-6, *75*, 78
Dulles, John Foster, 128

E

Eagle Flights, 12, *29*
Eisenhower, Dwight D., 91, 128-9, *128*

F

Fall, Bernard, 14
Far East, 20, 58, 158
Farmgate, Operation, 134-5, *135*
Felt, Admiral Harry D., 86
Flaming Dart, Operation, 103, 169-71, *173*, 183
Forrestal, Michael, 82, 91
France, 81, 128, 131
French, 23, 63, 100, 104, 130, 174; agents, 100; ambassador to South Vietnam, 84; catastrophe of 1954, 90; colonial army, 81; colonial rule, 43, 75; efforts for settlement of war, 84; sympathizers in South Vietnam, 100; Vietminh struggle against, 34; war against, 32, 46, 68
French Indochina War, 22-3, *35*, 77
Freund, Colonel John, *151*
Fulbright, J. William, 160-1

G

Geneva; accords (1954), 6, 23, 34, 103, 128; agreements (1954), 84; Conference of 1962, 129-30
Giap, General Vo Nguyen, 22, *41*, 103, 114, 117
Gillespie, Captain Vernon, *146, 148*, 151, *151*
Goldwater, Barry, 124, 155, 164
Government of South Vietnam (GVN), 6, 14, 18, 38, 42, 58, 60, 62, 78, 84-6, 101, 106, 172, 178; defeat, 51
Grace, Captain William, *149*
Grant, Sergeant Gerald "Doc," *133*
Green Berets, 12-3, 136, 138-9, 143, 148 (see also Special Forces)
Gruening, Ernest, 161, 183
Guerrilla, 14-5, 19-23, 34, *39*, 40-1, 45, 48, 50-1, 53-5, *97*, 108, *108*, 114, 117, *140*, 141; attacks, 13, 90; bands, 130; bivouac, 144; camp, 97; fighting, *104*; forces, Communist, 129; gunfire, *50*, 51; leadership and training, 36, 169; recruits, 118; struggle, 97; tactics, 42, 53, *104*, 116-7; territory, 23; warfare, 12, *50, 128*, 134, 168 (see also Vietcong)
Guerrillas, 15, 24, *43*, 47, 96, 118, 163, 170-1 (see also Vietcong)
Gulf of Tonkin, 145, 152, *154*, 155-6, *155*, 158, *159*, 161-2, 164, 168, 173

H

Hades, Operation (see Ranch Hand, Operation)
Haiphong, 103, 160; Harbor, 101
Hai Yen (Sea Swallow), Operation, 18
Halberstam, David, 58–60, *61*, 62, 75, 77
Hanoi, 34, 36, 84, 94–5, 97, 102–3, 122–3, 130–1, 133, 154–5, 158, 163–4, 168–70, 181, 183
Harkins, General Paul D., 8–11, *9*, 24, 51, 56, 59–60, 62, 82, 85–6, 89, 94, 124
Harriman, W. Averell, 82, 130
Hastings, Operation, *31*
Hawaii, 50; Honolulu, 10, 62, 89, 94, 122–3, *159*
Helicopters, 12, 19–21, 24–31, *26*, *29*, *30*, *31*, 36, *50*, 51, 53, 59, *60*, 62, 134, 143, *149*, 163, 168, 173–5; CH-47 "Chinook," 31; CH-46, *31*; CH-34, 144; CH-37 "Jolly Green Giant," 31; CH-21, 26, *26*, 31, 50, 56, 62; evacuation via lifts, 11, 26, *30*, 50, 56, 174; Hueys, 21, *29*, 31, *50*, 55–6; UH-1, 31; UH-1A, 21, *29*, *50*, 55–6; UH-1B, 21, *29*, 55–6
Herrick, Captain John, 154–60, 162
Hilsman, Roger, 15, 24, 82–3, 104, 121
Ho Chi Minh, 34, 36, 84, 103, 132, 183
Ho Chi Minh Trail, 23, 118, 120–1, *121*, 129–30, 138–9, 142, *143*; American-led strikes against, 145
Hoa Hao sect, 34, *101*
Hon Gai, 160, *161*
Hon Mat Island, 154
Hon Me, 145, 152, 154
Hon Ngu, 145, 152, 154
Hop Tac, 122; Council, 122
Hope, Captain Leon, 130
Hotfoot, Operation, 126, 128; renamed Operation White Star, 129
Hue, 63, *64*, 75–6, 78–80, 84, 101, 133, 170

I

Indochina, 53, 59, 91, 95, 100, 128
International Control Commission (ICC), 84, 123, 155
International Volunteer Service, 12

J

James, Lieutenant Ralph, *160*
Japanese, 32, 34, 62
Johnson, General Harold K., 178
Johnson, Lyndon Baines, 92, 94, *94*, 100–2, 104, 124, *142*, 144, 155, *158*, 159–65, 168–72, 178, 183–4; civil rights bill of, 123; concept of foreign policy, 95; Great Society of, 123
Johnson, U. Alexis, 133, 168, 184
Joint Chiefs of Staff (U.S.), 18, 24, 59, 84, 100, 102, 124, 144, 154, 159, 172, 174, 178
Joint General Staff (South Vietnamese), 11, 100; headquarters, 86–7

K

Karch, Brigadier General Frederick J., 174–5, *178*
Kattenburg, Paul, 83–4, 102, 104
Kennedy, John F., 8, 15, 18, 23, 57, 60–3, 79, 81–2, 84–92, 94–5, 124, 128, 130–1, 134, 146; assassination of, 91–2; civil rights bill of, 123; commitment to South Vietnam, 26; inauguration of, 129; State of the Union address (1963), 56
Kennedy, Robert F., 12, 82–4, 124
Khanh, General Nguyen, 81, 96, 99–102, *99*, *101*, 106, 117, 122, 125, 162–3, 165, 168, 172, 173
Khiem, General Tran Thien, 81, 100, 162–3
Khiet, Thich Tinh, 76–7
Khrushchev, Nikita, 155
Kien Hoa Province, 14, 19
Kim, Le Van, 81, 96, 100
Kontum Province, 38–40, 112, 121, 142, 178
Kosygin, Aleksei, 103, 168–9
Krulak, Major General Victor, 84
Ky, Nguyen Cao, 131, 135, 163–5, 169, 172, *173*

L

Lao Dong party, 34–6, 42, 97, 103, 117 (see also Communist)
Laos, 10, *10*, 11, 21, 23–4, 94, 100, 102, 120–1, 123, 126, 128–32, *128*, *131*, 136, 138–40, 142, 144–5, 164
Layton, Gilbert, 12, 132, 136
Leaping Lena, Project, 142–3, 145
Lemnitzer, General Lyman, 18
Lodge, Henry Cabot, 79, 81–3, *83*, 85–9, 94, 97–8, 100, 102, 118, 122–4
Long An Province, 55, 98, 114, 120, 122
Long Thanh, 132–3, 145
Luc Luong Dac Biet (LLDB), 131, 138–40, 143 (see also Special Forces, South Vietnamese)

M

MacArthur, General Douglas, 164
McCone, John, 82, 94
McGarr, General Lionel, 15
MacGill, Captain Jim, *116*
McNamara, Robert, 18, 24, 56, 62, 82, 84–5, 89, 91, 94, 98–9, 101–2, *101*, 106, 118, 124–5, 132, 135, 144, 158–61, 165, 169, 178, 183–4
Mansfield, Senator Mike, 58–9, 91
Mao Tse-tung, 41–2, 114
Mecklin, John, 60, 63
Mekong River, 22
Mekong River Delta, 11, 14, 20, 22, 26, *29*, *39*, 42, 47, 54, 61, *67*, 94, 104, *104*, 106, *108*, 118, *118*, *138*
Mendenhall, Joseph, 84
Military Advisory Assistance Group (MAAG), 8, 12, 15, 106, 130
Military Assistance Command, Vietnam (MACV), 8–11, *9*, 19, 51, 57, 62, 86, 102, 115–6, 124–5, 132–3, 135, 138, 142–5, *144*, 145, 156, 172, 174
Minh, General Duong Van "Big," 19, 81–2, 85, 87–9, 94–6, *95*, 99–100, *99*, 117, 125, 162–3
Minh, General Tran Van "Little," 174
Montagnards, 12–3, 23, 136, *136*, 138, 146, *146*, 148, 151
Morning Star, Operation, 20–1, 52
Morse, Senator Wayne, 160–1, 183

N

Nam Dong, 140–2, *141*, 142
Napalm, 23, 57, *57*
National Liberation Front (NLF), 6, 24, 33–47, *35*, *39*, *40*, *47*, 91, 96–7, *104*, 117–8, 120, 123, 132, 136, 170, 183; first Congress of (February 1962), 34; liberation associations, 43–6; military planning, 97; organization of, 34; plan to overthrow Diem government, 35; political terrorism, 38; positive appeal of, 46; ten-point program, 34–5; territory, 140; units, 97, *118*, *121*; violence program of, 38–40 (see also Communist)
National Security Action Memorandum (NSAM) 273, 94, 100, 118
National Security Action Memorandum (NSAM) 288, 102, 106, 122
National Security Action Memorandum (NSAM) 328, 184
National Security Council (South Vietnam), 61, 102
National Security Council (U.S.), 82–5, 89, 125, 184
Navarro, Sergeant Robert, *138*, *139*
Nha Trang, 12, 80, 130–1, 169
Ngo family, 15, 53, 59, 62–3, *64*, 65, 81, 85–6
Nhu, Madame Ngo Dinh, 20, 54, 59, 63–5, *64*, 75–7, *78*, 79, 81, 82, 85, 88, 95–6, *96*
Nhu, Ngo Dinh, 15, 61, 63–5, 76–7, *77*, 79, 81–2, 84–5, 87–9, 100, 138
Nixon, Richard M., *123*
Nolting, Frederick, 57, 60, *77*, 78–9
North Vietnam (Democratic Republic of Vietnam), 35, 41, 64, 97, 102, 104, 120–1, 123, 125, 129–33, 144–5, 152, 154, 156, 162–4, 168–70, 172, 174, 178, 181–4; aggression from, 59; U.S. bombing of, 100–2, *154*, *158*, 160, *160*, 162, 164, 165, 169, 170, 171, 172–4, *173*, *175*, *180*, 181–2, 183, 184
North Vietnamese, 117, 121, 123, 130, 132, 143, 154–6, 158, 160, *161*, 162, 168, 173, 183; air attacks, 170; allies of Pathet Lao, 128; aptitude for detecting infiltrators, 142; army high command, 41–2; infiltration through Laos, 123; military activity along the DMZ, 130; training camps and industrial complexes, bombing of, 101
Norton, Dr. Robert, *124*
Nosavan, General Phoumi, 129
Nung tribe, 138–41, 145; soldiers, *121*
Nuttle, David, 12

O

Oanh, Nguyen Xuan, 165, 172
O'Donnell, Kenneth, 92
Ogier, Commander Herbert L., 154

P

Pathet Lao, 126, 128–30; troops, *128*
Penchenier, Georges, 44–5
Pentagon, 12, 57, 59, 62, 102, 135, 158–60, 162, 174
People's Action Team (PAT), 115–6, *115*, *117*; recruits, *116*; subsumed by Revolutionary Development Cadre program, 116
People's Army of Vietnam (PAVN), 103; soldiers, 120; 325th Division, 120
People's Liberation Army (PLA), 34, 40–2; Guerrilla Popular Army of, 40–1; Main Force battalion of, 41; Regional Force companies of, 40–1
People's Revolutionary party, 34–8, 46; background, 35–8; Political Bureau of, 41; structure, 35–7
People's Special Forces, 114–5
Personalism, 15, 18
Phat, Brigadier General Lam Van, 122, 163, 172
Phu My, *123*, 170
Phuoc Tuy Province, 44
Phuong Hoang (Royal Phoenix), Operation, 18
Phu Yen Province, 14, 18, 24
Pike, Douglas, 35–6
Plain of Jars, 129–30
Plain of Reeds, 19, 48
Pleiku, 112, 166, 168–70, *169*, 178
Popular Forces, 106, 115
Powers, Corporal Garry, 175
Psychological warfare, 15, 42, 94, 132, 135, 145

Q

Quang Binh Province, 120
Quang Khe, 160, 173
Quang Nam Province, 14
Quang Ngai Province, 18, 23, 112, 114–5, 122
Quang Tin Province, 106
Quat, Dr. Phan Huy, 172
Qui Nhon, 112, 170–1, *170*, *171*

R

Radio Freedom, 133
Radio Hanoi, 132, 170
Radio Saigon, 80, 87
Ranch Hand, Operation, 134
Rangers, 10, *13*, *108*, 117–8, 135, 144, 174; role in Operation Sunrise, 15
Regional Forces, 106, 115 (see also Civil Guardsmen)
Rhade tribe, 12–3, 23, *133*, *148*, *149*, *151*
Richardson, John, 82, 88
Rolling Thunder, 172–4, *175*, *180*–1, 183–4
Ron, 145, 156
Royal Laotian Army, 128, *129*
Rusk, Dean, 56, 87, 89, 94, 124–5, 144, 155, 158–60, 183–4

S

Saigon, 8, 10, 12, 14–5, 18–20, 22–4, *41*, 42, 44, 45, 51, 53–4, *53*, 56–65, 72, *74*, 79–82, *83*, 84–90, 95–102, 112, 114, *115*, 117–8, 122, *123*, 130, 132, 135, 145, 156, 162–5, *164*, 168, 170–2, 174, 184; American colony in, 118; –area interzone, 34; Buddhist demonstrations in, 76; defoliation flights north of, 11; demonstration against Diem, *80;* government, 13, 36–8, 41, 58, 60–1, 63, 77–8, *77*, 85, 89, 106, 108; Harbor, 118; night life, *95*, 96; pagoda at, *76;* people of, 6; press corps, 58; rebel troops deploy around, 86; River, 6
Scotton, Frank, 112, 114–5, *115*
Seaborn, J. Blair, 123
Sedang, 23
Self Defense Corps, *16*, 19, 53–4, 98, 106, 114, 118; renamed Popular Forces in 1964, 106
Senate (U.S.), 81, 95, 123, 161–2, 183
Shackleton, Captain Ronald, 12–3, 148
Shank, Jr., Captain Edwin, 135, *135*
Shaplen, Robert, 63, 88–9
Sharp, Jr., Admiral Ulysses S. Grant, 159–60, 168, 174 (see also CINCPAC)
Sheehan, Neil, 59–60, *61*, 62
Sihanouk, Prince Norodom, 24
Simons, Lieutenant Colonel Arthur D. "Bull," 126, 128–9
Skyhawk jets, 157, 160, *161*, 169, *180*
Skyraider jets, 135, 142, *154*, 160, 169, 171, 173, *180*, 181
Soc Trang, 11, 21, 135
South Vietnam, 10–2, 14, 18, 23–6, 35, 58–63, 75–6, 78, 83–4, 91, 94, 96, 100–3, 122–3, *125*, 130, 136, 143–5, *143*, 154, 160, 163–4, 170, 183; French ambassador to, 84; NLF's division of, 34; plan for removal of American advisers from, 57; U.S. ambassador to, 57, *77*, 79, 81, 86; U.S. dependents in, 122, 170; U.S. economic aid to, *124;* Vietcong controlled territory in, 131
South Vietnamese, 52, *64*, 66, 94, 103, 117, *118*, 132, 136, 145, 152, 161, 162, 168, 170, 183; air force pilots, 11; army, 12, 19, 36, 50–1, 170, 183; command, 20, 62, 144; confidence for victory, 24; countryside, 22, 34, 38, 54; forces, 8, 10, 11, 14, 19, *26*, *29*, *30*, 54, 56, 58–9, *79*, 115, 122; generals, 81–2; government, 12, 20, 38, 59, 91, 122; marines, 11, 19; officers, *164*; Special Forces troops, 81
Southeast Asia, 14, 57, 94, 122, 128, *128*, 159, 183; American conduct in, 160; arrival of CIA in, *50;* U.S. involvement in, 12, 58–9, 95, 128
Southeast Asia Resolution, 160–2, 183
Southeast Asia Treaty Organization (SEATO), 10
Soviet Union, 103, 129, 136, 155, 168–9, 183; Communist party in, 35; intervention in North Vietnam unlikely, 101; news agency, *161;* U.S. nuclear test ban treaty with, 57
Special Forces; A Teams, 136, 148; camps, 13, 148, 151, *151;* 5th Special Forces Group, 145; 1st Special Forces Group, 12; instructors, 12; soldiers, 126, 140; South Vietnamese, 81, 85, 118, 131, 136–8, 142–3, *144;* teams, 13, 21, *149;* U.S. advisers, 129; U.S. Army, 12, *13*, 24, *50*, 54, 114, *121*, 128–33, *128*, *131*, *133*, 136, 138, *138*, *141*, 142–3, *146*, *146*, 148, 151 (see also Green Berets, *Luc Luong Dac Biet*)
State Department (U.S.), 82, 84, 87, 89, 94, 102, 123, 130, 165, 183–4
Strategic Hamlet Program, 15, 18–9, 24, 54, 56, 61, 98, 104
Strategic hamlets, 10, 14–5, *16*, 18–9, 24, 40–2, *41*, 54, 56, 57, 75, *97*, 98, 106, 114, *149;* five overrun by Vietcong, 118; renamed "new life hamlets," 106
Strike force, 12–3, 140, 151
Studies and Observation Group (SOG), 128, 131–3, 139, 144–5, *145*
Sully, François, 59, *60*, 62

Sunrise, Operation, 15, *16*, 18
Suu, Phan Khac, 163, 165
Switchback, Operation, 138

T

Tan Son Nhut Airport, 8, 20, 62, 81, 88, 100, 118, 122, 134, 165, 170, 172, 178
Taylor, General Maxwell, 10, 15, 24, 59, 82, 84, 91, 94, 100–1, *101*, 122, 124–5, 162–5, 168, 172–4, 178, 182, 184
Tay Ninh Province, 20, 106, 136; provincial capital, 96
Tchepone, 121
Tet, 165; cease-fire, 166; offensive, post–, 166
Thach, Dr. Pham Ngoc, 121
Thai Nguyen, 103
Thanh, General Nguyen Chi, 117
Thanh Hoa Province, n. 132
Thanh Tam, 98
Thao, Colonel Pham Ngoc, 172
Thi, General Nguyen Chanh, 163–5, 174–5, *178*
Thieu, Nguyen Van, 163–5, 172, 174
34–Alpha, Operation, 132
Tho, Major Lam Quant, 51, 60
Tho, Nguyen Huu, 34, *35*
Tho, Nguyen Ngoc, 98
Thompson, Sir Robert, 14–5, 54, 85
Throckmorton, Lieutenant General John L., 174
Thuan, Nguyen Dinh, 66, 89
Thuc, Ngo Dinh, 63–5, 88
Times of Vietnam, 18, 54, 77, 85, 88; anti-American press campaign, 85
Timmes, Major General Charles, 24
Tra, Major General Tran Van, 42
Tri, General Do Cao, 81
Trueheart, William, 78, 102
Trug Ciang, 14
Truong Son Mountains, 23, 68
Tu Dam Pagoda, 80
Tung, Colonel Le Quant, 81, 85
Tu Nghia District, 114

U

U Minh Forest, 19, 117
United States, 24, *29*, 34, 36, 46, 59–63, 65, *77*, 78, 81–6, 88–9, 91, 94, 100–4, 118, 123, 125, *125*, 128–30, 134–5, 155–6, 159–62, 165, 168–9, *169*, 172, 178, 182, 183; advisers, 15, 20, 35, 58, 68, *70*, 84, 106, 115, 170–1; aid to South Vietnam, 8, 18–20, 24, 59, 60–1, 65, 81, 85, 106, *124;* air bases, 163, 174; dependents in South Vietnam, 122, 170; government, 6, 8, 18, 60, 61, 82, 84, 85–7, 123, 125; involvement in South Vietnam, 18, *26*, 42, 58, 60, 81, 94, *101*, 104, 114, 118, 122, 145, 170, 178, 183, 184; jets, 173; military aid to French, *35;* military arsenal, 134; military command, 48, 51, 57, 144; objectives, 102, 125; officers, 11, 58, 173; officials, 20, 24, 60, 85, 96, 98, 100; policy, 12, 78, 84, 135, 164, 184; recognition of Khanh regime, 100; relations with Diem, 75, 85; soldiers, 12, 85, 170, *170*; supplies, 61, *115;* training camps in, 53 (see also America)
U.S. Agency for International Development (USAID), 18, 59, 106, 114, *124*, *125*
U.S. Air Force, 134–5, *135*, 173
U.S. Army, 10, *13*, *116*, 178; 93rd Helicopter Company, 21; officer, *164*; pilots, 6; Special Forces, 12, *50*, 54, *128*, 146
U.S. Embassy, 58, 62, 87, 89, 91, 181–2, *182*
U.S. Information Service (USIS), 60, 86, 112, *115*
U.S. Marines, 21, *30*, 84, *108*, 168, 174–5, *178*, *179*, 184
U.S. Mission, 57–8, 60, *61*, 78–9, 85–6, 94, 125; Council, 125
U.S. Navy, 11, 145, *160*, 184
U.S.S. *C. Turner Joy,* 156–7, *159*, 162
U.S.S. *Card,* 118
U.S.S. *Constellation,* *154*, 160

U.S.S. *Coral Sea,* 168, 171, *180*
U.S.S. *Core,* 6
U.S.S. *Hancock,* 168, 171
U.S.S. *Maddox,* 152, 154–60, *155*, *159*, 162
U.S.S. *Mount McKinley,* 174
U.S.S. *Ranger,* 168, 171
U.S.S. *Ticonderoga,* 154–6, *159*, 160, *160*

V

Vann, Lieutenant Colonel John Paul, 48–51, 58–9, 62
Vietcong, 8, 11–5, *16*, 18–22, *21*, 23–4, *25*, *26*, 32–47, *34*, *39*, *41*, *47*, 50–62, *50*, *53*, *55*, *57*, 75, 84, 91, 94, *97*, 98–9, *98*, 102, 104, *104*, 106, 108, *108*, 114–5, 117–8, 120, *120*, 122, 135–6, *136*, 139–40, *140*, 142, 144–5, *146*, 148, *151*, 163, 165–6, 168, 170–1, *170*, *171*, 175, 178, 183; activity, 90, 114, 116; assault at Nam Dong, 141; attacks, 97–8, 102, *108*, 138, *163*, 168, *169;* casualty rate, 55; concentrations, 48; –controlled territory, 118, 131; defections, 61, 90; equipment, *43;* losses at Ap Bac, 51; Main Force guerrillas, 118, 142; 1961 offensive launched, 14; North Vietnamese aid to, 100; prisoners, *108*, *144;* propaganda, 106; recruit montagnards, 23; terror, 38, 107–9 (see also Communist, guerrilla, guerrillas)
Vietminh, 22, 34, 36, 42, 114
Vietnam, 12, 20–1, 23, 25–6, 34, 42, 43, 45, 56, 58–60, *60*, 62–3, 65, 68, 77, 83–4, 88–91, 94–6, 102–4, 106, 112, 114, 122–5, 130, 133–5, *135*, 138–9, 142–3, 145–6, 148, 151, 159–60, 166, 168–9, *168*, 174–5, 178, *178*, 182–4; American military personnel and advisers in, 8, 22, 24, 35, 94, 118, 131, 134, 142, 161; French control over, 75; U.S. Counterinsurgency Plan for, 128
Vietnamese, 20, 23, 36, 50, 56–7, 59, 62–3, 65, 68, 70, 72, 76, 81, 84–5, 87–9, 91, 97, 100, 112, 115, 132, 135–6, 138–41, 143, 145, 151, 159, 164, 174, 178, 184; air bases, 174; aircraft, 132, 134–5, 168; air force, 12, 51, 132, 172–3; armed forces, 24, 131, 178; army, 102, 108, 151; civilians, 59, 133; commandos, 142; council, 125; frictions with Americans, 12; navy, 11; officers, 53, 81, 84, 118; officials, 81–2, 85, 122; peasants, 45–6; pilots, 134, 173, *173;* police, 81
Vietnamese private air transport corporation (VIAT), 131
Viet Tri, 103
Vinh, 145, 160
Vinh Linh, 169
Vinh Long Province, 40, 120
Vinh Son, 181
Vung Tau Charter, 162
Vung Tau Peninsula, 115

W

Werbiski, Captain Philip, *116*
Westmoreland, General William, 59, 122, *123*, 124–5, 144, 164, 168–9, 172, 174, 178; daughter Katherine, 170
White House, 10, 79, 86–7, 89, 91–2, 128, 133–4, 155, 159, 168, 171, 183–4
White Star, Operation, 129–30, *131*
World War II, 8, 36, 104, 124, 126, 131, 134, 161, 168, 174

X

Xa Loi Pagoda, *74*, *75*, 80, 88
Xom Bang, 173
Xuan, General Mai Huu, 87, 96, 100

Y

Yarborough, Major General William P., 139
York, Brigadier General Robert, 60
Youngblood, Rufus, 92

Names, Acronyms, Terms

Agitprop—agitation-propaganda. Ideological indoctrination.

APC—armored personnel carrier.

ARVN—Army of the Republic of Vietnam. The army of South Vietnam.

A Teams—twelve-man units made up of Green Berets. (See Green Berets and Special Forces.)

Binh Xuyen—bandit army that at one time controlled half of Saigon.

Can Lao—the Can Lao Nhan Vi Cach Mang Dang, or Personalist Labor Revolutionary party. Diem's brother Ngo Dinh Nhu's private secret police force.

Cao Dai—religious sect formed in 1925 by a group of civil servants in southern Vietnam.

Caribou—De Havilland Canada C-7A Caribou, small cargo aircraft of the U.S. Air Force.

CIA—Central Intelligence Agency. Conducted clandestine sabotage operations in Laos and South Vietnam throughout 1961-65.

CIDG—Civilian Irregular Defense Group. Project devised by the CIA which combined self-defense with economic and social programs designed to raise the standard of living and win the loyalty of the mountain people. Chief work of the U.S Special Forces.

CINCPAC—Commander in Chief, Pacific Command. Commander of American forces in the Pacific region, which includes Southeast Asia.

DMZ—demilitarized zone. Established according to the Geneva accords of 1954, provisionally dividing North Vietnam from South Vietnam along the seventeenth parallel.

DRV—Democratic Republic of Vietnam. The government of Ho Chi Minh, established on September 2, 1945. Provisionally confined to North Vietnam by the Geneva accords of 1954.

Green Berets—nickname for soldiers of the U.S. Special Forces, derived from the green berets of their uniforms. (See Special Forces and A Teams.)

GVN—government of South Vietnam. Also referred to as the Republic of Vietnam. Provisionally established by the Geneva accords of 1954.

Hoa Hao—Vietnamese religious sect founded in the South in 1959.

Huey—nickname for UH-1 series utility helicopters, speedy and heavily armed, used to support larger, more vulnerable helicopters.

ICC—International Control Commission. Mandated by Geneva accords of 1954 to supervise implementation of the agreement. Consisted of representatives of Poland, India, and Canada.

Joint Chiefs of Staff—Consists of chairman, U.S. Army chief of staff, chief of naval operations, U.S. Air Force chief of staff, and marine commandant. Advises president, the National Security Council, and the Secretary of Defense. Created in 1949 within the Department of Defense.

JGS—Joint General Staff. South Vietnamese counterpart to MACV.

KIA—killed in action.

Lao Dong Party—Vietnam Worker's party (Marxist-Leninist party of North Vietnam). Founded by Ho Chi Minh in May 1951. Absorbed the Vietminh and was the ruling party of the DRV. Extended into South Vietnam as the People's Revolutionary party in January 1962.

LZ—landing zone.

MAAG—see MACV.

MACV—Military Assistance Command, Vietnam. Superceded the Military Assistance Advisory Group (MAAG), the U.S. military advisory program to South Vietnam begun in 1955 and dissolved in May 1964. First organized in 1962, MACV placed U.S. advisers in the South Vietnamese military.

montagnards—the mountain tribes of Vietnam, wooed by both the North and the South because of their knowledge of the rugged highland terrain.

napalm—incendiary used in Vietnam by French and Americans both as a defoliant and anti-personnel weapon. Shot from a flame thrower or dropped from aircraft, the substance adheres while it burns.

NCO—noncommissioned officer.

NLF—National Liberation Front, officially the National Front for the Liberation of the South. Formed on December 20, 1960, it aimed to overthrow South Vietnam's government and reunite the North and the South. The NLF included Communists and non-Communists.

NSAM—National Security Action Memorandum. Presidential policy statements determining action on national security issues.

NSC—National Security Council. Established in 1947 to "advise the president with respect to the integration of domestic, foreign, and military policies relating to the national security."

Its specific functions and membership changed under each president. President Kennedy used the NSC principally as a sounding board.

NVA—North Vietnamese Army. (See PAVN.)

PAVN—People's Army of Vietnam. North Vietnam's army, led by Vo Nguyen Giap. Also called Vietnam People's Army and North Vietnamese Army.

PRP—People's Revolutionary Party. Communist party that dominated the NLF. Founded on January 15, 1962, as the successor to the Lao Dong party in South Vietnam.

sapper—VC commando, usually armed with explosives.

SDC—Self Defense Corps, local militia of South Vietnam.

SOG—Studies and Observation Group. Under MACV, conducted "unconventional" warfare, including "cross-border" missions in Laos, Cambodia, and North Vietnam throughout the Vietnam War.

Special Forces—U.S. soldiers trained in techniques of guerrilla warfare. In Vietnam, carried out counterinsurgency operations, many of them covert. Also trained South Vietnamese and montagnards in counterinsurgency and antiguerrilla warfare. (See Green Berets and A Teams.)

Strategic Hamlet Program—begun in February 1962, concentrating rural villages into fortified villages to separate people from the Vietcong and to gain their allegiance.

USAID—United States Agency for International Development. Responsible for administering foreign aid in Vietnam from the early 1960s to 1972, USAID provided funds for the building and renovation of hospitals, maternity dispensaries, and physicians who served tours of duty in South Vietnam.

USIA—United States Information Agency, now called the International Communications Agency. Established in 1953 with the purpose of international dissemination of information about the U.S. Overseas, the agency was referred to as the USIS (United States Information Service).

USIS—See USIA.

VC—Vietcong.

Vietcong—derogatory reference to a member of the NLF, a contraction of Vietnam Cong San (Vietnamese Communist). In use since 1956.

Vietminh—founded by Ho Chi Minh in May 1941, coalition that ruled the DRV. Absorbed by the Lao Dong party in 1951.

VNAF—Vietnamese Air Force (South).

VPA—Vietnam People's Army. (See PAVN.)

WIA—wounded in action.